Diodorus Siculus

AND THE FIRST CENTURY

Diodorus Siculus

———— ✦ ————

AND THE FIRST CENTURY

———— ✦ ————

KENNETH S. SACKS

PRINCETON UNIVERSITY PRESS

PRINCETON, NEW JERSEY

Copyright © 1990 by Princeton University Press
Published by Princeton University Press, 41 William Street,
Princeton, New Jersey 08540
In the United Kingdom: Princeton University Press, Oxford

Library of Congress Cataloging-in-Publication Data

Sacks, Kenneth.
Diodorus Siculus and the first century / Kenneth S. Sacks.
p.   cm.
Includes bibliographical references (p.).
ISBN 0-691-03600-4 (alk. paper)
1. Diodorus, Siculus. Bibliotheca historica.
2. History, Ancient. 3. History, Ancient—
Historiography. I. Title.
D58.D563S23   1990
930—dc20   90-31253

Publication of this book has been aided by
the Whitney Darrow Fund of
Princeton University Press

This book has been composed in Linotron Bembo

Princeton University Press books are printed on
acid-free paper, and meet the guidelines for
permanence and durability of the Committee on
Production Guidelines for Book Longevity
of the Council on Library Resources

Printed in the United States of America by
Princeton University Press,
Princeton, New Jersey

2   4   6   8   10   9   7   5   3   1

For Jane

εἰς ἀεί

CONTENTS

ACKNOWLEDGMENTS

I AM indebted to several institutions. Funding from the Graduate School and the William F. Vilas Foundation at the University of Wisconsin allowed me to begin my work; a fellowship from the National Endowment for the Humanities permitted me to complete it. Much of my research and almost all of my creative thinking about Diodorus occurred while I was a visiting fellow in the Department of Classics at Princeton University. I am most thankful to members of that department for their warm hospitality and a deeply stimulating environment. That this book is being published by Princeton University Press is a satisfying remembrance of a happy time spent there.

Thanks are due to Mr. Vincent Burns, who caught numerous errors in the bibliography, and to Mr. Randall Smith, who helped me run the *TLG* machine-readable tape of Diodorus until the University of Wisconsin purchased an Ibycus computer. Many scholars discussed and refined portions of this book, though they may still disagree with its conclusions: Professors Richard Billows, Stanley Burstein, Frank Clover, Robert Connor, Emilio Gabba, Erich Gruen, Christian Habicht, Sidney Halpern, John Pollini, Kurt Raaflaub, Matthew Santirocco, Philip Stadter, Sir Ronald Syme, and Frank Walbank. Three deserve special note, for their perseverance and inspiration: Catherine Rubincam, James Luce, and especially Arnaldo Momigliano—that he could not read and help improve the completed version is the least of our loss.

ABBREVIATIONS

ABBREVIATIONS of journals conform to the style of *L'année philologique*, and those of ancient works and modern scholarly collections conform generally to the list of abbreviations in the *Oxford Classical Dictionary*². Additional or differing abbreviations include:

ANRW   *Aufstieg und Niedergang des römischen Welt: Geschichte und Kultur Roms im Spiegel der neueren Forschung.* Edited by H. Temporini and W. Haase. New York, 1972–.

CHCL   *Cambridge History of Classical Literature, II: Latin Literature.* Edited by E. J. Kenney and W. V. Clausen. Cambridge, 1982.

DS   Diodorus Siculus.

FGH   F. Jacoby. *Die Fragmente der griechischen Historiker.* Vols. I-IIIc. Berlin/Leiden, 1923–.

Gruen, *HWCR*   E. S. Gruen. *The Hellenistic World and the Coming of Rome.* 2 vols. Berkeley, 1984.

MRR   *The Magistrates of the Roman Republic.* Edited by T.R.S. Broughton. 3 vols. Cleveland and Atlanta, 1951, 1952, and 1986.

Nock, *Essays*   *Arthur Darby Nock: Essays on Religion and the Ancient World.* 2 vols. Edited by Z. Stewart. Oxford, 1972.

RE   *Real-Encyclopädie der classischen Altertumswissenschaft.* Edited by A. Pauly, G. Wissowa, W. Kroll, and K. Mittelhaus. Stuttgart, 1893–.

Rostovtzeff, *SEHHW*   M. Rostovtzeff. *The Social and Economic History of the Hellenistic World.* 3 vols. Oxford, 1941.

Theiler   W. Theiler. *Poseidonios: Die Fragmente.* 2 vols. Berlin, 1982.

TLG   *Thesaurus Linguae Graecae*, machine-readable tape
(see under "Texts" in the Bibliography).

Walbank, *Commentary*   F. W. Walbank. *A Historical Commentary on Polybius*. 3 vols. Oxford, 1956–1979.

Walbank, *Selected Papers*   F. W. Walbank. *Selected Papers: Studies in Greek and Roman History and Historiography*. Cambridge, 1985.

Diodorus Siculus

AND THE FIRST CENTURY

INTRODUCTION

The Argument

"a compilation only as valuable as its authorities"[1]

WRITING during the last years of the Republic, Diodorus Siculus produced a universal history entitled the *Bibliotheke*.[2] Of its forty original books, only fifteen are completely extant, with most of the others surviving in various fragmentary states. The history's claim to universality is established by its range, both geographic and chronological. Along with the myths of the barbarians and Greeks, it covers the affairs of mainland Greece, Sicily, Rome, and surrounding areas, from the time of the Trojan War until 60 B.C.

With his net cast so widely, Diodorus relied heavily on written accounts for his information. Except for some fragments, most of these earlier histories are now lost. Thus the *Bibliotheke*, as the primary medium of survival for much of Greek historiography, provides important testimony for substantial portions of antiquity. In fact, Diodorus's obvious contribution is in preserving rather than in creating historical traditions.

Over the past century and a half it has been virtually axiomatic that the *Bibliotheke* directly reflects the works of the earlier, more critical historians whom Diodorus used.[3] When ap-

[1] *Oxford Classical Dictionary*[2], s.v. "Diodorus Siculus."

[2] Pliny, *NH praef.* 25. On the title, see esp. H. Stephanus in N. Eyring, *Diodori Siculi Bibliothecae Historicae Libri Qui Supersunt, e recensione Petri Wesselingii, etc.* I, vi–vii; also J. Hornblower, *Hieronymus of Cardia*, 22–24. The word usually means a bookcase or library.

[3] A summary of the methodology is in J. Palm, *Über Sprache und Stil des Diodoros von Sizilien*, 11–14; a recent example is W. Peremans, *Historia* 16 (1967), 432–55. It was put forth by B. G. Niebuhr and T. Mommsen (cited by J. Seibert, *Das Zeitalter der Diadochen*, 27–28), but argued in detail by C. Volquardsen, *Untersuchungen über die Quellen der griechischen und sicilischen*

3

plying the axiom to the narrative, scholars have achieved some success in judging the merits of material in the *Bibliotheke* and in identifying sources that are on the whole otherwise lost.[4] But the *Bibliotheke* also contains discussions of politics, historiography, and moral and natural philosophy, the contents of which are similarly attributed to earlier authorities. When Diodorus's source is not obvious, scholars speculate freely, choosing from an array of writers. Rarely is Diodorus himself considered capable of contributing such ideas to his work. Even the scholar most responsible for showing Diodorus's independence in style rules out a similar independence in thought.[5]

The notion that Diodorus is incapable of intruding into the text to any significant degree has its roots in nineteenth-century scientific positivism. But within modern theories of literary composition it is simple-minded and naive. Thoroughly cannibalized, with parts assigned to a variety of authors and traditions of the previous four centuries, the *Bibliotheke* has lost its integrity as a unified work and its place within the history of ideas.

This loss would be lamentable for any piece of literature but is especially so for the *Bibliotheke*. Despite the massive expansion in history writing during the Hellenistic period, precious

---

Geschichten bei Diodor, Buch xi bis xvi. The idea grew because of E. Schwartz's articles in *RE* and F. Jacoby's commentary to *FGH*.

[4] Although that approach is constantly confronting the *Einquellen-theorie*. For a brief history, see Hornblower, *Hieronymus of Cardia*, 20–22; most recently supported by L. Pearson, *The Greek Historians of the West*, 135–36.

[5] "Die Frage ist, *wie* ein Gedanke ausgedrückt wird, nicht *welcher* Gedanke," according to Palm, *Über Sprache und Stil*, 64 (his emphases). Most recently, e.g., Hornblower, *Hieronymus of Cardia*, 28, and F. Bizière, *Diodore* XIX, Budé edition, ix, write of Diodorus's "slavish dependence on his sources." Important exceptions include C. [Reid] Rubincam, R. Drews, W. Spoerri, M. Pavan, and J. de Romilly, on whose works, see the Bibliography. No note could be taken of the important articles published in *Aevum* 61 (1987). In 1890, R. Neubert, *Spuren selbständiger Thätigkeit bei Diodor*, effectively refuted Volquardsen's influential arguments regarding Diodorus's lack of originality (see n. 3), but his brief essay has been virtually ignored.

little remains. Only the writings of Polybius, Dionysius of Halicarnassus, and Diodorus are sufficiently preserved to be of much use; and Diodorus's work is the only large-scale history written in the late Republic, by either a Greek or Roman, to survive.

Diodorus Siculus and the First Century offers a reappraisal. In the following chapters, I argue that Diodorus himself, influenced by contemporary political and aesthetic considerations, is responsible for much of the nonnarrative material and determined the overall shape and main themes of the history. This does not mean that all such thoughts are original with him. Diodorus echoes contemporary ideas and also preserves in his text certain attitudes of his sources. But these, it will be demonstrated, are generally compatible with his personal beliefs. What emerges from this investigation is that the *Bibliotheke* was not composed by rote, nor is it an arbitrary collection of thoughts derived from whatever source Diodorus happened to be following at that moment. It is, instead, a document substantially reflecting the intellectual and political attitudes of the late Hellenistic period.[6]

This book involves three overlapping areas of investigation. The first concerns selected conventions in history writing. Most historical works in antiquity contained introductory prologues (prooemia), organizational markers, speeches, and polemics against earlier authors. These conventions are also found in the *Bibliotheke* and, predictably, are usually considered to come from Diodorus's sources rather than arising from his own creativity. Chapters 1 and 4 (separated from one another because the latter is based substantially on findings from the two intervening chapters) argue that for the composition of these aspects of historiography Diodorus himself is largely, perhaps entirely, responsible. Themes expressed within these conventions are internally consistent and also intersect with ideas developed throughout the narrative of the

---

[6] "Diodor ist ein Kind seiner Zeit"—so Neubert, *Spuren selbständiger Thätigkeit bei Diodor*, 10.

work. Selective rather than exhaustive, the discussions of historiographical conventions suggest that the general understanding of how Diodorus composed the *Bibliotheke* ought to be reconsidered.

Chapters 2 and 3 deal with five broad themes of historiography in the *Bibliotheke*: character assessments, the power of fortune, and a pattern for the rise and fall of empires in the former; and explanations of human progress and the idea of universalism in the latter. These themes are also found, in various forms, in Diodorus's sources. But Diodorus has modified these ideas to fit his own notion of history and to voice a contemporary message. Sentiments throughout the *Bibliotheke* are consistent and intertwined. Such could not be the case if the work were merely a random compilation of older traditions. Surviving fragments from Diodorus's sources serve as controls on his method of excerption. These outside checks prove that, while paraphrasing factual narrative, Diodorus freely invents asides on politics, philosophy, and historiography. Broadly moralistic, the central feature of the *Bibliotheke* is its call to peoples and nations to act clemently and with moderation.

The third area of investigation concerns Diodorus's attitude toward Rome (Chapter 5) and the effect that had on the shape and bias of the *Bibliotheke* (Chapter 6). A close examination of Diodorus's life is reserved for the final chapter, in order to show the relationship between the author's personal experiences and his work. Diodorus grew up in the Sicilian town of Agyrium, lived in Egypt from about 60 to 56 B.C., and then resided in Rome from about 56 to at least 30 B.C., during which period he researched and wrote the *Bibliotheke*. These were violent times that brought an end to the Republic and turned Italy and the provinces alike into battlefields; Diodorus's homeland of Sicily suffered especially. Such experiences inevitably condition a writer's outlook. Although most Greek emigrants, anxious to be part of the new order, praised Rome, Diodorus often cast the imperial power in a worse light by slanting the narrative of his sources. Fear and animosity also

influenced the structure of his work. Diodorus eventually decided to avoid treating events that occurred between 60 and 46
B.C., instead offering oblique judgments in narrating earlier
periods. From his use of historiographical conventions, to his
development of broad themes, to his shaping of the *Bibliotheke*
in response to contemporary politics, it is apparent that Diodorus had far more control over his work than is generally
assumed.

ANY investigation of the *Bibliotheke* requires an initial decision about *Quellenforschung*. After more than a century of attempting to define Diodorus's sources,[7] a good deal of progress has been made, but not much of it has come recently.
There are parts of the *Bibliotheke*—for example, book xvi and
much of the Sicilian material—for which it appears there will
never be general agreement. The demonstration that Diodorus has smoothed over different accounts with his own style
of writing[8] and the present attempt to show that he has infused
the work with his own thoughts make the future identification
of sources all the more difficult. This book as much as possible
avoids the practice of *Quellenforschung*. The emphasis here is
not on discovering which particular traditions he followed,
but on demonstrating that at specific moments Diodorus
must have written independently of all of them. Consequently, the most probable source behind a given passage, as
agreed on by most scholars, is accepted in order to show that
thoughts found there also occur in parts of the *Bibliotheke* in
which scholars have identified another tradition. Or again, a
suspected source is noted if there exists material from that historian outside of what is preserved in the *Bibliotheke* that
might illuminate Diodorus's method of composition. But the

---

[7] Volquardsen's *Untersuchungen über die Quellen der griechischen und sicilischen
Geschichten*, published in 1868, is the watershed in modern *Quellenforschung* of
Diodorus, but even he was responding to work of the previous century: see
his p. 2, n. 1.

[8] Palm, *Über Sprache und Stil*, was partially anticipated, however, in methodology and findings by Neubert, *Spuren selbständiger Thätigkeit bei Diodor*.

practice of determining Diodorus's source by comparing the alleged *Tendenz* of the *Bibliotheke* with the hypothetical *Tendenz* of the suspected source is generally sterile. Of many of the works Diodorus might have used, very little survives outside of what is supposedly found in the *Bibliotheke*. Until that fact is faced, source investigation of Diodorus will grow increasingly obscure.

Finally, a word about translations. Translations are commentaries. To use one's own renderings is to run the risk of altering the evidence in one's favor. Wherever possible the standard Loeb translation is employed, with the translator's name given in parentheses; any changes from that version are noted alongside the citation.

ONE

Prooemia

ALL STUDIES of Diodorus have been dominated implicitly or explicitly by the overarching concern to identify the sources behind the *Bibliotheke*. Still influenced by nineteenth-century methodology, scholars believe that Diodorus followed previous histories so closely that through diligent inquiry the original authors can usually be identified. Plagiarism, too strong a term in its modern sense to use in judging ancient practices,[1] is, in fact, the word customarily applied to Diodorus's method of composition.[2] In particular, the prefaces to the individual books of the *Bibliotheke* are mechanically ascribed to Diodorus's sources. With few exceptions (books ii, iii, and xi have only tables of contents), every completely extant book of the *Bibliotheke* contains a full prooemium, as do a few of the only partially preserved books. The proems generally concern either moral and didactic questions pertaining to the books they introduce[3] or historiographical questions.[4] Rich in pronouncements on history and philosophy, the prologues contain some of the most important nonnarrative material in the *Bibliotheke*. A study of the prooemia is an appropriate place to begin examining the degree of Diodorus's own invention.[5]

[1] See M. Hadot, *Leçon inaugurale*, 34.

[2] E.g., S. Mazzarino, *Il pensiero storico classico* I, 322.

[3] Those to books i, xii, xiii, xiv, xv, xviii, xix, xxi, xxv, xxvi, xxxii, and xxxvii.

[4] Proems to i, iv, v, xvi, xvii, and xx; from M. Kunz, *Zur Beurteilung der Prooemien in Diodors historischer Bibliothek*, 41, with modifications. The proem to book xxvi is only Diodorus's acknowledgment that his *Bibliotheke* thus far may not have found favor with everyone. There is no certain proem to xxxii, but it is perhaps chaps. 2 and 4; on which see my Chapter 2. The prologue to xx is considered in Chapter 4.

[5] Much of the following is a revision of K. Sacks, *Hermes* 110 (1981), 434–

9

The proem to book i is the longest passage in the extent *Bibliotheke* in which are found discourses on the nature of history and history writing. Much of it must certainly be Diodorus's own creation, for it includes a discussion of the efforts required in composing his work and the resources available to him (4.1–5), a brief outline of events contained within (4.6–5.1), and the argument that the summary of contents is intended to discourage the cannibalization of work by others (5.2). All of this pertains to his work specifically. The authorship of the first part of the proem, containing discussions of a general nature, is, however, more open to question. It begins with a praise of history and historians, particularly universal historians: history teaches by vicarious experience (1.1–5); historians (of universal histories) reflect Divine Providence, which has been moving toward a commonality of mankind (1.3); and history, by judging historical figures, can affect future actions (1.5, 2.1–5). It concludes with a chapter devoted to the advantages of the genre of universal history (3.1–8).

As early as 1746, Wesseling, noting the correspondence between certain of these sentiments and material in Polybius, suggested that Diodorus drew his material from that historian.[6] While Polybius long remained a favorite candidate for much of Diodorus's main proem,[7] the case was also frequently made for Ephorus and Posidonius.[8] Echoes of various Hellenistic philosophies are certainly evident in the *Bibliotheke*; still,

---

41; permission by the editors of *Hermes* for its inclusion is here gratefully acknowledged.

[6] As discussed by Hornblower, *Hieronymus of Cardia*, 19. The best edition of Wesseling's great commentary is the 1793 reprint by Eyring, *Diodori Siculi Bibliothecae Historicae Libri*, which incorporates (and identifies) the comments of Wesseling and others.

[7] Kunz, *Zur Beurteilung der Prooemien*, 73–82. Hornblower's (*Hieronymus of Cardia*, 25, n. 28) list of parallel sentiments in Diodorus's first prooemium and in Polybius contains some inappropriate comparisons.

[8] Ephorus: R. Laqueur, *Hermes* 46 (1911), 161–66; Jacoby, *FGH* IIc, 43; G. Barber, *The Historian Ephorus*, 70. Posidonius: see discussion in R. Laqueur, *Hermes* 86 (1958), 289; most recently, J. Malitz, *Die Historien des Poseidonios*, 412–16.

the past few decades have witnessed a growing realization that a specific and direct influence is impossible to identify. Diodorus may have drawn on one or several historians for inspiration, but modern authorities now generally concede that the substance of the prooemium is his own.[9] The shift in opinion has come about because, once scholars put aside the belief that Diodorus could not possibly have taken the trouble nor had the talent to compose the main prooemium, they discovered, through study of syntax and vocabulary, that indeed he must be its author. The language is representative of the late Hellenistic period[10] and, therefore, generally similar in vocabulary to that of the rest of the *Bibliotheke*.[11] Numerous phrases of philosophical import found in the proem are echoed throughout the *Bibliotheke*,[12] and, it will be argued in Chapter 3, the central points of the proem establish the most significant tenets of Diodorus's historiography. Although scholars remain heavily influenced by the belief that Diodorus is merely a compiler, investigation into the authorship of this prologue has suggested differently.

[9] Kunz herself paved the way here (*Zur Beurteilung der Prooemien*, 73–82), but acceptance came slowly. See now Palm, *Über Sprache und Stil*, 139ff.; A. Nock, *JRS* 49 (1959), 4–5 = Nock, *Essays* II, 860; R. Drews, *AJP* 83 (1962), 383, n. 3; A. Burton, *Diodorus Siculus Book I: A Commentary*, 35–38; Hornblower, *Hieronymus of Cardia*, 24–26; C. Fornara, *The Nature of History in Ancient Greece and Rome*, 116, n. 35; most completely discussed by M. Pavan, *RAL* 16 (1961), 19–52. Laqueur, in *Hermes* 46 (1911), 161–62, originally argued for Ephorus, but a half-century later claimed only that i 1.3 is Posidonian (*Hermes* 86 [1958], 209); on the passage, see Chapter 5, n. 1.

[10] Hornblower, *Hieronymus of Cardia*, 263–66.

[11] Palm, *Über Sprache und Stil*.

[12] E.g., ἅπαντα τὸν αἰῶνα: i 1.3, 2.3; xviii 59.6; history as προφῆτις τῆς ἀληθείας: i 2.2 and xxi 17.4; cf. Dion. Hal., *Thuc.* 8.334 (ἱέρεια τῆς ἀληθείας); μητρόπολις: i 2.2; xxi 1.1; xxv 1 (on which, see later in this chapter); ὠφελῆσαι τὸν κοινὸν βίον: i 1.1, 8.8, 15.9, 20.3; 87.1; ii 38.5; iv 64.1; v 64.1; x 12.1; xxxi 15.1; similarly: i 2.1–2, 13.5; iv 1.5, xxvii 18.2; on its Stoic antecedents, see W. Spoerri, *Späthellenistische Berichte über Welt, Kultur und Götter: Untersuchungen zu Diodor von Sizilien*, 194, n. 30; διὰ τῆς δόξης ἀθαντισμῷ: i 1.5; xv 1.1; μεσολαβηθέντες τὸν βίον ὑπὸ τῆς πεπρωμένης: i 3.2; xi 26.8; xvi 1; cf. xii 29: from Neubert, *Spuren selbständiger Thätigkeit bei Diodor*, 4, n. 22.

11

If the main prooemium to the *Bibliotheke* is finally being attributed to Diodorus, the proem to book xxxvii—frequently termed the "second main prooemium" because of its length and the obvious energy Diodorus puts into it—has long been considered his work. An introduction to the Italian Social War, it compares that conflict with the preceding wars of Greco-Roman history in order to show its magnitude. The proem is customarily attributed to Diodorus because it is thought that its arguments are too specious to have been composed by Posidonius, who is the source for the narrative part of that book.[13] For example, the assertion that the Italian Social War was the greatest conflict of all time is crude and embarrassingly reminiscent of Thucydides' opening remarks. But a better reason for attributing the proem to Diodorus is the similarity of sentiment between it and other parts of the *Bibliotheke* in which Diodorus is not following the account of Posidonius.[14] And in the references to Gelon's great victory over the Carthaginians in 480, all three figures for troops, ships, and casualties accord perfectly with Diodorus's earlier description of the event in book xi.[15]

It is for the other prooemia that the question of authorship remains unresolved. In nearly every instance, the notion persists that Diodorus copied these passages from the historians on whose narrative material he was also drawing. The charge of plagiarism rests substantially on Diodorus's use of the fourth-century historian, Ephorus of Cyme. Writing a history of Greeks and barbarians, from just after the Trojan War to around 340 B.C.,[16] Ephorus composed what may be called the first universal history.[17] Within that tradition of universal-his-

---

[13] See Chapter 5.

[14] Cf. xxxvii 1.6 with passages in Chapter 2, n. 66.

[15] xi 20.2–4, thought to be Timaean: K. Meister, "Die sizilische Geschichte bei Diodor von den Anfängen bis zum Tod des Agathokles: Quellenuntersuchungen zu Buch IV–XXI," 42–44; Jacoby, *FGH* IIc, 88.

[16] Jacoby *FGH* IIc, 24, 28–29, and Drews, *AJP* 83 (1962), 389.

[17] Polybius v 33.2; cf. Diodorus iv 1.2, v 1.4. Jacoby, *FGH* IIc, 22–23,

tory writing stand Diodorus and some of his most important sources: Posidonius, Polybius, and Agatharchides. Ephorus is Diodorus's main source for books xi–xv and, it is often argued, a source for book xvi.[18] Because Diodorus seems to have followed him closely in constructing much of the narrative of these books, it is assumed that he also used the Cymean for the prooemia to these same books. And because Ephorus wrote an epideictic prooemium for each book of his thirty-volume world history,[19] Diodorus could have drawn on many of those prologues when he was writing on a period not covered by Ephorus. Even in cases where the prooemia do not seem to be the work of Ephorus, Diodorus might still have been inspired by Ephoran material or practice.[20]

The attribution to Ephorus of most of the *Bibliotheke*'s proems is an extreme version of early source criticism. A subtler interpretation is that Diodorus took the prooemia not solely from Ephorus, but from any of the various sources he used throughout the *Bibliotheke*. This random procedure created contradictions between the narrative of a book, which might be based on one tradition, and its prooemium, which could be taken from another source detailing different events.[21] This hypothesis has proved particularly influential and needs to be tested first.

The prooemia that supposedly involve the most flagrant

---

agrees with Polybius's assessment. For an analysis of the Polybian passage, see K. Sacks, *Polybius on the Writing of History*, 96–110.

[18] Beginning with Volquardsen, *Untersuchungen über die Quellen der griechischen und sicilischen Geschichten*. On the Sicilian material see esp. Meister, "Die sizilische Geschichte"; on book xvi, see most recently, M. Sordi, *Diodori Siculi Bibliothecae liber sextus decimus*. The attempts to attribute the Sicilian material to the intermediary Silenus are aptly criticized by F. Walbank, *Kokalos* 14–15 (1968–1969), 476–98.

[19] *FGH* 70 T 10 = DS xvi 76.5; cf. T 23 = Polybius xii 28.10.

[20] Originally proposed by Laqueur, *Hermes* 46 (1911), 204–6; supported most recently by W. Theiler, *Poseidonios: Die Fragmente* II, 85.

[21] Originally argued by Kunz, *Zur Beurteilung der Prooemien*, 37–39; most recently by Fornara, *The Nature of History*, 116, n. 35. Others noted in Sordi, *Diodori Siculi Bibliothecae liber sextus decimus* xv, n. 4.

contradictions with their narratives are those to books xvi and xvii, books that contain the lives of Philip II and Alexander the Great respectively. It is argued that the proems promise that the books they introduce will contain material that is not in fact found there. Consequently, Diodorus must have drawn his prooemia from a different source than that from which he took his narrative.[22]

Book xvi begins:

> In all historical expositions it is incumbent upon the historian to include in his books events about cities or kings that are αὐτοτελεῖς from beginning to end. . . . For events that are ἡμιτελεῖς and are not continuous from their beginnings to their conclusion interrupt the attention of avid readers; but actions [that are αὐτοτελεῖς], encompassing a continuity of narrative up to the conclusion, achieve a complete exposition of events. Whenever the very nature of the events cooperates with the historian, then most of all he must not deviate in any way from this principle. For this reason, we too, arriving at the actions of Philip of Amyntas, shall try to include the deeds performed by this king within the present book. (xvi 1.1–3; my translation)

To many, this proem suggests that the life of Philip and, whenever possible, all other single, self-contained themes should be the lone subjects (αὐτοτελεῖς) of entire books, to the exclusion of all other material. Because the narrative of book xvi does include material that has nothing to do with Philip, Diodorus would then be guilty of a contradiction. This would reflect Diodorus's practice of mechanically copying the prooemium from one source and his narrative from another.

Such an interpretation, however, rests on a misunderstanding of the term αὐτοτελεῖς. Rather than suggesting events that preclude the detailing of other material, it describes events with well-defined end points—that is, ones that can be

---

[22] Kunz, *Zur Beurteilung der Prooemien*, 88–89, 100.

told completely in a single book. Diodorus uses the term that way in the prooemium to book i,[23] and here he states that the historian should not deviate from the principle "whenever the very nature of the events cooperates with the historian." Any material could, of course, be narrated continuously and without interruption, if the author so chose. Consequently, the notion of events that lend themselves to being αὐτοτελεῖς must mean something else. And when Diodorus concludes with his promise to "try to include the deeds performed by this king within the present book," it is clear that he has in mind stories that are brought to completion within one book. In that way, the reader can appreciate the full significance of Philip, whose life begins with the proem and ends with the conclusion of the book. Elsewhere Diodorus indicates that synchronized events are included within the αὐτοτελεῖς deeds of that monarch. At the very end of book xv, in a passage demonstrably of Diodorus's own composition,[24] he announces that in the next book he will include "all the achievements of [Philip] until his death, encompassing also the other events in the known parts of the world" (xv 95.4); and the beginning of book xvii (1.1) confirms that he had accomplished his plan. It seems certain that Diodorus, at least, thought that the proem to xvi was consistent with the narrative contents of that book.[25]

[23] Diodorus states that nonuniversal historians have written about ἑνὸς ἔθνος ἢ μιᾶς πόλεως αὐτοτελεῖς πολέμους. Because ἑνός and μιᾶς already indicate exclusivity, αὐτοτελεῖς must mean something else. These writers of αὐτοτελεῖς events are juxtaposed to universal historians, who record the κοιναὶ πράξεις from the earliest times down to their own day (i 3.2); thus accounts of αὐτοτελεῖς wars are contrasted with histories of unlimited expanse and time; cf. Wesseling in Eyring, *Diodori Siculi Bibliothecae Historicae Libri* (i, 299). Note also the force of αὐτοτελεῖς at i 10.7, but at xii 1.1 it does suggest exclusively, where it is an echo of a philosophical sentiment: cf. Plato, *Phaedrus* 250c, with the similar use of ὁλόκληρον. Dionysius of Halicarnassus uses ἡμιτελεῖς twice within a similar context to mean "half-completed" (*Thuc.* 9.337).

[24] See Laqueur, *Hermes* 86 (1958), 281–85.

[25] Sordi, *Diodori Siculi Bibliothecae liber sextus decimus*, xiv–xxii, like Laqueur and others, argues for Ephorus, or at least for his son and continuator, Demophilus, as the original source behind the proem to book xvi on the basis

The second important contradiction between prooemium and narrative involves the opposite organizational philosophy. In the prologue to book xvii, Diodorus promises to include the life of Alexander the Great, from his accession to his death, but also contemporaneous events occurring throughout the known world (xvii 1.2). Yet, in the narrative of book xvii Diodorus includes only the events surrounding Alexander, leaving aside the usual coverage of Sicily and Italy. Thus again Diodorus is alleged to have drawn his proem and his narrative from different sources.[26] Such a contradiction, admittedly present, pales, however, in light of Diodorus's general practice in the selection of material for his history. The approximate number of chapters devoted to the various spheres of interest in each of Diodorus's completely extant historical books is given in Table 1. Egyptian and Persian affairs are included with the Greek category, as the events re-

TABLE I

SPHERES OF INTEREST BY CHAPTER IN
DIODORUS'S *BIBLIOTHEKE*, BOOKS XI–XX

Book	Greece		Sicily	Roman Italy
xi	68.5		22.5	1
xii	56.5	4[a]	17	6.5
xiii	43.5	33[a]	37.5	b
xiv	45.5		62.5	7
xv	83		8	b
xvi	69.5		25.5	b
xvii	117		none	none
xviii	74		none	none
xix	85.5		19.5	4
xx	52		52	7

[a] Chapters on the Athenian invasion of Sicily.

[b] Indicates brief allusions of a few lines to consular elections.

that they are Diodorus's source(s) for the narrative. But see R. Drews, *AJP* 84 (1963), 251–52, and Sacks, *Polybius*, 115, n. 42. The argument that Diodorus took his prooemia from Ephorus will be discussed.

[26] Kunz, *Zur Beurteilung der Prooemien*, 100.

corded inevitably affected Greece, and the chapters concerning Greek Italy alone or the Sicilian invasions of Italy are listed under Sicilian affairs. As the table shows, until the third century, Rome held little interest for Diodorus (see also Chapter 5). Additionally, Diodorus tended to include Sicilian affairs only at sensational moments: the material in xiii–xiv (excepting the Athenian expedition) pertains to the Carthaginian invasion, accompanied by the rise of the tyrant Dionysius; book xvi contains the exploits of Dion and Timoleon; and books xix and xx refer to events surrounding Agathocles. Only in book xi and the first part of book xii does Diodorus attempt a more synchronic account, recording Sicilian material that lacks a central theme. Otherwise, as in book xv, he virtually ignores Sicily.

Now Diodorus deals exclusively with Greek affairs not only in book xvii, but also in book xviii (perhaps acknowledged at xviii 1.5). He returns to Sicilian events at the beginning of xix, when he reviews the early life of Agathocles. Possibly Diodorus began book xvii as he did xvi, intending to include a central and completed character, but also other nonrelated material. In fact, xvii begins with Alexander's accession, rather than his boyhood, indicating that Diodorus thought of it as a history of a period rather than a complete biography of the Macedonian.[27] But as he notes, Alexander conquered much of Europe and nearly all of Asia.[28] And, as it turned out, aside from what concerned Alexander and mainland Greece, nothing of note occurred in the period covered by book xvii, the same being the case for the *diadochoi* and book xviii.[29]

[27] Though Diodorus probably is following Cleitarchus, who began his work with the accession of Alexander (Jacoby, *FGH* IIb, 484–85; for the current state of the question, see A. Bosworth, *From Arrian to Alexander: Studies in Historical Interpretation*, 7–13), Diodorus could have drawn on another source for Alexander's early years. Diodorus discusses Macedonian genealogy down to Alexander at vii 15.

[28] xvii 1.4, 113.1–2, 117.5.

[29] Unlike Arrian, Plutarch, and Justin/Trogus, Diodorus moves from the

There may be an even simpler explanation. Twice at the beginning of book xix (3.3, 10.3), Diodorus alludes to his discussion of Syracusan and Italian affairs in the previous book. Book xviii, however, contains no material at all on Sicily or Italy. Some believe that the references in xix were in Diodorus's source, which he mindlessly copied into his own narrative. But, compared with other contemporary authors, Diodorus was especially precise with his cross-references, and allusions to earlier discussions in the *Bibliotheke* are nearly always accurate. More likely, then, book xviii originally contained material on Sicily and Italy, which Diodorus later eliminated, forgetting at the same time to remove the references in book xix.[30] The same might be the case for book xvii, where the prooemium refers to material in the narrative that may later have been excised.[31]

Contradictions between prooemia and narrative, then, do not prove Diodorus's dependence on various sources. The other, more long-standing theory is that Diodorus took most or all of his prologues from Ephorus alone. Yet even in those books for which Ephorus is his main source, such an attribu-

---

figure of Alexander to events in mainland Greece, consciously dividing his narrative to cover affairs of both theaters: e.g., xvii 5.1, 5.3, 47.6, 63.5, 73.4–5, 83.3–4, 108.3–4, 111.1. Consequently, he preserves important details found nowhere else, such as those concerning Agis's war against Antipater, the decree for the return of the exiles, and Harpalus's flight.

[30] Discussed in Chapter 4, pp. 88–91.

[31] Kunz, *Zur Beurteilung der Prooemien*, 100–1, suggests another major contradiction in the proem to book v, where Diodorus announces that whenever possible he will organize each book κατὰ γένος (v 1.4)—that is, by geography: Drews, *AJP* 84 (1963), 244–55, and *Hermes* 104 (1976), 497–98; cf. G. Schepens, "Historiographical Problems in Ephorus," in *Historiographia antiqua: commentationes Lovanienses in honorem W. Peremans Septuagenarii editae*, 116. Although keeping to this method in the first six books (see Chapter 3), he subsequently treats material annalistically. There is no contradiction: when recounting myths in the first six books, he acknowledges the difficulty in establishing a relative chronology for these disparate stories (i 5.1, 9.2–4; iv 1.1; xl 8), so the κατὰ γένος approach proves better here. Later, he turns to a different approach. The sentiments of v 1.3 are echoed at xxi 17.1, on which see Chapter 4.

tion of proems is far from certain. No one should want to claim credit for the proem to xii. In introducing a book that covers the *Pentekontaetia*, the author includes among the most illustrious men of that extraordinary half-century Aristotle, Isocrates, and his students (xii 1.5). It is doubtful whether Ephorus, a fourth-century historian who may well have been Isocrates' student (see Chapter 2), would have written this. Indeed, in the later narrative for the year 366/5, for which Ephorus is almost certainly the source, the place of Isocrates, his disciples, and Aristotle is put correctly (xv 76.4). Moreover the theme of παράδοξον, on which this proem is based, pervades the *Bibliotheke* and may be Diodorus's own sentiment.[32]

The prooemium to book xiii, attributed to Ephorus, contradicts Ephoran methodology. Its author asserts that the practice of writing long prooemia is incompatible with his attempt to include as much factual information as possible within each book. Since Ephorus was famous for his elegant prooemia, as Diodorus testifies,[33] it is doubtful whether he composed the statement. If anything, the proem to xiii may be a polemic against Ephorus.

Finally, the ascription to Ephorus of the prologues to books xiv and xv faces a major hurdle: both prooemia discuss and moralize on combinations of events found in their respective books, although in Ephorus's work these events were spread throughout many different books. For example, the prooemium to xiv declares that the actions of the Thirty Tyrants of Athens and the life of Dionysius I confirm the author's sentiments on tyranny; these events of Athens and Sicily are naturally contained within book xiv of the *Bibliotheke*, but were not so combined in Ephorus's work.[34] Moreover, the senti-

---

[32] See Chapter 2. Kunz, *Zur Beurteilung der Prooemien*, 85–87 and 104–6, attributes the proem to Agatharchides. But for this period, Diodorus does not use Agatharchides, whose work mainly concerns the Hellenistic period (*FGH* IIc, 150–51).

[33] *FGH* 70 T 10 = DS xvi 76.5; T 23 = Polybius xii 28.10.

[34] R. Drews, "Historiographical Objectives and Procedures of Diodorus

ment found in the prooemium to xiv—that ruling states that treat their subjects unjustly risk losing their empires (xiv 2.1)—is part of a model for empire found throughout the Bibliotheke and attributable to Diodorus himself (see Chapter 2). And the first sentence of the prologue to book xv, that the author has been employing frank speech (παρρησία) for the betterment of society, is also a Diodoran topos.[35] The argument that Diodorus took from Ephorus the prooemia for the books in which he employs Ephorus as his main source, xi–xv, is the bedrock of all arguments that Diodorus plagiarized his proems. It should now be apparent that it has little force—a finding that has profound significance for the study of Diodorus. For, if Diodorus, while largely basing his narrative of books xi–xv on Ephorus, did not draw his prooemia from him as well, the logical conclusion is that Diodorus created these passages himself.[36] The examination of a few other prologues will indicate that it is best to attribute these also to Diodorus.

In the proem to xxi, Diodorus states that πλεονεξία is the μητρόπολις . . . τῶν ἀδικημάτων, and in the introduction to book xxv, after paraphrasing Epicurus concerning the virtues of a just life, Diodorus goes on to declare that ἀδικία is the μητρόπολις τῶν κακῶν. Μητρόπολις is also found in the opening prooemium, where Diodorus refers to history as the mother-

Siculus," 113–16. Neubert, Spuren selbständiger Thätigkeit bei Diodor, 7, shows the general thematic connections between Diodorus's proems and their respective books. Laqueur himself became more circumspect about the attribution to Ephorus of the proem to xiv, later suggesting only that Ephorus was the "inspiration" (Hermes 86 [1958], 285). See also Pavan, RAL 16 (1961), 117–25, for a defense of the proem to xv as Diodorus's own work.

[35] See Chapter 2, pp. 33–35.

[36] Two other prooemia attributed to Ephorus can quickly be disposed of. For that to book xviii, see Hornblower, Hieronymus of Cardia, 61–62, with n. 141, for a congruence of vocabulary between the proem and the rest of the Bibliotheke, and Pavan, RAL 16 (1961), 141–43, for a congruence of thought. For the prologue to xix, the arguments about democracy (1.1–8) are also found at xv 58.1 and xxv 8; and the theme is stressed in the narrative of the same book (xix 5–10), regarding events occurring well after the death of Ephorus. The proem to book xx is discussed in the section on speeches in Chapter 4.

city of philosophy (i 2.2). The metaphoric use of μητρόπολις is quite rare, occurring outside of Diodorus only in philosophical literature.[37] Because Agatharchides is thought to have been influenced by Epicurus,[38] and because Diodorus in the early books of the *Bibliotheke* used Agatharchides,[39] it has been suggested that Diodorus must have been following Agatharchides for the prooemia to i, xxi, and xxv.[40] But the sentiment that greed is the root of evil in the prologue to xxi (1.4a) has led to a different identification. As the term πλεονεξία is also found within surrounding material for which Diodorus follows Hieronymus of Cardia, the proem to xxi has been treated as Hieronymus's creation.[41]

Both arguments show the extreme of *Quellenforschung* in analyzing the *Bibliotheke*. The word πλεονεξία is thematic to Diodorus's work, occurring nearly fifty times, of which in only seven instances Hieronymus could have been the source. It is a term Diodorus demonstrably employs on his own.[42] Nor is the incidence of μητρόπολις indicative of "plagiarism" from Agatharchides. In the opening prooemium, μητρόπολις is used in a positive context; in the prologues to xxi and xxv it is connected with evil. In xxi 4a.1, greed brings great misfortunes to private citizens and even to great kings; in xxv 1 injustice brings misfortunes to private citizens and collectively on nations and kings. The proems are meant to establish themes for the subsequent narrative, as they frequently do in the *Bibliotheke*. The prologue to xxi assuredly connects with the greed of Antigonus and the impieties of Agathocles, which cause their deaths (xxi 1, 16.5); that of xxv anticipates Carthaginian misdeeds in the Mercenary War that lead to the defeat in the Second Punic War (xxv 2–3). And the idea that personal greed can bring destruction on an entire people re-

---

[37] See Kunz, *Zur Beurteilung der Prooemien*, 92–93.

[38] Most recently, P. Fraser, *Ptolemaic Alexandria* I, 547; but Peripatetic influence is frequently noted: e.g., *FGH* IIc, 151.

[39] Schwartz, *RE* 5, 670–73.

[40] Kunz, *Zur Beurteilung der Prooemien*, 104–5.

[41] Hornblower, *Hieronymus of Cardia*, 50, n. 104.

[42] See my comments at the end of Chapter 5.

curs in the history. Although he generally follows Posidonius for the late Republic, in discussing the death of Marius Diodorus departs from the tradition preserved by the Apamean.[43] He concludes with an extended argument that personal greed can bring collective destruction, in this case to the Italian peoples (xxxvii 29.4–30.1). Thus the sentiments expressed in the prooemia are consistent with material found within their respective books and elsewhere in the *Bibliotheke* as well.

The entire question of intellectual influence upon Diodorus has been prejudiced by early presumptions. By the middle of the past century, the now-standard case was made that books xi–xv represented not just the substance but the spirit as well of Ephorus's treatment of classical Greece.[44] The thesis is demonstrably incorrect (see Chapter 2), and the most that can be said is that Diodorus *may* have been influenced by Ephoran practice. The same should hold true for the prooemia. When Diodorus puts into his own words[45] and introduces by his own volition discussions of historiography and philosophy within his prooemia, the influence of his sources may occasionally be discernible, but Diodorus's own contribution is certainly far greater than mere plagiarism. The practice of creating prooemia for narrative became widespread in the first century,[46] and Diodorus may well have been influenced by contemporary practice. In the absense of any proof of direct copying, all that can be asserted is that some of Diodorus's thoughts were possibly influenced by the sources he employed.

---

[43] xxxvii 29.4: death by suicide, rather than pleurisy: Plut. *Mar.* 45.4 = *FGH* 87 (Posidonius) F 37; cf. Pavan, *RAL* 16 (1961), 146–47.

[44] Above, n. 18.

[45] In his study of Diodorus's style, Palm, *Über Sprache und Stil*, throughout sees the prooemia as consistent with the narrative in syntax and vocabulary: e.g., pp. 152 (xii), 149 and 154 (xv), 131 and 150 (xvi), 128 (xviii), 154 (xx).

[46] Hornblower, *Hieronymus of Cardia*, 26. Even Herodotus used the prooemium as more than just a main introduction, for he gives a proem to his Egyptian digression: ii 64; cf. H. Immerwahr, *Form and Thought in Herodotus*, 80.

TWO

Themes in Historical Causality

THREE important forces or historical patterns help to shape Diodorus's narrative: benefit, chance, and the decline of empires. As with his prooemia, it is usually argued that Diodorus simply took these ideas from his sources without considering their contemporary relevance or internal consistencies. Yet these concepts pervade the *Bibliotheke*, providing thematic unity and structure. A reexamination of the concept of benefit will show that Diodorus has imposed his own beliefs in stating the principle that history can be useful to its readers. The role of chance and the theory of the decline of empires are then considered, with similar results emerging. Although Diodorus may have drawn on his sources in presenting these themes, he has modified or enlarged them to fit his own notions of history writing.

By the Hellenistic period, the most prominent justification for writing history was the bestowal of benefit (ὠφέλεια) or utility (τὸ χρήσιμον) on the reader. The first indication that Greek historiography was to be didactic is perhaps found in Herodotus's pervasive theme of arrogance and retribution, but Herodotus nowhere states outright that his aim is to warn the reader against folly. Thucydides actually discusses ὠφέλεια in his passage on methodology (i 22.4) and by implication in his description of the plague (ii 48.3); yet his precise intent is also somewhat vague. Sometime between Thucydides and the later Hellenistic authors, however, the notion grew that historians had to justify their narrative by the benefit afforded the reader.[1] Absent in Xenophon's *Hellenica*, though implicit within his *Cyropaedia* and *Agesilaus*, utility plays a prominent role in the stated theories of all three Hellenistic historians whose works are substantially extant: Polybius, Diodorus, and Dionysius of Halicarnassus. Benefit holds center stage in the *Bibliotheke*, and, for the past century, the consensus has been firm that the notion of moral benefit was taken nearly in its entirety from Diodorus's main source for the classical period, Ephorus.

In discussing the nature of benefit, perhaps what should be stated first is the interpretation not found in Diodorus. Polybius, Dionysius of Halicarnassus, and possibly Thucydides believe that history can be of use in supplying facts and their causes, so that the student of history can perhaps learn to avoid the mistakes and imitate the successes of the past.[2] The historian does not aim at influencing future behavior, but merely hopes that the reader will find the knowledge useful in his own life.

Diodorus, however, desires to improve the moral attitudes of his clientele, pronouncing frequently in his work that:

> I shall make mention of certain men to serve as models, both because they merit my praise and for the good it

[1] For the ancient testimony and discussion, see G. Avenarius, *Lukians Schrift zur Geschichtsschreibung*, 22–26, and P. Scheller, *De Hellenistica Historiae Conscribendae Arte*, 73–83.

[2] On the difficulties in Thuc. i 22.4, see W. Pritchett, *Dionysius of Halicarnassus: On Thucydides*, 72–73, n. 9, and A. Parry, "Logos and Ergon in Thucydides," 103–13. On Polybius, see Sacks, *Polybius*, 133–44; of the numerous references to utility in Polybius, only one seems to refer unambiguously to moral utility: xxiii 14.12. On Polybius x 21.2–4, see F. Walbank, *JHS* 105 (1985), 211. A useful episode for contrasting Diodorus's and Polybius's perceptions of ὠφέλεια is Polybius i 35 and DS xxiii 15; cf. Walbank, *Commentary* I, 93. On Dionysius, see *AR* v 56.1 and esp. xi 1.4–5. These historians may praise and condemn particular figures (see, e.g., Scheller, *De Hellenistica Historiae Conscribendae Arte*, 74–76; Sacks, *Polybius*, 133–36; F. Walbank, *Polybius*, 91–96), but there is little indication that amid these judgments and character sketches their aim was to improve the reader morally. An example from the Latin side is Livy, in theory (*praef.* 10) and practice (e.g., xxvii 8.4–10).

does to society, in order that the denunciations of History may lead the wicked to turn from their evil course, and the praises that its enduring glory confers may persuade the good to aspire to high standards of conduct.[3]

For Diodorus, history tries to modify the behavior of the reader and influence the future. Diodorus is not concerned with improving the general's strategic skills and the politician's powers of diplomacy. Rather, the historian encourages the noble deeds of all peoples through the emphasis on civic virtue.[4] Not so much practical, Diodorus's notion of judging a historical figure with the hope of urging readers toward better lives can be termed "moral utility."[5] For Diodorus, benefit is much more than a mere consequence of studying the historical narrative: it is an active force that Clio directs at her readers. History, according to Diodorus, has the responsibility to act as moral suasion, condemning the worst in people and encouraging the best. Consequently, it is the duty of historians to allow Clio to speak through the historical narrative for the betterment of humanity.

Ephorus, through the influence of Isocrates, is usually credited with introducing moral utility into history writing. As part of effective style, Isocrates filled his set speeches with moral judgments in the form of praise and condemnation. Whether Ephorus was actually Isocrates' student is not certain; but it is clear that Ephorus was very much in the orator's

---

[3] xxxvii 4 (Walton). Similarly, e.g., i 1; ii 2.1–2; x 12; xi 38.5–6; xxiii 15.1; xxxi 15.1; xxxviii/xxxix 18.1.

[4] E.g, i 1.1–5. Compare this, or e.g., x 12, to Polybius, ix 9.9–10, who says that his praise is intended to extol practical successes and implies that it is aimed at political leaders, not readers generally.

[5] At times, Diodorus discusses only the act of judging: e.g., xi 11.2, 46.1, 59.4, 82; xiii 35.5; xiv 1.1; xv 81.1–4, 88.1; xviii 38.4; xx 1.2; xxvi 24.2; and xxxvii 7. At other times he includes his hope of future moral improvement: e.g., i 1.5, 2, 93; x 12; xi 3.1; xv 1; xx 2.2; xxiii 15; xxx 15; xxxii 26; xxxvii 3; xxxviii/xxxix 18. The two ideas are related in Diodorus, but can also be independent: Avenarius, *Lukians Schrift zur Geschichtsschreibung*, 22–26, 157–63.

intellectual debt.[6] Consequently, it appears that at least to some degree the moralizing tendency developed by Isocrates was in turn adopted by Ephorus.[7]

Now the *Bibliotheke* is filled with sentiments of moral utility. Because Diodorus uses Ephorus extensively, it is naturally assumed that he drew the notion of moral utility with its ethical assessments from the Cymaean. Certainly Ephorus was the main source for much of the material in the *Bibliotheke* where such assessments are found. Outside controls of existing Ephoran material, including a papyrus fragment[8] and other short quotations, make it clear that Diodorus employed Ephorus as one of many sources for the archaic period of Greek history[9] and then began using him as the primary source for factual information in his narrative of classical Greece to 340.[10] Determining how much Diodorus drew on

[6] Schwartz (*RE* 6, 1–2) sought to disprove the tradition of Ephorus as student of Isocrates, but he is not wholly convincing: see Jacoby, *FGH* IIc, 22–23. For testimony and discussion, see Barber, *The Historian Ephorus*, 3f.

[7] The ancient testimony to Ephorus's writing style is contradictory: Ephorus's style is like that of Isocrates (*FGH* 70 TT 24a and b); it is similar to Theopompus's wordy style (TT 21, 25, and 26); it is, in contrast to Theopompus's, clear (TT 28a and b; cf. T 22). Yet, contra Fornara, *The Nature of History*, 109–12, and Drews, "Historiographical Objectives," 118–19, Ephorus employed paradigms: Polybius xii 28.10 refers to Ephorus's ἐπιμετροῦντες λόγοι (on which, see Sacks, *Polybius*, 142, n. 44), and excerpts of Ephorus's history were collected in imperial times and entitled Περὶ ἀγαθῶν καὶ κακῶν (cf. Schwartz *RE* 6, 16). For an analysis of *FGH* 70 F 42, see the discussion in this chapter; also C. Reid [Rubincam], "Diodorus and His Sources," 90–92, for evidence of rhetoric in the papyrus fragment usually attributed to Ephorus (B. Grenfell and A. Hunt, *The Oxyrhynchus Papyrus* XIII, 1610).

[8] *P. Oxy.* xiii 1610 = *FGH* 70 F 191. Generally accepted as Ephoran: most recently by C. Rubincam, *Phoenix* 30 (1976), 357–66. The doubts of T. Africa, *AJP* 83 (1962), 86–89, are excessive, but worth noting.

[9] There is non-Ephoran material in the earlier books (Schwartz, *RE* 5, 678–79, 690–91, Drews, *AJP* 83 [1962], 392, n. 30), though Ephorus's presence seems probable as well (Schwartz, ibid.; Barber, *The Historian Ephorus*, 4–5).

[10] In its standard formulation by Volquardsen, *Untersuchungen über die Quellen der griechischen und sicilischen Geschichten*, and Schwartz, *RE* 5, 679. Ephorus's relationship to the Sicilian material is much more difficult to determine: Meister, "Die sizilische Geschichte," 10–11.

Ephorus for his subjective expressions, however, has proved more difficult. No fragment containing Ephorus's complete thoughts on moral utility exists outside of the *Bibliotheke*. Nor does Diodorus himself attribute such a notion to his source, mentioning Ephorus only infrequently, and then more often to criticize. Despite the scanty remains of Ephorus's work, the view has persisted for more than a century that the pronouncements on moral utility contained in books xi–xv are near-verbatim extracts from Ephorus's history, which in turn reflects the ideas of Isocrates.[11] Even in sections of the *Bibliotheke* for which Diodorus could not have drawn on Ephorus, his influence is usually suspected, and such ethical assessments as appear to be Diodorus's own words are termed "pathetic attempts."[12] It is time for a reevaluation.

Isocrates, the alleged creator of moral utility, never gives any hint of the concept as fully detailed in the *Bibliotheke*, nor does he indicate an obligation to make moral judgments. He does occasionally state that his recitation of virtuous deeds may cause others to emulate them,[13] but, unlike Diodorus, he makes no claim that such praise necessarily improves the lis-

[11] First elaborated by Volquardsen, *Untersuchungen über die Quellen der griechischen und sicilischen Geschichten*, 48–50; quickly supported, e.g., by Schwartz, *RE* 6, 7, and *RE* 5, 681; Laqueur, *Hermes* 46 (1911), 343–53; Jacoby *FGH* IIc, 23 and 38; Barber, *The Historian Ephorus*, 102–3; Kunz, *Zur Beurteilung der Prooemien*, 20–21; Avenarius, *Lukians Schrift zur Geschichtsschreibung*, 23–24; Scheller, *De Hellenistica Historiae Conscribendae Arte*, 49 and 74–75; P. Pédech, *La méthode historique de Polybe*, 502, n. 43; R. Sinclair, *PACA* 6 (1963), 37; Meister, "Die sizilische Geschichte," 10, and passim. Some recent doubts have been expressed by Drews, "Historiographical Objectives," 88–100, and *AJP* 83 (1962), 388–89; Reid, "Diodorus," 47–49; Pavan, *RAL* 16 (1961), 19–52, 117–50.

[12] Barber, *The Historian Ephorus*, 102.

[13] i 11, 51; v 113; vii 84; ix 73–76; xii 137. He also maintains that fathers should be models for the virtues of their sons and other such concepts: i 9, 11; ii 31; iii 37; vi 83; viii 49; ix 12; cf. Scheller, *Die Hellenistica Historiae Conscribendae Arte*, 77–78. This does not mean that Isocrates never criticized or cast blame in his epideictic speeches (on which, see Arist., *Rh.* iii 14, 1414b), but simply that he did not envisage moral improvement through these negative examples.

tener. And Isocrates does not present criticisms in order to deter similar behavior. In contrast, Diodorus's purpose in presenting exempla is strictly teleological, so that negative character assessments have just as much influence as positive ones.[14]

Isocrates' approach of presenting only paradigms of virtuous behavior may be reflected in the one surviving fragment of Ephorus involving moral assessments:

> Now the other writers, [Ephorus] says, tell only about [Scythian] savagery, because they know that the terrible and the marvelous are startling, but one should tell the opposite facts too and make them patterns of conduct [παραδείγματα ποιεῖσθαι], and [Ephorus] himself, therefore, will tell only about those who follow "most just" habits, for there are some of the Scythian nomads who feed only on mare's milk, and excel all men in justice.[15]

Ephorus argues here that the historian should not seek to dissuade the reader by presenting examples of improper behavior, for the recounting of violent Scythian habits is simple sensationalism. In practice Ephorus must have included examples of evil and impropriety, for at some point in the Roman empire his stories of both good and evil were excerpted and published as a separate work.[16] But by including examples of evil, Ephorus did not necessarily intend to offer them as warnings for the ages. Isocrates, an expert on the epideictic essay, was more inclined to offer praise, as was Aristotle in his discussion of epideixis.[17] Ephorus may have been similarly disposed. In

---

[14] For examples of censure in Diodorus, see Drews, "Historiographical Objectives," 23, 32, 39–46.

[15] FGH 70 F 42 = Strabo vii 3.9 (Jones' translation). Fornara, The Nature of History, 110–12, in attempting to break the link between Ephorus and Isocrates, renders παραδείγματα ποιεῖσθαι as "to give examples [of the opposite facts]." But that makes a pleonasm out of stating (λέγειν) and giving (ποιεῖσθαι) examples; see also Walbank, JHS 105 (1985), 211.

[16] Schwartz, RE 6, 16.

[17] He analyzes only actions worthy of praise (Rh. i 9), being content to state that the opposite of these characteristics deserves blame (1367a 20).

fact, his belief that the presentation of praiseworthy deeds alone has benefit is akin to the approach of Polybius[18] and of Diodorus's contemporaries, Dionysius of Halicarnassus and Strabo.[19] All three praised Roman rule, and Dionysius and Strabo are especially significant, because they looked with favor on the Augustan spirit. Augustus, significantly, stressed the education of the young based on positive exempla.[20] Much later, Tacitus, less fooled by the trappings of absolutism, reasserted the historian's duty to present examples of both the positive and the negative.[21] Diodorus could be critical of Roman rule (see pp. 44–52 and chapters 5 and 6). It may be that different variations in the use of moral suasion tended to be more appropriate to particular political expressions.

Diodorus's understanding of moral utility, therefore, appears to differ somewhat from that of Isocrates and Ephorus, and a close examination will reveal that Diodorus does not rely on Ephorus for his main philosophical inspiration. Within the books in which Ephorus was Diodorus's main source there are found six extensive judgments of individuals or events.[22] Four of these also contain statements reminding the reader that the assessment, in fulfilling the duty of history, is intended to be didactic. All are thought to represent a "rhetorical" approach to history and to be the work of Ephorus.[23]

---

[18] ii 66.11, though this may be special pleading: see Sacks, *Polybius* 143, n. 47. He tends to criticize historians who dwell on the negative (vii 7–8; xv 34–36) and offers instead a positive figure who would be more beneficial for the reader to learn from (vii 7–8). Frequently, too, he says that history should praise brave deeds: references in Avenarius, *Lukians Schrift zur Geschichtsschreibung*, 159–61; cf. R. Heinze, *Virgils Epische Technik*[3], 476, on the whole question. In practice, Polybius does bring numerous charges against historical figures.

[19] Dion. Hal., *AR* i 1.2–3 and Strabo i 1.23. Most recently, see A. Woodman, *Rhetoric in Classical Historiography*, 40–42.

[20] Z. Yavetz, "*Res Gestae* and Augustus' Public Image," in *Caesar Augustus: Seven Aspects*, ed. F. Millar and E. Segal, 19–20.

[21] *Ann.* iv 33.2.

[22] Thermopylae: xi 11; Pausanias and Aristides: xi 46–47; Themistocles: xi 58–59; Myronides: xi 82; Pelopidas: xv 81; and Epaminondas: xv 88.

[23] Volquardsen, *Untersuchungen über die Quellen der griechischen und sizilischen*

Yet spread throughout the *Bibliotheke* are many such judgments, some containing the didactic pronouncement and some lacking it.[24] Many of these fall outside the books for which Ephorus was the main source; some that are in the Ephoran books concern Sicilian affairs, where the source was possibly Timaeus.[25] Surely the extended praise of the Roman Lucretia—complete with a sentiment concerning the relationship of epideixis to history writing—cannot have been the work of Ephorus (x 21). The eulogy, moreover, indicates a connecting characteristic throughout the *Bibliotheke*: acknowledgment of noble acts by women. Literary interest in women became especially pronounced in the Hellenistic world, after the time of Ephorus.[26] Nevertheless, the literary style of all these moral assessments remains remarkably constant.[27]

From his very first books, Diodorus may have believed such moralistic assessments to be a principal part of history. In book xi, Diodorus writes: "Throughout the entire historical work [παρ' ὅλην τὴν ἱστορίαν] we have been accustomed [εἰ-

---

Geschichten, 47–51; Scheller, *De Hellenistica Historiae Conscribendae Arte*, 49; Avenarius, *Lukiens Schrift zur Geschichtsschreibung*, 159; those of xi 82 do not contain such statements. To the list in the preceding footnote, xi 38.5–6 might be added: it has all the necessary sentiments but is less long-winded; cf. also xi 3.1.

[24] E.g., iv 1–2; x 3, 21; xi 67; xii 62.1–5, 74; xiii 35; xviii 38.4; xix 19, 59.3, 67; xx 24.6–25, 92; xxx 15; xxxvii 4, 7; xxxviii/xxxix 18; and especially xxxii 27.3 on Julius Caesar. There are also numerous final encomia and censures when Diodorus is about to move a character permanently out of his history. These occur throughout the *Bibliotheke*: e.g., x 12; xi 38, 58.4–59.4; xv 81.4, 88.1–4; xvi 95.2; xvii 117.5; xx 10.5, 19; xxi 25–26; and xxxiii 22.1–2; cf. Drews, "Historiographical Objectives," 33, and especially Neubert, *Spuren selbständiger Thätigkeit bei Diodor*, 14–22.

[25] For example, xi 38; cf. Meister, "Die sizilische Geschichte," 44. Even if Diodorus's main source in books viii–x for Sicily were instead Hippys of Rhegium (E. Manni, *Kokalos* 17 [1971], 131–45) or Silenus (discussed in Walbank, *Kokalos* 14–15 [1968–1969], 486–92), that would not change the present argument.

[26] See the discussion in Chapter 3.

[27] Neubert, *Spuren selbständiger Thätigkeit bei Diodor*, 19–22; Reid, "Diodorus," 48.

ωθότες] to increasing the glory of good men by means of pronounced praise" (xi 46. 1; Oldfather). Ephorus was Diodorus's occasional source for books viii–x and nearly full-time thereafter until book xvi, but the force of this sentence implies more than infrequent judgments in viii–x; it says outright that Diodorus has been making such assessments all along. Certainly in the earlier, fragmentary historical books, such practices are evident where Diodorus is not likely to have been following Ephorus.[28] But even when considering myths in the earliest books, Diodorus was aware of the importance of moral utility. For example, although the myths concerning Hades are fictitious, they are said to greatly increase piety and justice (i 2.2). And, if not so presumptuous as to assess the worth of each god or hero, Diodorus does state that Hercules gained eternal glory for his deeds and Jason received his just punishment.[29] The narrative of the prehistorical East is also full of such ethical judgments.[30] Because Ephorus specifically chose not to include myth as a formal part of his history,[31] this material could not have been drawn from him.

Judging the worth of a historical figure or event is obviously not the exclusive characteristic of the so-called Isocratean "school of history." Brief biographical sketches began with Thucydides and the lesser-known fifth-century writers, Ion of Chios and Stesimbrotus.[32] Thucydides' portrait of Cleon, for example, shows he could offer a subjective judgment, and the Periclean Funeral Oration can be understood as consciously didactic.[33] Literary portraiture seems to have received its greatest impetus not from the students of Isocrates

[28] E.g., ix 1–2 and x 3–4; cf. Schwartz, *RE* 5, 678–79, and Meister, "Die sizilische Geschichte," 39. On the independence from Ephorus of moral sententiae in books vi–x, see further Drews, "Historiographical Objectives," 106ff.

[29] Heracles: iv 8.5, 53.6–7; Jason: iv 55.1.

[30] Listed in M. Sartori, *Athenaeum* 62 (1984), 505, n. 70.

[31] DS iv 1.3.

[32] See, e.g., Walbank, *Polybius*, 91–92.

[33] Scheller, *De Hellenistica Historiae Conscribendae Arte*, 79.

CHAPTER TWO

but from the Peripatetics.[34] Aristotle himself discusses which
types of actions deserve praise and blame (voluntary ones) and
which condonation and pity (involuntary ones).[35] The practice was too widespread in the Hellenistic world to justify the
tracing of its presence in the *Bibliotheke* directly and necessarily back to Isocrates.

To be sure, there is an extremely close correspondence between some material in the *Bibliotheke* and the works of Isocrates. It is a reasonable conclusion that Ephorus's history reflected the sentiments of Isocrates and served as a conduit for
ideas that reappear in Diodorus.[36] But one of these verbal echoes reveals the extent of Diodorus's creativity. In describing
the heroism of the Spartans at Thermopylae, Diodorus or his
source has clearly borrowed the wording of Isocrates' *Panegyricus*.[37] In the *Bibliotheke*, however, the statement is prefaced
with a sentiment not found in Isocrates: "Consequently what
man of later times might not emulate the valour of those war-
riors" (Oldfather). When the notion of moral utility is found
in Diodorus and is absent in Isocrates, there is no reason to
believe it was introduced by Ephorus.[38] In fact, a similar sen-

[34] Walbank, *Polybius*, 91–92.

[35] *Eth. Nic.* iii 1109b 30.

[36] Volquardsen, *Untersuchungen über die Quellen der griechischen und sicilischen
Geschichten*, 47ff. *Paneg.* 95 = DS xi 1.1; *Paneg.* 92 and *Archid.* 9 = DS xi
11.2; and *Paneg.* 174 = DS xiv 23.4. That Ephorus was the intermediary for
these passages is shown by the further equation of *Paneg.* 125 with Ephorus F
211 and DS xv 23.5 (see Barber, *The Historian Ephorus*, 76). Barber (184) adds
two more parallel passages, less similar in style: *Paneg.* 38–39 = DS xiii 26.3,
and *Paneg.* 156 = DS xi 29.3. Verbal similarities between DS ix 1–2 and the
Panegyricus are noted by M. Mühl, *WS* 69 (1956), 203–5. Certain interpretations of events in Diodorus, such as the Panhellenism of the Greeks during
the Persian Wars, may have come ultimately from Isocrates: Barber, 76–83,
88–102. Similarly, Isocratean influence on Androtion may be echoed in Aristotle's *Constitution of Athens*: P. Rhodes, *A Commentary on the Aristotelian* Athenaion Politeia, 20.

[37] *Paneg.* 92: οἱ μὲν διεφθάρησαν καὶ ταῖς ψυχαῖς νικῶντες τοῖς σώμασιν
ἀπεῖπον (οὐ γὰρ δὴ τοῦτό γε θέμις εἰπεῖν, ὡς ἡττήθησαν· οὐδεὶς γὰρ αὐτῶν φυ-
γεῖν ἠξίωσεν); cf. *Arch.* 9; DS xi 11.2: οἵτινες τῷ μεγέθει τῆς περιστάσεως
κατεσχημένοι τοῖς μὲν σώμασιν κατεπονήθησαν, ταῖς δὲ ψυχαῖς οὐχ ἡττήθησαν.

[38] In another essay, Isocrates does suggest that men will praise and be

timent is found in the opening prooemium to the *Bibliotheke*, considered to be Diodorus's own.[39] Diodorus certainly composed a similar discussion about the benefit brought about by history when following the account of Polybius. Prusias, king of Bithynia, won dubious fame in antiquity for groveling before Rome both during and after the Third Macedonian War.[40] Polybius records this with obvious scorn (xxx 18), and Diodorus maintains the Polybian spirit in his paraphrase (xxxi 15). But in the middle of his account, he adds:

> For when the virtue of good men is praised, many in later generations are guided to strive for a similar goal; and when the poltroonery of meaner men is held up to reproach, not a few who are taking the path of vice are turned aside. Accordingly the frank language [παρρησία] of history should of set purpose be employed for the improvement of society.[41]

Precisely the same addition to Polybian material can be found later as well,[42] proving that Diodorus himself expresses the philosophy of moral utility. Moreover, the moralistic passages found outside of the "Ephoran" books are far more than what have been termed "pathetic attempts." Of the major statements defining moral utility, only two fall within Ephoran books (xi 3.1; xv 1), whereas the other instances (n. 24) appearing from the beginning of his work (i 45.2) to near the end (xxxviii/xxxix 18), do not.

An important subordinate aspect of the praise-blame ap-

---

amazed at the battle (*Panath.* 187). But Isocrates is not urging the emulation of outstanding behavior, an idea central to the moral utility aimed at in the *Bibliotheke*.

[39] i 1.4–5; cf. Pavan, *RAL* 16 (1961), 25–29.

[40] The embassy *to* Prusias should be dated to 172: Walbank, *Commentary* III, 441, is more convincing than D. Braund, *CQ* n.s. 32 (1982), 353–54.

[41] DS xxxi 15.1 (Walton); cf. Drews, *AJP* 83 (1962), 383–92.

[42] DS xxxii 27.3 = Polybius xxxviii 12. Diodorus may also have added the more significant passage at xxx 15, but the possibly corresponding Polybian passage is no longer extant.

proach to writing history should also be viewed as part of Diodorus's own conception of benefit. The term παρρησία, or frankness of expression, is frequently employed in the *Bibliotheke*. In its five historiographical instances, it involves the duty of the historian to praise the deeds of good men and condemn those of evil men with candor.[43] A historian who properly employs παρρησία, then, involves himself in a most subjective aspect of history: the judging of individuals rather than the analysis of events. This convention involves moralistic and biographical aspects of history that began even before Xenophon but were later developed more fully by Polybius.[44] Among contemporaries of Diodorus, Dionysius of Halicarnassus judged παρρησία a characteristic of Theopompus's work,[45] while Philodemus wrote a treatise on the subject, perhaps with political overtones.[46]

Despite its popularity with Hellenistic authors, its presence in the *Bibliotheke* is thought to be due to Ephorus. In particular, it occurs in the prooemia of books xiv and xv, often considered to be Ephorus's work.[47] These prooemia, though, should now be considered Diodorus's own composition (see Chapter 1). The term παρρησία also occurs in passages of the *Bibliotheke* where Ephorus cannot be Diodorus's main source. It is found once in the story of the Roman matron, Lucretia (x 21.2). Twice more, when Diodorus follows the account of Polybius and where the Polybian text is extant to serve as a control, it is Diodorus who introduces the term.[48] Other uses of παρρησία similarly suggest Diodorus's independence.[49]

[43] x 12.1; xiv 1.2; xv 1.1; xxi 17.3; xxxi 15.1.

[44] Polybius xxxviii 4.3; Sacks, *Polybius*, 122–70.

[45] *Mim.* 428; and, without using the actual term, in *Pomp.* 785. Also in Lucian, *Hist. Conscr.* 41, 44, and 66; cf. Avenarius, *Lukians Schrift zur Geschichtsschreibung*, 40, 46.

[46] *Philodemi* Περὶ παρρησίας *Libellus*, ed. A. Olivieri (Leipzig, 1914), cols. 22–23, p. 62.

[47] Laqueur, *Hermes* 46 (1911), 346; Avenarius, *Lukians Schrift zur Geschichtsschreibung*, 46.

[48] DS xxix 21 = Polybius xxiii 14; DS xxxi 15.1 = Polybius xxx 18.

[49] It appears in Diodorus's attack on Timaeus (xxi 17.3), a passage that may

Παρρησία, an intricate aspect of moral assessment, belongs to Diodorus's own philosophy of history.

Diodorus's understanding of moral utility is, then, somewhat independent and different from that of Ephorus. Diodorus includes exempla involving condemnation, which appear to be absent in Isocrates and Ephorus. He adopted moralistic judgments found in Ephorus, but only because they were compatible with his own particular theory of history. An interesting case is his assessment of Epaminondas (xv 88). Diodorus probably drew upon either non-Ephoran traditions or his own resources in shaping part of the eulogy,[50] and the emphasis on moderate behavior (ἐπιείκεια) is a telltale sign of Diodorus's intrusion.[51] Yet within that discussion is found the interpretation that the death of Epaminondas marked the eclipse of Theban power (xv 88.4). This agrees with a statement in the *Bibliotheke* where Diodorus is following Ephorus and with an Ephoran fragment preserved outside the *Bibliotheke*.[52] But it conflicts with Diodorus's analysis when he is later following Hieronymus of Cardia, in which Thebes remains strong until its destruction by Alexander the Great (xix 53.8). Although Diodorus supplied at least the moral yardstick of ἐπιείκεια, he must have built some of the eulogy on the framework found in Ephorus. For the books in which Diodorus drew on Ephorus, he could use or modify much of the ethical material. But for the rest of the *Bibliotheke*, Diodorus was on his own. In turning to another important concept in his history, it will again be evident that, though

be based on Polybius xii 15 (Walbank, *CR* 39 [1945], 41, is still fundamental), but Polybius does not use παρρησία there. Twice where Diodorus's sources are unknown, Diodorus says of Solon and Plato that παρρησία is the duty of the philosopher: ix 2.2: Schwartz, *RE* 5, 678–79; xv 7.1: ibid., 681–82. That notion became especially prominent in the first century: see A. Momigliano, *JRS* 31 (1941), 157 = *Secondo contributo*, 388.

[50] See Drews, *AJP* 83 (1962), 383–92.
[51] xv 88.1 and 88.3; see below, pp. 42–44, and Chapter 3.
[52] xv 79.2, *FGH* 70 F 119 = Strabo x 2.2; cf. C. Vial, *Diodore* xv, Budé edition, 162.

Diodorus may draw on his sources for inspiration, much of the substance is his own work.

Aristotle lists four types of forces at work in the world: human agency (τὸ δι' ἀνθρώπου), divine intellect (νοῦς), nature (φύσις), and fortune or chance (τύχη).[53] Of these, human agency is clearly the most active in the Bibliotheke. But from the opening prooemium, Diodorus indicates that forces unseen and unexpected also play a considerable role. Diodorus argues that historians, especially writers of universal histories, serve as representatives of the Divine Providence (ἡ θεία πρόνοια) by bringing together historical narratives of disparate lands and times, thus uniting mankind (i 1.3). This sort of sentiment has encouraged scholars to identify a Stoic influence in Diodorus's work,[54] though his stress on an unseen mover could reflect several different philosophies current in the late Hellenistic period.[55]

Diodorus frequently refers to some divine plan at work, manifested by the appearance of πρόνοια, δαίμων, and especially θεός. The term θεός occurs about one thousand times in the Bibliotheke; most of its uses, however, are noncausative.[56]

---

[53] Eth. Nic. iii 3, 7. His fifth force, ἀνάγκη, is the law of the inanimate world: see H. Rackham, The Nicomachean Ethics (London, 1926), 134, n.; Diodorus uses it in at least one passage along with τύχη, suggesting there a Stoic understanding (xv 2.1); cf. also his use of νέμεσις (xxvii 15.2).

[54] G. Busolt, Neue Jahrbücher für Philologie und Paedagogik 140 (1889), 297–315.

[55] Ibid., 298; see also Spoerri, Späthellenistische Berichte, 163, and E. Rawson, Intellectual Life in the Late Roman Republic, 223. The use of πρόνοια in history is found as early as Herodotus: e.g., iii 108.2. Diodorus's diverse and casual employment of τύχη and divine forces resembles the practice of Polybius, to whom no specific philosophy can be ascribed: Walbank, Commentary I, 16–26.

[56] Statistics from the TLG machine-readable tape, or J. McDougall, Lexicon in Diodorum Siculum, for the nonfragmentary books. Examples of divine causality: viii 15, 32, 2; xi 13.1, 14.4; xiii 112.2; xiv 70.4; xvi 57.2, 58.5, 61, 66.3, 79.5; xx 70.1, 70.4; xxxvi 13; xxxviii/xxxix 6, 19. If book xvi has a greater concentration, several of the references are to the Phocian sack of Delphi in the Third Sacred War, for which divine vengeance as a theme would be

The divine agency need not act by itself, for τύχη may also participate,[57] and there may be a concomitant human explanation as well (αἰτίαι: xiv 70.4). Divine forces appear in so many contexts throughout the work that it is impossible to see the direct influence of a particular source.

Nature, or φύσις, has a more restrained presence in the *Bibliotheke*. Despite occurring nearly three hundred fifty times in the work, it is only infrequently portrayed as a distinct force that intrudes into human actions. As with θεός, this use of φύσις does not seem to derive from any particular source. It is found, for example, in passages where Diodorus follows Agatharchides[58] and Posidonius,[59] in an analysis of Alexander the Great,[60] and where Diodorus accurately follows Polybius, who has introduced the word himself.[61] One especially interesting use of φύσις is as self-taught (αὐτοδίδακτος) human nature, which needs no help from civilization in deciding proper behavior. That notion is formulaic in parts of Diodorus where he is suspected of drawing on Posidonius; there it is applied to barbarians and slaves whose behavior is consequently ennobled.[62] Nowhere else in the extent *Bibliotheke* is the force of nature so employed, but Diodorus does use self-taught φύσις perhaps independently of his current source to demonstrate how nature on its own drives man toward improvement.[63] In

---

expected. Sordi, *Diodori Siculi Bibliothecae liber sextus decimus*, xxiv, attributes this to Diodorus's use of a pietist source, Diyllus of Athens.

[57] E.g., xx 70; xxxiv/xxxv 18. Despite being drawn from different sources, these passages have much in common: note especially the use of ὥσπερ ἐπίτηδες.

[58] iii 31.2; cf. Schwartz, *RE* 5, 673. Not in the parallel Phot., *Codex* 250, 60, 453b.

[59] v 27.1: see Schwartz, *RE* 5, 678; cf. v 39.2 = *FGH* 87 F 118.

[60] xvii 107.2; here it is separated from τύχη. Cf. xvi 1.6. For a brief discussion of the current state of the question of the sources for xvii, see R. Kebric, *In the Shadow of Macedon: Duris of Samos*, 64–66.

[61] DS xxx 17 = Polybius xxviii 21.

[62] xxxiii 7.3–5; xxxiv/v 2.40; xxxviii/xxxix 21.1: on the Posidonian character, see, e.g., Malitz, *Die Historien des Poseidonios*, 136, n. 12.

[63] Photius provides a rough control on one passage based on Agatharchides:

one application, Posidonian influence is evident, but in another it is part of Diodorus's own philosophy of culture.

Although it occurs "only" about two hundred fifty times, τύχη is the most prevalent and variable force found in the *Bibliotheke*. It plays so many different roles in the narrative that, as in Polybius's history,[64] it ranges from a rhetorical device to a true goddess. Τύχη can be employed off-handedly, without a specific force in mind: "but as for the vows which we made for the victory, inasmuch as Fortune has prevented our paying them. . . ."[65] Perhaps with as much casualness, Diodorus qualifies τύχη with ὥσπερ;[66] this, like Polybius's qualifiers,[67] may indicate almost an embarrassment in ascribing a true presence to τύχη. At the other extreme, τύχη becomes a determining factor in events, in the way in which Aristotle thought of it: "That their plans were soundly conceived was generally agreed, yet it was Fortune who beyond their hopes presided over the course of events and unexpectedly brought to a happy issue an understanding that appeared impossible and fraught with peril."[68] The deterministic application of τύχη, however, is not so long-range as Polybius's. The latter can see the rise of the Roman Empire as brought about by the will of Fortune (i 4). It is not just that Diodorus would not attribute Roman success to divine will (see Chapter 5); it is also that his approach to political and military actions is far less synthetic. Recording events annalistically and drawing on

---

DS iii 19.2—not in Phot., *Codex* 250 43, 450b (see Chapter 3); cf. iii 10.6, also Agatharchidean: Schwartz, *RE* 5, 673. On the theme generally, see Chapter 3.

[64] Walbank, *Commentary* I, 16–26.

[65] xiii 102.2 (Oldfather). Also xiv 23.5; xvi 1.6; xviii 13.4; xxxi 11.3; xxxiv/xxxv 19, 27; xxxvii 12.2, 29.3.

[66] xi 24.1, 63.3; xiii 53.2; xv 80.3 (χρέων); xvi 92.2; xx 13.3, 70.2; xxv 5.2, where Diodorus is quoting Polybius i 86.6; xxvii 15.3; xxxii 17.2; xxxiv/v 9.1, 18.1; xxvi 7.2; xxxvii 1.6, 2.3.

[67] Ziegler, *RE* 21, 1538–40.

[68] xii 1.2 (Oldfather). Other examples: ix 2.2; xi 71.5; xii 1.2; xiii 90.5; xiv 46.4, 76.1; xvii 20.1, 101.2; xviii 8.7; xix 42.5, 108.2; xx 99.1; xxi 11; xxii 13.6; xxvi 24.2; xxxi 12; xxxii 10.5; xxxiv/xxxv 28.2–3, 30c; xxxvi 5.3, 7.2.

disparate sources for his entries, Diodorus rarely accounts for long-term causes and developments. Consequently, for Diodorus the force of τύχη is more particularistic and ephemeral. It is most prevalent as a reflection of individual temperament and holds an important place in his notion of moral utility. In judging the character of individuals in order to provide moral lessons for the reader, Diodorus frequently examines how people behave while enjoying good fortune. Polybius had already made the examination of individuals caught in μεταβολαί and περιπέτειαι a central feature of his work, arguing that it is beneficial for the reader to learn how statesmen and generals could survive and even succeed amid unpredicted turns of events.[69] Diodorus as well mentions the great reversals of fortune[70] but is less interested in the practical benefits derived from such an examination. His main concern is demonstrating that, because τύχη is capricious, an individual ought to avoid arrogance when blessed with good fortune: "Most men are made proud by their successes because of their good fortune and, becoming arrogant in their success, are forgetful of the common weakness of mankind."[71] Occasionally, Diodorus will inject a practical message: intelligent people, enjoying good luck, will always take precautions against the inevitable shift of fortune.[72] This only somewhat approximates Polybius's emphasis on teaching the reader how to maintain equanimity, and so to succeed, when luck changes. Finally, often combined or associated with the god-

---

[69] Sacks, Polybius, 132–70.

[70] E.g., iv 34.1, 82.3; viii 10.3; xii 1.3, 62.6; xiv 112.5; xvi 70.3; xvii 27.7; xviii 53; xix 53.3; xxvi 6; xxx 23; xxxi 12.1 (= Polybius xxix 22; cf. Schwartz, RE 5, 689), 18.3; xxxii 10.2 (on which, see Schwartz, RE 5, 690); xxxiv/xxxv 2.41.

[71] xvii 38.4–6 (Welles). See also, e.g., ix 33.3; xiii 21–30, passim; xiv 76.1; xv 33.3; xvi 70.2; xvii 38.5–6; xix 95.6–7; xx 13.3; xxiii 12.1, 13; xxvi 16; xxvii 1.2; xxxi 1.3–4 (= Polybius xxix 27; Schwartz, RE 5, 690); xxxiii 7; xxxvii 29.3. Some of these passages refer to a divine force other than τύχη, but with the same sense.

[72] E.g., xi 71.5; xv 54.5; xvii 108.6; xx 93.7; xxi 11; xxiii 12; xxix 8.2.

head, τὸ δαιμόνιον, τύχη for Diodorus performs the task of moral retribution upon those who turn arrogant.[73] Despite similarities to Polybius's understanding of τύχη, none of Diodorus's different interpretations is concentrated in any one book or in material drawn from a particular source. Τύχη is found as often in the later, highly fragmentary books as in books that are completely extant,[74] which might suggest that originally τύχη occurred even more frequently in these final books. But the main collections of excerpts were done by Byzantine scholars who searched for passages involving moral sentiments. Many of Diodorus's references to chance are encased in such *sententiae*, and therefore may have been disproportionately preserved by the Constantinian editors.

Most of the various facets of τύχη in the *Bibliotheke* cannot be traced to a particular source. Around the figure of Eumenes, the *diadochos*, however, an almost unique aspect of τύχη emerges, which may help to elucidate how Diodorus reacts to the influence of his authorities. In the midst of troubles, Eumenes remembers that his bad luck is sure to change. He takes heart, avoids acting rashly, and eventually wins out.[75] Instead of a situation where good fortune must be borne with modesty, here Diodorus stresses that in the darkest hour one must remember that good fortune may yet come. Diodorus supplies this optimistic reasoning to explain Eumenes' actions, intending it as a practical lesson for other generals in

[73] The compensatory power of τὸ δαιμόνιον or τύχη at xi 24.1, xiii 21.1, 21.5, xiv 76.1, 76.4, xx 13.2–3, and 70.1–4 is attributed to Timaeus: Meister, "Die sizilische Geschichte," 66, 95. Yet the sentiment also occurs when Diodorus is following Polybius (DS xxv 5.1 = Polybius i 84.10; DS xxv 5.2 = Polybius i 86.7; DS xxviii 3 = Polybius xv 20) and where no controls exist: vii 5.11, 7; x 16.2; xiii 90.5; xiv 76.4; xv 48.4 with xvi 61–64; xxiii 12, 15.2; xxiv 9.2; xxvii 6.2, 12.1, 15.2, 17.2; xxviii 4; xxxix 18; xxxi 11.3, and xxxiv/xxxv 9, 17.1. It is present in iii 40.6–7, where Diodorus is following Agatharchides, but absent in Photius's abbreviated parallel text (*Codex* 250, 82, 456b).

[74] See, e.g., the index to F. Walton, *Diodorus of Sicily* XII, Loeb edition, s.v., "Fortune."

[75] xviii 41.6 and 42.1.

similar positions. A short while later, when contrary to all expectations the Macedonian Silver Shields pledge their loyalty to Eumenes and his luck begins to change, Diodorus is led to say that such is the purpose of history: to explain the changes in τύχη (xviii 59).

The source for this episode is Hieronymus of Cardia, the friend and probable relative of Eumenes.[76] Although there is evidence of Diodoran language in the passage,[77] it may have been Hieronymus who produced this slant on τύχη. Yet while different in precise force from Diodorus's other applications, it is not inconsistent with his general understanding of τύχη. The need to remain optimistic amid ill fortune is only the underside of the need to be cautious while enjoying good fortune. Moreover, Diodorus manages to interpose in his discussion of Eumenes an aspect of the more conventional interpretation of τύχη: after Eumenes' luck changes for the better, he begins taking precautions against the time when it will once again sour (xviii 60.1).

This novel aspect of τύχη, that bad fortune must be borne with equanimity, is present only one other time in the *Bibliotheke*, when the narrative is based upon Philinus in book xxiv.[78] Diodorus may have taken the specific passage directly from Philinus, or, once this view of τύχη was introduced by Hieronymus, it may have become part of Diodorus's own philosophy. Just as with his use of moral assessments, when Diodorus was influenced by his current source to include the sentiment, the alteration is one only of emphasis, not of fundamental philosophy.

[76] On Hieronymus's life and relationship to Eumenes, see Hornblower, *Hieronymus of Cardia*, 8–16; on Hieronymus as the main source for Diodorus xviii–xx, Hornblower, 32–34.

[77] Hornblower, *Hieronymus of Cardia*, 62, n. 141, draws attention to πάντα τὸν αἰῶνα and ὁ κοινὸς βίος, reminiscent of the opening prooemium: see Chapter 1, n. 12.

[78] xxiv 13: it refers back to the Regulus/Xanthippus episode of xxiii 12–15, which goes back to Philinus (from whom Polybius too drew the story: Walbank, *Commentary* 1, 92–93). This standard of courage amid ill fortune is a consideration for Polybius: iii 4.5.

The process by which Diodorus is influenced by his sources can be examined in another significant theme in the *Bibliotheke*: the explanation for the rise and fall of empires. Diodorus's thoughts on the subject are clear and consistent. When analyzing the Athenian Empire of the fifth century, he attributes the disaffection of the subject states to a change in the way Athens treated them. By the 460s, after gaining so much power, Athens no longer behaved moderately (ἐπιεικῶς),[79] but acted harshly (βιαίως καὶ ὑπερηφάνως). Consequently, many allies discussed rebellion and even began to act on their plans (xi 70.3–4). Similarly, in the early fourth century the Spartans threw away their empire, which their ancestors had won by acting ἐπιεικῶς καὶ φιλανθρώπως. The later generation behaved βιαίως καὶ χαλεπῶς; hence when the Spartans were defeated at Leuctra, all their former subjects held them in contempt.[80] Athens and Sparta built their empires on goodwill; they then turned to acting harshly toward their subjects and ceased demonstrating moderation; because of this new attitude, the subject states rebelled. Applied to Athenian and Spartan behavior separately,[81] the model is also used to explain the fall of Athens in conjunction with the rise of the short-lived Spartan empire: in 421, the future of the two powers moved in different directions, as Sparta treated its allies moderately (ἐπιεικῶς), while Athens applied terror (xii 76.2–3).

Although these judgments on Athenian and Spartan governance occur in the part of the *Bibliotheke* in which Ephorus is the main source, it is unlikely that Diodorus drew the interpretation from him. No Ephoran material outside of that in Diodorus contains a similar model for empire. And Isocrates, whose ideas are sometimes found in the Ephoran parts of the

---

[79] Ἐπιείκεια can mean *clementia*: M. Gelzer, *Philologus* 86 (1931), 270–71, n. 22 = *Kleine Schriften* II, 47, n. 22; cf. DS xxiii 27.3 and Plut., *Caes*. 57, on Caesar's ἐπιείκεια. Evolution of the term is discussed by J. de Romilly, *La douceur dans la pensée grecque*, 53–61.

[80] xiv 2.1–2; xv 1.1–5.

[81] xii 67.2; xv 28.2–4, 29.8, 30.3–31.1

Bibliotheke (as noted previously), never offers this analysis.[82] Though arguing generally that Athenian moderation is praiseworthy,[83] he stresses a different explanation for the decline of empire, one that Diodorus quite intentionally does not follow. Most important, Diodorus's paradigm is not limited in application to Athens and Sparta. He uses it in diverse contexts, which stretch far beyond the Ephoran material: in mythology, in the accounts of early Egyptian and Median history, in a fictitious speech by a Sicilian in 413, in describing the behavior of the *diadochoi*, and in nearly two dozen other circumstances spread throughout the *Bibliotheke*.[84] Further, the key concept of moderate behavior, expressed in the terms ἐπιείκεια and φιλανθρωπία, is also a hallmark of Diodoran thought generally. He employs the words with extraordinary frequency, using them about three hundred times to describe and judge the behavior of individuals or nations.[85] Where a papyrus fragment of Ephorus provides a control, it is clear that Diodorus himself substitutes the notion.[86] The belief that only clement

[82] The closest are *On the Peace* 99–115 (hybris can cause the loss of an empire); *Plat.* 39–40 (the advantages of a ruling state acting πραότερον); and *Antidosis* 121–22 (Athens won its empire through φιλία and lost it by inspiring μίσος). See also *On the Peace* 140, and cf. J. de Romilly, *JHS* 78 (1958), 95 and 97. Isocrates never employs ἐπιεικῶς and βιαίως or (contra J. de Romilly, *The Rise and Fall of States According to Greek Authors*, 66) applies ἐπιείκεια to the subject of empire maintenance. Εὔνοια, so important to Isocrates, for Diodorus is only one obvious result of ἐπιείκεια/φιλανθρωπία/εὐεργεσία: i 51.4, 64.9, 71.4; ii 28.6; xi 26.4, 41.4; xiii 27.4; xiv 44.3; xvi 79.2; xvii 94.4; xix 62.2; xxvii 16.2; xxxi 32.1; xxxvii 13.2; at xi 67.2–4, a complex argument, the terms might be synonymous.

[83] De Romilly, *La douceur dans la pensée grecque*, 159–65.

[84] i 55.10–12, and with modifications at i 60.1–5; ii 28.5–6; iii 61.4, 71.3; iii 72.4; v 81.5; viii 30 (modified); xi 67; xiii 21.6–25: see the section on speeches in Chapter 4; xiv 90.2; xv 31.1, 57.1, 61.2; xvi 54.4 (cf. 60.4); xix 86.2–5, 90.2; xx 24.3–25.2; xxii 2.4; xxvii 16.1: see the section on speeches; xxxiii 12, 18; xxxiv/xxxv 3.

[85] *TLG* machine–readable tapes; cf. McDougall, *Lexicon*, for the nonfragmentary books.

[86] xi 59.3 and *P. Oxy.* xiii 1610 FF 4–5 (Ephorus); see the discussion at the end of this chapter. Busolt already recognized ἐπιείκεια as part of Diodorus's own understanding of empire in *Neue Jahrbücher für Philologie und Paedagogik*

behavior could assure the loyalty of subject states became topical as Rome started treating its subjects harshly. Polybius and Sallust suggested a similar theory, and Cicero argued that empires cannot be controlled through fear, using Sparta as an example of a state that lost its rule because of arrogance. A discussion by the contemporary Epicurean philosopher Philodemus, who even uses the term ἐπιείϰεια, can be similarly interpreted.[87] For inspiration, then, Diodorus may well have drawn on contemporary sentiments. The notion so pervades the *Bibliotheke*, applied even to events involving Diodorus's hometown of Agyrium (xxii 2.4), that it must reflect his own attitude and not simply that of a specific source.[88]

This model is spelled out with only slight modification in fragments found at the beginning of book xxxii:

> Those whose object it is to gain dominion over others use courage and intelligence to get it, moderation and consideration for others [ἐπιειϰείᾳ ϰαὶ φιλανθρωπίᾳ] to extend it widely, and paralyzing terror to secure it against attack. The proofs of these propositions are to be found in attentive consideration of the history of such empires as were created in ancient times as well as of the Roman domination that succeeded them. (xxxii 2; Walton)

In a related passage, the narrator goes on to discuss Philip and Alexander, who, like Rome of his day, had not surrendered

---

140 (1889), 302, as did Neubert, *Spuren selbständiger Thätigkeit bei Diodor*, 24, the following year. H. Strasburger's belief that ἐπιείϰεια in Diodorus is a Posidonian thought (*JRS* 55 [1965], 47, n. 70) and O. Murray's (*JEA* 56 [1970], 161, n. 7), that it is Hecataean, do not take this into account. Where Posidonius's own words survive, he puts little emphasis on the notion of philanthropy (ἐπιείϰεια itself is not found): de Romilly, *La douceur dans la pensée grecque*, 212, n. 2, 249–50. On Diodorus and Hecataeus, see also de Romilly, 254, n. 4.

[87] Polybius x 36.6–7; Sall., *Catiline* 2.4; Cic., *De Off.* 2.26–29; on Philodemus, see O. Murray, *JRS* 55 (1965), 177. On Polybius and ἐπιείϰεια generally, see de Romilly, *La douceur dans la pensée grecque*, 235–49.

[88] See de Romilly, *La douceur dans la pensée grecque*, 249–56, who, however, strongly overstates Diodorus' optimism about Rome: see below, n. 121.

their empires either and had shown the greatest moderation toward their subjects (xxxii 4.1–3; ἐπιείχεια is used three times). He concludes by reaffirming that Rome used valor to win its empire, was quite reasonable (ἐπιειχέστατα) in extending it, to the point of treating its subjects as benefactors (εὐεργέται), but finally imposed rule by terror with the destruction of Corinth, Macedonia, and Numantia (xxxii 4.4– 5). This analysis of the Roman Empire has long been attributed to Polybius. Certainly Diodorus followed him for the narrative events in book xxxii, and it is possible to connect this discussion with Polybius's belief that, after the Third Macedonian War, Rome became so thirsty for power that it began treating its subjects harshly.[89] But the discussion appears to be part of the proem,[90] an area of particular Diodoran creativity (see Chapter 1). Moreover, the examples of moderate behavior involving Philip and Alexander have little to do with the arguments Polybius makes elsewhere in his history.[91] Nor is the reference to Corinth strictly relevant to the proposed Polybian context.[92] The passage, with its stress on ἐπιείχεια and terror, is more compatible with the model for empire found throughout the *Bibliotheke*.[93] Yet the analysis differs in some detail from the earlier pattern: instead of representing the final stage of empire, terror is now seen as a method for preserving

---

[89] Gelzer, *Philologus* 86 (1931), 285–95 = *Kleine Schriften* II, 60–68; cf. Walbank, *Polybius*, 179, and E. Gabba, *RSI* 86 (1974), 638, n. 34, for bibliography.

[90] Cf. Walton, *Diodorus of Sicily* XI, Loeb edition, 411, n. 2.

[91] J. Touloumakos, *Zum Geschischtsbewusstsein der Griechen in der Zeit der römischen Herrschaft*, 28–29, n. 28; cf. F. Walbank, *Polybe*, Fondation Hardt, *Entretiens* 20, 18–20 = Walbank, *Selected Papers*, 289–90. De Romilly, *La douceur dans la pensée grecque*, 250, puts too much stress on Polybius v 10: the discussions of Philip are somewhat close, but not those concerning Alexander; it shows that Diodorus may have refashioned some of Polybius's arguments.

[92] Polybius xxxvi 9; cf. Walbank, *Polybius*, 179.

[93] The connection of εὐεργέται and ἐπιείχεια is also frequently found in the *Bibliotheke*: see Chapter 3.

it. The difference probably arises because here Diodorus is discussing Rome, a hegemon that has not yet lost its empire. Consequently, he modified the paradigm slightly to fit a contemporary situation.

Beginning two books later, however, a new model for the decline of empires is proposed. On the eve of the Third Punic War, Cato the Censor and Scipio Nasica argued over the fate of Carthage, which had already been defeated twice by Rome. Cato urged that it be annihilated; Nasica countered by predicting that, if Carthage were destroyed and there were no other strong force in the Mediterranean, then, first, Roman magistrates would act rapaciously toward subject states and, second, Rome would suffer civil war at home. Cato won the debate, and Nasica's warnings came true (xxxiv/xxxv 33). The predicted effects of the Third Punic War were finally felt when the Italian Social War occurred, because "the Romans abandoned the disciplined, frugal, and stern manner of life that had brought them to such greatness, and fell into the pernicious pursuit of luxury (τρυφή) and license" (xxxvii 2.1; Walton). Roman mores had declined so greatly that to illustrate his point the historian supplied vignettes of Romans who still reflected the older virtues (xxxvii 3–8). Nearly all of this analysis of Roman decline can with confidence be traced back to Posidonius.[94]

In fact, the consideration of social decay takes Diodorus far from his simple model for the decline of empire. Explanations involving the morality of a citizen body are virtually absent in the rest of the Bibliotheke. Only rarely does Diodorus apply

[94] xxxiv/xxxv 33 = FGH 87 F 117; F 178 (Theiler). On all details, see Gelzer, Philologus 86 (1931), 261–99 = Kleine Schriften II, 39–72; most recently, Gruen, HWCR I, 352, n. 189. xxxvii 2–8 = FF 211–16, 223, 235, 238–40, 242 (Theiler), and is identified as Posidonian, e.g., by Strasburger, JRS 55 (1965), 47, and P. Desideri, RIL 106 (1972), 481–93. It contradicts in spirit the immediately preceding passage (xxxvii 1), which is Diodorus's own attempt to prove the bravery of the Romans and Italians: see Chapter 1. xxxiii/xxxiv 33.5 contains the Diodoran sentiment that Rome had ruled the best way, ἐπιεικῶς, but the Carthaginian constraint on Roman behavior is foreign to his model.

the theme of decadence to Rome. At one point, in departing from the Polybian text, he accuses contemporary Rome of increasing greed (πλεονεξία)[95] but does not specifically connect it with moral decay. The few times that he does discuss Roman decadence, he closely follows his sources, Polybius and Posidonius.[96] Yet these two writers, in making that part of their themes, had included much material illuminating Roman decadence. Polybius, perhaps influenced by Scipio's use of moral issues in his political program, wrestled with the disturbing features of Roman behavior.[97] Posidonius, who generally included examples of social excess throughout his history,[98] inevitably was drawn to discuss the growing Roman decadence also.[99] Diodorus's account of the late Republic survives only in a highly fragmentary condition, and it may be that precisely the passages on social decay have been lost. But the second half of the Bibliotheke, for whose existence the Constantinian excerpters are almost entirely responsible, is replete with moral sententiae of various kinds.[100] Among those passages are all the discussions of decay from Posidonius and Polybius found in Diodorus's work.[101] The process of selection cannot account for the small number of passages on Ro-

[95] xxxi 26.2; not in Polybius xxxi 22.

[96] DS xxxi 24 = Polybius xxxi 25.5–6 and DS xxxi 26.7 = Polybius xxxi 25.6. DS xxxvii 3.1–6 = Pos. F 211b–c (Theiler): from Polybius xxxi 25.5–6; cf. Athen. vi 273a–275b = FGH 87 F 59, F 81 (Theiler). On the First Sicilian Slave War, see Chapter 5: Posidonius accused the Sicilians of decadence. Diodorus follows Posidonius on the decadence of the Tyrrhenians: v 40.4 = FGH 87 F 119.

[97] E.g., Walbank, Polybe, Fondation Hardt Entretiens 20, 3–31; esp. vi 57.

[98] E.g., FGH 87 FF 2, 5, 6, and 10; all from Athenaeus (where there are numerous other possible examples) to avoid circularity. See also Sen., Ep. 90.36, and H. Heinen, "Die Tryphè des Ptolmaios VIII. Euergetes II," in Althistorische Studien: Hermann Bengtson zum 70. Geburtstag dargebracht von Kollegen und Schülern, 121, n. 16.

[99] E.g., FGH 87 F 59. See further, Strasburger, JRS 55 (1965), 43–47.

[100] E.g, xxi 1.1, 1.4, 21; xxv 2–3, 5.3; xxvii 4.8, 5; xxviii 3, 7; xxix 31; xxx 17, 18.2, 21.2; xxxi 5.2b; xxxvii 17.1, 30; xxxviii/xxxix 6, 19. See also Reid, "Diodorus," 9, and E. Badian, RFIC 96 (1968), 208.

[101] See n. 96.

CHAPTER TWO

man decay found in the *Bibliotheke*. The changing values of the
imperial city required examination, and the theme is found in
nearly all historians of the period.[102] Despite Diodorus's own
negative feelings toward Rome (see Chapter 5), he generally
avoids the emphasis found in his sources on the increasing social decay.

Illuminating is Diodorus's treatment of the Roman Social
War. It is contained in a book introduced by a prooemium of
his own creation.[103] He briefly mentions how the conflict came
about, ascribing it to the strife and ambition (ἔρις καὶ φιλο-
τιμία) of the Italians (xxxvii 1.6). The subsequent narrative
begins with Photius's paraphrase of the war reflecting the account of Posidonius.[104] Here blame is laid directly at the feet
of the Romans, who have fallen into decadence (τρυφή: 2.1).
Thus, where it is reasonably certain that the words are Diodorus's own, decadence is not associated with empire; when
the narrative appears dependent on Posidonius, decadence
plays a prominent role.

The idea of moral decay was not limited to historians who
wrote on Rome. Ephorus is the main source for Diodorus's
narrative of the classical period, and the fragments of his work
indicate decadence was for him an important theme.[105] In particular, Ephorus suggested that only so long as they avoided
moral decay (ἕως μὲν οὐκ ἐτρύφων) were the Milesians powerful.[106] Diodorus is probably echoing something of this passage

[102] A. Passerini, *SIFC* 11 (1934), 52–56; Walbank, *Commentary* III, 500;
A. Novara, *Les idées romaines sur le progrès d'après des écrivains de la République*
I, 57–74. Diodorus's discussion of the decadence of Hannibal's army (xxvi 11)
is part of an annalistic tradition: cf. Livy xxiii 18.10–16.

[103] Busolt, *Neue Jahrbücher für Philologie und Paedagogik* 141 (1890), 321ff.;
Kunz, *Zur Beurteilung der Prooemien*, 59–61; discussed at the beginning of
Chapter 1, and in Chapter 5, n. 36.

[104] xxxvii 2; on the identification, see above, n. 94. Photius mentions the
first cause (πρώτη αἰτία: 2.1) of the war; Posidonius may have offered a
lengthy analysis: cf. *FGH* 87 T 15b = Strabo ii 3.8, on Posidonian etiologies.

[105] F 149 = Strabo x 4.16; discussion of moral decay may also have been
present in the original of F 29 = Athen. vi 263f, and F 119 = Strabo ix 2.2.

[106] Μιλήσιοι δ᾽ ἐνίκων Σκύθας . . . καὶ τάς τε ἐφ᾽ Ἑλλησπόντῳ πόλεις ἔκτισαν

48

when he recounts how, though the Milesians had grown soft (Μιλησίων τρυφώντων), a traveler had recounted that Miletus was the one free city he had seen.[107] But if Diodorus is following Ephorus's narrative and his description, he does not include his explanation that τρυφή caused weakness. Only twice is τρυφή found within Ephoran material in the *Bibliotheke*. The Spartan regent, Pausanias, is condemned for following the decadent habits of the Persians, thus causing Sparta to lose control (ἡγεμονία) of the sea.[108] Here, Ephorus's use of decadence to explain the Spartan loss of power focuses on the individual rather than society. Diodorus, ever interested in biography to demonstrate history's moral utility, preserves the emphasis on τρυφή in a final judgment after Pausanias's death (xi 46.1–3). The other usage also involves Sparta. In describing the Lycurgan reforms, Diodorus writes that after four hundred years the Spartans finally did succumb to τρυφή, were corrupted by money, and so lost their empire (ἡγεμονία).[109] Ephorus, whose work may have been slanted against the Spartans,[110] probably used decadence as a causative force for their decline. Isocrates had argued something similar, that both Athens and Sparta lost much of their social and political cohesion when they made bids for empire.[111] Ephorus appears to have adopted this association between inner decay and loss of empire. Diodorus, however, chose to follow the analysis only once, instead emphasizing the role of moderate and harsh behavior in accounting for the Athenian and Spartan hegemonies.

. . . *FGH* 70 F 183 = Athen. xii 523a. Jacoby (*FGH* IIc, 88) associated the passage with the Ionian revolt, but it should be dated to the 550s and is probably derived from the tradition behind Hdt. v 28–29.

[107] viii 20; Ephoran: Jacoby, *FGH* IIc, 34.

[108] xi 46, cf. 47.3, 50.1.

[109] vii 12.8; Ephorus as source: Schwartz, *RE* 5, 678; Jacoby, *FGH* IIc, 33.

[110] Most recently, Pavan, *RAL* 16 (1961), 31–32.

[111] *On the Peace* 77, 79, 82, and 96; cf. *Paneg.* 140–52; *To Philip* 124; perhaps *Plat.* 25. *On the Peace* 75–131 is revealing: Athens has lost its empire partly because of its insolence toward allies (something Diodorus might argue), but that attitude is tied to the moral values of its citizens.

Timaeus also employed τρυφή to describe social malaise and the decline of political power.[112] One example, preserved in lurid detail by Athenaeus, concerns the Sybarites, who "were exhausted by an eager rivalry among themselves in self-indulgence, and the whole community also contended with all other states in luxury. And so, not long afterward . . . they were destroyed [by Croton]."[113] Diodorus, too, includes material on Sybaris. In a passage drawn from Timaeus, Diodorus discusses τρυφή, but makes no connection between it and Sybaris's subsequent catastrophe.[114] In two later passages, possibly from Timaeus also,[115] Diodorus retails the destruction of Sybaris. In the first (x 21) it is caused not by τρυφή, so graphically rendered by Timaeus, but by the inability of the Sybarites to live moderately with their εὐδαιμονία and εὐτυχία. Strabo (vi 1.13) also claims that the Sybarites ignored their εὐδαιμονία and εὐτυχία, but specifically adds that their defeat was caused by τρυφή and ὕβρις. The echo of εὐδαιμονία and εὐτυχία makes it probable that Diodorus and Strabo followed the same source, but only Strabo included the notice about τρυφή. In his other, more extended account of their destruction, Diodorus notes the extraordinary wealth of the Sybarites, but makes no connection between that and the taking of their city.[116]

Finally, Diodorus and Photius preserve a parallel part of Agatharchides' work, one passage from which is relevant here. Sabae was an abundantly wealthy Arabian city located too far from the centers of world power to fear an invasion.

---

[112] Meister, "Die sizilische Geschichte," 9; Novara, *Les idées romaines sur le progrès* I, 56–67.

[113] *FGH* 566 F 50 = Athen. xii 519b–520c (Gulick's translation). Also FF 48, 49, and 51 = Athen. xii 518b–f, 523c.

[114] viii 18–19, on which see Jacoby *FGH* IIIb, 560, and Meister, "Die sizilische Geschichte," 39. Manni, *Kokalos* 17 (1971), 131–45, posits an intermediate source between Timaeus and Diodorus.

[115] Jacoby, *FGH* IIIb, 560 on x 23 and xii 9–10.1; Meister, "Die sizilische Geschichte," 53, on xii 9–10.1.

[116] xii 9–10.1; see also M. Casevitz, *Diodore* XII, Budé edition, 97–99; to which add G. de Sensi Sestito, *RIL* 110 (1976), 243–50.

Diodorus, however, omits the sentiment found in Photius's version, that a lazy state (τῆς ῥᾳθυμίας) cannot maintain its freedom for long.[117] Again the equation of internal decay and loss of power held little interest for Diodorus. Had the theme of decadence been important to Diodorus, there were numerous historical accounts, in addition to those of Ephorus and Timaeus, on which he could have drawn. The weakening of the Persian Empire through moral decay and its implications for imperial Athens were, of course, one of Herodotus's grand themes. In what is likely a Spartan speech before the battle of Thermopylae, Diodorus reflects Herodotus's dichotomy between the enslaved but wealthy Persians and the poor but free Greeks (x 34.7–11). Here, Diodorus is probably following Ephorus, who in turn took his material from Herodotus.[118] Where the narrative is fully preserved for the remainder of the Persian Wars (book xi), however, only in the condemnation of Pausanias (xi 46) is there an allusion to Persian decadence. Theopompus and Duris, too, strongly emphasized the theme of moral decay,[119] and both are thought to be Diodorus's occasional or frequent sources.[120] Diodorus could have exploited their use of τρυφή, had he wished to do so.

Diodorus's model for empire demonstrates his independence in matters of interpretation. Most of his sources argued that ruling states grow weak as imperial power corrupts their social values. But Diodorus preferred to stress the relationship

[117] DS iii 47.8 and *Codex* 250, 102, 459b.

[118] On Ephorus's use of Herodotus and Thucydides, see Jacoby, *FGH* IIc, 31; Pavan, *RAL* 16 (1961), 19–52, however, argues that Diodorus at times drew directly on Thucydides and Herodotus.

[119] *FGH* 115 (Theopompus) T 20a = Dion. Hal., *Pomp.* 6. On Ephorus and Theopompus on luxury, see also K. Trudinger, *Studien zur Geschichte der griechisch-roemischen Ethnographie*, 62ff., 139ff. and Passerini, *SIFC* 11 (1934), 44–52. On Duris of Samos: Kebric, *In the Shadow of Macedon*, 20–23; Phylarchus also exhibits an interest: *FGH* 81 F 44 = Athen. iv 141f–142f.

[120] Theopompus: N. Hammond, *CQ* 32 (1938), 137–51, and C. Welles, *Diodorus of Sicily* VIII, Loeb edition, 4. Duris: Kebric, *In the Shadow of Macedon*, 60–66, 70–79.

between rulers and subjects by explaining that kind actions bring loyalty, harsh ones rebellion. The pervasive use of the schema may have been intended as a warning to Rome. Diodorus held ambivalent feelings for the imperial power (Chapter 5), and he indicates that Rome reached the point of terrorizing its subjects. In failing to make the obvious prophecy, Diodorus perhaps felt more comfortable allowing the reader to draw his own conclusions about Rome's fate.[121] If that was his motive, then his preference for the ruler-subject paradigm over the stress on τρυφή is clarified. Diodorus was a provincial, with strong allegiance to Sicily; he was less concerned with what occurred within Roman society than with how Rome treated its subjects.

Despite his apparent departure from his sources when analyzing empires, Diodorus does not force the narrative to conform to his model. For example, he follows Polybius in condemning Perseus for his part in the Third Macedonian War, but later, when stressing the terrorizing tactics Rome employed in maintaining its empire, he himself makes the Macedonian king a victim.[122] The case of Athens is especially striking. Diodorus offers his explanation that Athens moved from clement behavior to terror while describing events of the 460s (xi 70.3–4). At that moment, however, his source, Ephorus, is denouncing the enemies of Athens and extolling its achievement.[123] Diodorus's pattern of decline creates a definite dissonance in the narrative, as Ephorus clearly meant to condemn Aegina, but Diodorus criticizes Athens.[124] In one of the rare instances in which the original words of Ephorus apparently survive, the reconstructed text describes the Athens of

---

[121] De Romilly, *La douceur dans la pensée grecque*, 53–61, stresses Diodorus's use of ἐπιείκεια in suggesting he was generally optimistic about Rome. But many passages do not support this: e.g., xxx 21.1; xxxii 4, 26–27; xxxiii 26.2; xxxiv/xxxv 23 (end); on which see Chapter 5.

[122] DS xxxi 8–9 and Polybius xxxvi 17.13; compare DS xxxii 4.5; see Chapter 5.

[123] For Ephorus on Athens and Sparta, see Pavan, *RAL* 16 (1961), 31–32.

[124] xi 70.2; cf. 78.3 and xii 28.1 on the phrasing. On the probable doublet, see R. Meiggs, *The Athenian Empire*, 51.

ten years earlier, in 470 B.C., as δικαιοτάτην, or a similar compliment.[125] Diodorus, however, substitutes ἐπιεικεστάτην (xi 59.3). The change is minor, but, in declaring that Athens was most clement, Diodorus sets up his charge of a few chapters later that Athens ceased acting ἐπιεικῶς and resorted to terror. Diodorus follows the account and the general interpretation of his source, in this case Ephorus, but makes his own moral point.[126] In examining the three concepts that Diodorus understood as forces of and within history, it becomes clear how he responded to the influence of his sources. For a Greek living within the Roman Empire and feeling devoid of practical power, moral improvement offered an avenue for personal fulfillment. Diodorus readily exploited a similar, though not identical, application of moral assessments in the Ephoran source material. But as it was part of his own philosophy of history, the practice is evident in books for which Ephorus was not his source. Similarly, certain aspects of fortune were part of Diodorus's own outlook. Unlike Polybius, Diodorus does not portray chance as a great power guiding the destiny of Rome and the Mediterranean. Somewhat ill-disposed toward Rome and its worldly success, Diodorus usually applies τύχη to individual circumstances, as a litmus test for moral character. One special application—that one should not despair amid misfortune—is perhaps a sentiment due directly to his sources. But as it was close enough to his own thoughts on fortune, it found its way into the *Bibliotheke*.[127]

[125] *P. Oxy.* XIII 1610 FF 4–5 = *FGH* 70 F 191; Hornblower, *Hieronymus of Cardia*, 28–29, 278. What can be read is [σο]φ[ωτάτην καὶ δικαι]οτά[την . . .], but its otherwise close relationship to Diodorus's account (see Grenfell and Hunt's comparison of the texts in *Oxyrhynchus Papyrus* XIII, 103) shows that Athens is being described, but not by the term ἐπιεικεστάτην. Isocrates, from whom Ephorus gets some of his material, refers to Athens as δικαιοτάτην: e.g., *On the Peace* 140.

[126] Diodorus later may have changed a Timaean sentiment from καλῶς to φιλανθρώπως to conform to his moral program: cf. xiii 19.5 with Plut., *Nic.* 28.3 = *FGH* 566 F 100b; see Chapter 4, n. 84.

[127] For Diodorus's independent use of such terms as φόβος and ψυχή as

The third historical concept examined here, the theory of empire, has more controls within the original sources. Diodorus set out a mechanistic explanation for the rise and fall of empires that generally avoided the question of social decay. Uninterested in the materialistic and institutional causes for empires,[128] Diodorus argues only that clement behavior earns states empires and that arrogant actions cause rebellions by their subjects. This moralistic structure is closely related to a facet of τύχη, for the ability to remain modest amid good fortune (εὐτυχία) is important to the maintenance of empire.[129] It has already been shown how chance and judgments involving moral utility interrelate. Although moral utility may be understood as Diodorus's main purpose in writing history, and τύχη and ἐπιείκεια as forces within history that act on events, all three concepts are for Diodorus interlocking. They also fit well into the picture of Diodorus's political outlook, as described in Chapters 5 and 6.

---

forces typical of the Hellenistic period, see Palm, *Über Sprache und Stil*, 167–71

[128] On which, see de Romilly, *Rise and Fall of States*, 20–41.

[129] i 60.3; xvii 14, 17.2, 17.4.

THREE

Culture's Progress

IN THE prooemium to book i, Diodorus announces that he will begin the *Bibliotheke* with a systematic treatment of the mythologies of the world (i 3.2). Though also including in the early books studies of topography, zoology, ethnography, and paradoxography, he considers the first six books devoted primarily to the recitation of myth and legend prior to the Trojan War.[1] Their organization is simple. Books i–iii cover the "barbarian" (i 4.6) East and books iv–vi treat the West. The Egyptians are discussed in book i; the Assyrians, Medes, Indians, Scythians, Amazons, and some eastern islands in book ii; and various aspects of Africa, including the Amazons, Atlantis, and the African version of Dionysus in book iii. Moving to Europe, book iv is devoted to the standard Greek myths; book v contains the mythologies and ethnographies of the islands of the Mediterranean and Red Seas and of Gaul, Spain, and northern Italy; and book vi, of which almost nothing survives, includes Euhemeran material on the Greek gods and originally went down to the Trojan War.[2]

A striking aspect of Diodorus's treatment of myth is that the first three books, covering the eastern lands, bear no obvious relationship to the historical portion of the *Bibliotheke*. Diodorus says that he had access to research materials in Alexandria and Rome,[3] where travelogues and local histories were certainly available. The histories of eastern lands were then becoming fashionable, as witnessed by the works of Alexander Polyhistor, Timagenes, and Pompeius Trogus. Yet

[1] i 3.2, 4.6; iv 1; xl 8.
[2] i 4.6; xiii 1.2; xiv 2.4; xl 8.
[3] i 4.2–4; iii 38.1; xvii 52.6.

55

CHAPTER THREE

Diodorus mentions no eastern peoples after book iii, unless they are directly involved with Greeks or Romans. In fact, in the first three books, Diodorus does not confine himself to pre-Trojan War material, but includes a few references to later history, as if to signal that he will not systematically treat the eastern lands later in the historical books.[4] In a practical sense, then, Diodorus's claim to universality is empty boasting. But an investigation into his view of progress reveals that books i–iii are philosophically connected to the rest of Diodorus's work and that they do help establish the universalism of the *Bibliotheke*. Once again it will be seen that material traditionally ascribed to Diodorus's sources is, in fact, of his making. His treatment of eastern mythologies and his view of progress are intricately connected to other themes in the *Bibliotheke* already established as being his own.

CHAPTERS 6–8 of book i form a transition between the proem and the Egyptian mythology and ethnography that take up the rest of that book. In chapters 6 and 7, Diodorus, acknowledging that he is following earlier authorities,[5] discusses different theories of the formation of the universe and life on earth. One theory, obviously of Peripatetic origin, held that the cosmos was always in existence and would remain so forever.[6] The other explanation, rendered in much greater detail, is that the cosmos formed out of indiscriminate mass through the interplay of heat and water (i 7). In chapter 8, Diodorus gives an account, again saying that it is found in his sources (i 8.1, 8.10), of the earliest generations of mankind. Humans came into a hostile world, having no notion of hoarding food or seeking shelter in the winter. Because necessity (χρεία) is the teacher (διδάσκαλος) of humanity, they learned not only to survive, but to develop important technical and social skills.

For much of this century, it was thought that a large part of

---

[4] Cf. C. Rubincam, *EMC/CV* 31, n.s. 6 (1987), 315–16; e.g., i 44–68.6, 83.8, 95.4–5; ii 32–34, 44.
[5] i 6.3, 8.1, and the indirect discourse of chap. 7.
[6] i 6.3; see most recently Burton, *Diodorus Siculus Book I*, 44.

chapters 7 and 8 derived from the fifth-century philosopher Democritus. It was argued that Diodorus took the discussion from his main source for the Egyptian narrative of book i, Hecataeus of Abdera, and transposed it to serve as an introduction to the entire *Bibliotheke*.[7] The chapters have subsequently been accepted as fragments of Democritus in standard editions.[8] But others believe there is some Posidonian material here, and part of chapter 7 is also now identified as a fragment from his work.[9] A third possibility, gaining acceptance, is that Diodorus, as he seems to suggest, found these ideas in some type of collection, perhaps modifying them to fit his own taste. The origins of the material and Diodorus's own contribution to them are then open to question.[10] But whether Diodorus took the discussion directly from a single source or drew on a variety of traditions and infused them with his own ideas, his descriptions of the cosmogony and zoogony find striking parallels in contemporary writers, especially Lucretius and Ovid.[11] At the very least, in using this material to preface his *Bibliotheke*, Diodorus was in step with current trends. Ideas expressed in chapters 6–8 of book i, in fact, are found throughout the history and are closely tied to other important themes.

The main sentiment of chapter 8 is that the human race started with nothing and was forced to learn through necessity

[7] Initially argued by K. Reinhardt, *Hermes* 47 (1912), 492–513; most recently, Murray, *JEA* 56 (1970), 169–70. On the transposition, see esp. T. Cole, *Democritus and the Sources of Greek Anthropology*, 174–92.

[8] E.g., H. Diels, *Die Fragmente der Vorsokratiker*[6], F 68 B5.

[9] DS i 7.3–6 = F 306 (Theiler); most recently, Fraser, *Ptolemaic Alexandria* I, 497.

[10] Drews, *AJP* 83 (1962), 108; E. Dodds, *The Ancient Concept of Progress and Other Essays on Greek Literature and Belief*, 10–11; Burton, *Diodorus Siculus Book I*, 44–51; S. Blundell, *The Origins of Civilization in Greek and Roman Thought*, 176–77, on chap. 8.

[11] Spoerri, *Späthellenistische Berichte über Welt, Kultur und Götter*, 34–38, 117–18, on DS i 7, and Ovid, *Met.* i 5f., 416f.; Cole, *Democritus and the Sources of Greek Anthropology*, 24–46, on DS i 8 and on Lucretius, Posidonius, and Vitruvius.

(χρεία), which is the teacher (διδάσκαλος) of humanity. The notion is common enough to many philosophies,[12] and Diodorus uses it repeatedly. A similar sentiment is found twice later in book i, both when Diodorus is following Hecataeus and when he is thought to be intruding into the text himself.[13] Later (ii 38.2), when generally following Megasthenes' history of India,[14] but exhibiting demonstrable independence in doing so, he quotes the very words of i 8. Then, in a part of the Bibliotheke based on Agatharchides, he recurrently employs the philosophy that χρεία is the teacher of mankind.[15] Another text of the same material from Agatharchides is transmitted by Photius, where the notion of necessity compelling humanity to learn is completely missing.[16] Either Photius excised all references to the idea from the Agatharchidean text, or Diodorus has added them himself. And in discussions where Posidonius is Diodorus's apparent or possible source, there is found again a similar sentiment.[17] The thought occurs too often in the Bibliotheke to be merely the contribution of one of Diodorus's sources. Moreover, the necessary precondition for development through χρεία—that the human race was born into a harsh and uncivilized condition—is found in a speech that Diodorus clearly helped shape.[18] Although that

[12] Spoerri, Späthellenistische Berichte über Welt, Kultur und Götter, 144–48, on Epicureanism and Stoicism. Χρεία can mean need/necessity or use/experience, and contains both ideas here, as πεῖρα at i 8.7 indicates: see Spoerri, 144–48, and K. Thraede, RhM 105 (1962), 167–69; see also i 43.1, discussed later in this chapter.

[13] i 60.9, 90.1; on which, Murray, JEA 56 (1970), 146.

[14] FGH 715 F 4 = DS ii 35–42.

[15] iii 15.7, 18.7, 19.2, 24.4.

[16] DS iii 15.7 = Phot. Codex 250 31, 449a; DS 18.7 = Phot. 42, 450b; DS 19.2 = Phot. 43, 450b. Palm, Über Sprache und Stil, 15–26, vigorously defends Photius's reliability as a preserver of the original, though others do not; factual parallels between the accounts in Diodorus and Photius are discussed most recently by W. Peremans, Historia 16 (1967), 432–55.

[17] v 39.2 = FGH 87 118; xxxviii 24.1; but cf. xxvi 11.1.

[18] xiii 25.3; see Chapter 4.

sentiment was particularly popular in the fifth century,[19] it was again topical in Diodorus's time.[20] Diodorus may have been influenced by a combination of source material and contemporary interest.

Other ideas found in chapter 8 also recur throughout the *Bibliotheke*. Diodorus knows of two explanations for the cosmogony. The first, that the universe has always existed, he again employs in his Babylonian version of the cosmogony (ii 30.1), which includes echoes of his opening prologue (i 1.3: the organizing force of divine πρόνοια). The second explanation, involving the natural generation of the universe and of life, he twice uses when following different sources.[21] Diodorus explains that the earliest social groupings resulted from the need to rid the land of wild animals (i 8.1–2). The overcoming of wild animals as a requirement for civilization occurs twice more in the books on mythology,[22] and Heracles is often described as performing this benefaction for mankind.[23] Diodorus may also have drawn on this theme in composing a speech urging the destruction of Carthage at the end of the Second Punic War.[24] The only other Greek known to stress this aspect of social development was Protagoras, and he, or Plato, associated it with Prometheus's gift of fire.[25] The theme may have been of particular interest to Diodorus, whose homeland faced Libya, a country especially infested by wild animals;[26] and the emphasis on Heracles as tamer of wild

[19] J. de Romilly, *Annali della Scuola Normale Superiore di Pisa* 35 (1966), 143–91.

[20] Spoerri, *Späthellenistische Berichte über Welt, Kultur und Götter*, 144–48, on Horace, Virgil, Lucretius, and Posidonius.

[21] iii 2.1 (Schwartz, *RE* 5, 673, argues for Artemidorus as the source) and v 56.3 (Schwartz, *RE* 5, 678, suggests a compilation).

[22] i 24.5–6; iii 25.1.

[23] i 24.5–6; ii 39.2; iv 17.4–5; v 76.1.

[24] xxvii 18; see Chapter 4.

[25] Plato, *Protag.* 322; Cole, *Democritus and the Sources of Greek Anthropology*, 34, 51.

[26] E.g., i 30.2; xx 40.

beasts may reflect the high esteem in which Agyrium, Diodorus's hometown, held that hero (iv 24. 1–6). The next stage in the development of civilization, as stated in book i, was the acquisition of language (i 8.3–5, 9). That was a theme stressed by other first-century writers: Lucretius, Cicero, Horace, and Vitruvius. And even if Diodorus and Vitruvius drew on a common source,[27] Diodorus also emphasizes the importance of language in his opening prooemium (i 2. 5–8), which is now taken to be Diodorus's own work (see Chapter 1).

The late first century was a period of great expansion in the quantity and genres of literature, as Rome became a magnet attracting almost all literati. Even a writer on the fringes of society, as Diodorus appears to have been (see Chapter 6), would be attuned to the intellectual currents. Certain notions, perhaps already voiced in an earlier period, became fashionable (perhaps again) in the first century. A pattern of contemporary individuals raising comparable questions and offering similar answers is a paradigm for intellectual and scientific progress.[28] Ideas Diodorus acquired were in the air.

Moreover, Diodorus wrote a universal history beginning with the mythologies of the world. It is, of course, appropriate to place a discussion of the origins of the cosmos and human society precisely at the beginning of such a work. The subject was of interest to earlier historians,[29] and Sicilian historians traditionally began their works with an *archaeologia*.[30] There is no reason to doubt that, whatever his sources, Diodorus had substantial control over the material he employed in the early chapters of book i[31] and that he saw χρεία as greatly contributing to human progress.

[27] Most recently: Cole, *Democritus and the Sources of Greek Anthropology*, 60–69; yet see Blundell, *The Origins of Civilization in Greek and Roman Thought*, 194–95.

[28] So T. Kuhn, *The Structure of Scientific Revolutions*; but see S. Toulmin, *Human Understanding* I, 98–123.

[29] Cole, *Democritus and the Sources of Greek Anthropology*, 4.

[30] Fornara, *The Nature of History*, 36–38.

[31] Cf. E. Havelock, *The Liberal Temper in Greek Politics*, 73–86, who sees pre-Socratic material behind book i.

Beside necessity or experience, there is another civilizing force. Throughout the early books and in all the lands of the earth, there emerged culture heroes, who, for their benefactions to humanity, were subsequently immortalized by mankind. For example:

Of Osiris they say that, being of a beneficent turn of mind, and eager for glory, he gathered together a great army, with the intention of visiting all the inhabited earth and teaching the race of men how to cultivate the vine and sow wheat and barley; for he supposed that if he made men give up their savagery and adopt a gentle manner of life he would receive immortal honors because of the magnitude of his benefaction [εὐεργεσία]. And this did in fact take place.[32]

Diodorus's early books are filled with the names of inventors, lawgivers, founders, originators of the arts and sciences, and great achievers who later gained immortality because of their benefactions (εὐεργεσίαι).

Necessity and benefaction are the two explanations for progress that Diodorus and many other ancient writers employed. Necessity, or χρεία, reflects a general condition and is a notion that an author inclined toward anthropological explanations might use. But the identification of culture heroes and their benefactions captured the greater curiosity of the ancients. By the fifth century B.C. individual studies listing society's benefactors and culture heroes were being produced.[33] History writing and the identification of these first discoverers were closely associated. The influential historian Ephorus even wrote a work on discoveries, Περί εὑρημάτων, which was employed by Diodorus.[34] Although little of his mono-

---

[32] i 17.1–2; that these are Diodorus's own words, see Murray, *JEA* 56 (1970), 149; cf. Schwartz, *RE* 5, 671.

[33] Cole, *Democritus and the Sources of Greek Anthropology*, 5; more recently A. Momigliano, "The Origins of Universal History," in *Settimo contributo*, 83–84 = *On Pagans, Jews, and Christians*, 37–38.

[34] *FGH* 70 FF 2–5, 104–6; DS v 64.4 = F 104.

graph survives, it seems that in ignoring Lacedaemonian claims to the benefactions of their ancestors, Ephorus furthered his polemic against the Spartans. The identification of culture heroes thus could have political consequences.[35] But Greeks could not rely solely on individual benefactors to account for progress. The barbarian East had a longer tradition than did Europe and consequently asserted that culture heroes arose in that environment.[36] The explanation that society advanced instead through χρεία came to be used by Hellenistic writers who wished to minimize that claim.[37]

Although both notions of progress might have political implications, some ancients had no problem reconciling them. Protagoras argued that the gifts bestowed by culture heroes were a direct response to the need (χρεία) of society. Similarly, for Diodorus the need might remain only that without the intervention and inspiration of benefactors.[38] To be sure, Lucretius, Diodorus's contemporary, could explain the development of civilization through both forces.[39] Χρεία meant not only need or necessity, but also experience (see n. 12). As want or need drives humanity to gain experience, the environment is established for the appearance of a benefactor. In Diodorus's account, Demeter does not bestow the gift of wheat on the Sicilians and Athenians until she is well received by both peoples: there are preconditions for the appearance of a benefactor (v 4.3–4).

The coexistence of necessity and benefactors can also be found in Diodorus's explanation of early Egyptian development. Initially Egyptians subsisted on roots and branches, learning which to eat through experience (πεῖραν: i 43.1).

---

[35] A. Kleingünther, *ΠΡΩΤΟΣ ΕΥΡΕΤΗΣ: Untersuchungen zur Geschichte einer Fragestellung, Philologus* suppl. 26.1 (1933), 148–49. On Ephorus's hostility toward Sparta, see further Pavan, *RAL* 16 (1961), 31f.

[36] E.g., B. Perry, *Aesopica* I, 4ff.

[37] K. Thraede, *RhM* 105 (1962), 178.

[38] Cf. de Romilly, *Annali della Scuola Normale Superiore di Pisa* 35 (1966), 155.

[39] Lucr., *DNR* v 1028f., 1104f. On progress, see also v 332f.

This is precisely the method for the development of all civilizations Diodorus describes earlier (i 8.5–7). After experience finally taught them to build houses and domesticate animals, Egyptians turned to eating bread, the discovery of which was attributed by some to Isis (cf. i 14.1), but by the priestly tradition to mortal men who were picked to be kings because of their benefactions (i 43.5–6). Egyptian culture developed using both methods: initial evolution through need and experience prepared civilization for the gift of its benefactors.

The issue of who introduced writing and when again exemplifies Diodorus's tendency to combine explanations of progress. Early in book i, he argues that myth is nonhistorical, because the events it purports to describe occurred before the development of writing (i 9.2; cf. i 29.5–6); he later notes that the creation of writing is important to establishing historical accuracy (v 57.3–5). Diodorus attaches the greatest significance to literacy: "for it is by means of [reading and writing] that most of the affairs of life and such as are most useful are concluded, like votes, letters, covenants, laws, and all other things which make the greatest contribution to orderly life" (xii 13.1; Oldfather). In determining the inventor of this essential tool, Diodorus keeps an open mind. He allows claims by various peoples that they were the first—the Egyptians (i 69.4), Ethiopians (iii 3.4–5), and Phoenicians (iii 67.1)—and he credits the Etruscans with helping to perfect the alphabet (v 40.2). These attributions of writing to a particular civilization are consistent with the belief that it is a recent innovation, as argued elsewhere (i 9.2). Here Diodorus associates writing with χρεία, or gradual cultural development. But he is also prepared to include the claims that writing was a gift of a mythological benefactor: either Hermes (i 16.1) or the Muses (v 74.1). Diodorus sees no inconsistency in including explanations of civilizations developing on their own and those accelerated by beneficent individuals.[40]

[40] For other traditions as to who gave writing to humanity, see Kleingünther, ΠΡΩΤΟΣ ΕΥΡΕΤΗΣ, 130–31, and Thraede, *RhM* 105 (1962), 179.

In reconciling the two explanations for civilization's progress, Diodorus had a less partisan though no less passionately held intention than some earlier theorists. The uncovering of Diodorus's particular motive for stressing human progress in both its forms will help account for the inclusion of eastern myth in books i–iii. In the prooemium to book i, Diodorus connects the writing of history with expressions of universality. He talks about "all men . . . united one to another by their kinship" and of Providence which "brought the orderly arrangement of the visible stars and the natures of men together into one common relationship" (i 1.3; Oldfather). There is Stoic influence here, and it used to be thought that Diodorus took the proem from Posidonius. Now it is recognized for what it is: Diodorus's own composition and a modest reflection of *koine* sentiment (see Chapter 1). In fact, Diodorus voices a similar expression later in his work where Posidonius could not be the source (xii 26.2–4) and where it is directly preceded by material almost certainly of Diodorus's creation.[41] Though not a Stoic thinker, Diodorus chose material that embodied many such sentiments,[42] and his frequently employed standard of judgment—whether someone or something benefited humanity (ὠφελῆσαι τὸν κοινὸν βίον)—is well founded in Stoicism.[43]

Diodorus's dual explanations for progress help further this universalism. Necessity was a force common to all societies, but the existence of individual culture heroes could inspire racial competition. Diodorus spent his early career in Alexandria, where particularistic strife among Egyptians, Jews, and Greeks abounded. One intellectual response by all groups was to argue for the chronological primacy of their own founding legends and hence of their respective races.[44] In contrast, Dio-

---

[41] On xii 26.1, see M. Casevitz, *Diodore* xii, Budé edition, xi, n. 1.

[42] E.g., the voyage of Iambulus (ii 55–60), on which see most recently, J. Ferguson, *Utopias of the Classical World*, 124–29, and Sartori, *Athenaeum* 62 (1984), 513–14.

[43] See Chapter 1, n. 12.

[44] E.g. K. Thraede, *RAC* 5, 1242–45; B. Wacholder, *HTR* 61 (1968), 451–81; M. Hadas, *Hellenistic Culture: Fusion and Diffusion*, 83–104.

dorus emphasizes that all legends involving such benefactors are valid. In the rest of the *Bibliotheke*, Diodorus arranges material annalistically, designating years by Olympic victors, Athenian archons, and Roman consuls. But when dealing with mythology, he claims not to know of any table that puts that material in proper chronological order. Rather than dating myths, he simply divides them by East (books i–iii) and West (books iv–vi). Diodorus may be reacting against a recent influential work. Castor's *Chronological Epitome*, appearing soon after 60 B.C., was perhaps the first important attempt in more than two centuries to order the mythologies of the world and attach dates.[45] In that respect alone it might produce contention among intellectuals. But it also reversed the general trend of Greek chronographers who had acknowledged the exceptional antiquity of the barbarians. Castor's chronology ignored certain accepted eastern mythologies and put Greek origins as far back as the barbarian.[46] Varro used Castor's study when writing *De Gente Populi Romani* in 43 B.C.[47] But Diodorus, starting to compose the *Bibliotheke* just three years earlier, specifically denies the existence of a trustworthy chronology of myths. He does this in the prooemia to books i (5.1) and iv (1.1), at the close of the *Bibliotheke* (xl 8), and when beginning his study of mythology.[48] His emphatic denial may be a po-

---

[45] Fraser, *Ptolemaic Alexandria* I, 456–57.

[46] Most recently, Wacholder, *HTR* 61 (1968), 464–65.

[47] *FGH* 250 F 9 = Augustine, *De Civ. Dei* xxi 8; L. Taylor, *CP* 29 (1934), 221–29.

[48] i 9.2–4. Jacoby (*FGH* IIc, 43) suggests that that is from Ephorus, because of his famous distinction between history and myth (T 8 = DS iv 1.3) and his statement that, while contemporary events can be reported accurately, it is unlikely that old events can be remembered through such a long time (F 9). But the latter statement says nothing of myth or even a time before historians; it refers simply to events (πράξεις) of long ago, and Jacoby rightly points to Thuc. i 20.1 as a parallel. Moreover, Diodorus anticipates i 9.2–4 with i 6.2, and at i 9.5 actually attacks Ephorus for accepting prehistorical traditions as historical! Diodorus may well have been inspired by an Ephoran sentiment without copying from him directly. That Diodorus did not use Castor, see Schwartz, *RE* 5, 665; Jacoby *FGH* IIb, 816; F. Càssola, *ANRW* II 30.1, 828.

lemic against Castor: though acknowledging the issue of racial primacy, he refuses to join in the debate (i 9.3). The only occasion when Diodorus accepts the claims about the early date of certain myths is when, predictably, they concern Sicily (v 1.4).

In another way as well Diodorus worked to defuse the inherent competition regarding the earliest civilization. In the first six books (though book vi is highly fragmentary), Diodorus notes the benefactions of dozens of individuals, most of whom were deified for their service to humanity. These are divided fairly evenly between books i–iii and iv–vi.[49] By including the myths of the East, Diodorus can give credit to both sides.

He also presents barbarian myths sympathetically. In at least four instances, Diodorus may have added to the account of Hecataeus a notice that a particular Egyptian figure had benefited humanity and received divine honors in return.[50] Two of these concern Osiris while on his great expedition (i 17–20). Inconsistencies indicate that the entire story was not part of Hecataeus's original narrative, and similarities with a later event that was in Hecataeus suggest the model Diodorus may have used to invent his version.[51] Osiris is portrayed as a great conqueror and benefactor to humanity, who commanded the likes of Hermes, Heracles, and Apollo. The Egyptian etiology for the discovery of ivory (by Osiris) is juxtaposed and given equal weight with the Greek claim (by Dionysus), and Diodorus appears to favor the Egyptian over the Greek version of how Prometheus was saved.

---

[49] i 13.1, 17.2, 18.5, 24.7, 90.2–3; ii 34.5, 38.5; iii 9.1–2, 56.5, 61.5–6, 64.2, 70.8; iv 1.4, 1.7, 8.5, 82.5; v 64.2, 66.3, 68.1, 73.3, 74.3, 76.1–2; vi 1.2, 2.1.

[50] i 17.2, 18.5, 24.7; 90.2–3; on which see Murray, *JEA* 56 (1970), 144. Murray is only slightly less radical than E. Schwartz, *Hermes* 40 (1885), 223–62, and Jacoby (*FGH* 264 FF 2 and 25) in arguing that book i is substantially Hecataeus's work rather than Diodorus's. Far more conservative are Spoerri, *Späthellenistische Berichte über Welt, Kultur und Götter*; Burton, *Diodorus Siculus Book I*; and Sartori, *Athenaeum* 74 (1984), 492–536.

[51] See Murray, *JEA* 56 (1970), 149–50.

In writing on India, Diodorus generally follows the account of Megasthenes,[52] but again departs to stress his own cosmopolitanism. Diodorus says simply that Dionysus came from "regions to the west."[53] Arrian, however, following Megasthenes more faithfully,[54] depicts Dionysus as being Greek and an invader,[55] as does Strabo, who quotes Megasthenes here.[56] There was, in fact, another tradition that claimed Dionysus came to India from Assyria,[57] which Diodorus perhaps was here acknowledging. But in any case, by remaining ambiguous about Dionysus's place of birth, Diodorus avoids referring to a possible Hellenic origin. Both Diodorus and Arrian maintain Megasthenes' allusion to an Indian account that Heracles was born in India,[58] and discuss what the two gods taught the Indians and the reverence in which they were held. But Diodorus employs a formula frequently found in the *Bibliotheke* that, by ruling so wisely and making so many benefactions, they were also immortalized there.[59] Also, whereas Arrian makes Dionysus—the fate of Heracles is undiscussed—depart the country,[60] Diodorus emphasizes the local tradition in stating that they both died in India.[61]

As part of his anthropology of India, Diodorus includes the legend of the Indian region named *Meros*, which locals claimed was responsible for the subsequent Greek belief that Dionysus was nurtured in the thigh (μηρός) of Zeus (ii 38.4). The story had already been criticized by Theophrastus (*HP* iv 4.1), and, when Arrian tells it in the *Anabasis* where he is not

---

[52] DS ii 35–42 = *FGH* 715 F 42.

[53] ἐκ τῶν πρὸς ἑσπέραν τόπων: ii 37.3.

[54] Cf. O. Stein, *RE* 15.1, 254.

[55] *FGH* 715 F 12 = Arr., *Ind.* 7.4–5.

[56] *FGH* 715 F 11a = Strabo xv 6.1.

[57] P. Wesseling, in Eyring, *Diodori Siculi Bibliothecae Historicae Libri* II, 444, on ii 37.3.

[58] DS ii 39.1; Arr., *Ind.* 8.4 = *FGH* 715 F 13. Strabo, xv 6.1 = *FGH* 715 F 11a, depicts him as a foreigner.

[59] ii 38.5, 39.4: on the construction, see above, n. 49.

[60] *FGH* 715 F 12 = Arr., *Ind.* 8.1.

[61] ii 38.6, 39.4. Dionysus returns from India in another tradition: iv 3.1.

following Megasthenes,[62] he puts it in the mouth of Indian envoys to Alexander.[63] To Arrian, or his source, the explanation was related by Indians who are only anxious to secure Alexander's cooperation. Diodorus, on the other hand, adds legitimacy to the account by making it part of his ethnological narrative.[64] At every place where the treatments of Diodorus and Arrian differ, Diodorus's version is more sympathetic to non-Greeks.

The universalistic treatment of benefactors fits well with Diodorus's anthropology. Underlying human development is χρεία, which is common to all mankind and drives civilization. Arising out of emerging societies are exceptional individuals who offer important gifts to humanity. The historicity of these individuals is not important to Diodorus, for he makes known his own skepticism about all myth.[65] But his particular application of Euhemerism provides the logical bridge between χρεία and the unique individual. If gods were humans deified for their gifts to mankind, their acts of benefaction occurred while they were members of that evolving civilization. Χρεία and εὐεργεσία mutually contribute to the development of society: necessity was a general condition for all humans, while culture heroes arose in specific locations to help every civilization progress. As Diodorus carefully celebrates the accomplishments of all culture heroes, Greek and barbarian, necessity and individual benefactors work in harmony and emphasize his universalistic sympathies.

[62] Cf. Curt. viii 10.12.

[63] Anab. v i 5; cf. v ii 5.

[64] It is argued that Diodorus there augments Megasthenes with another source (Stein, RE 15.1, 252ff.), but this is merely denying the possibility of Diodorus's own creativity: cf. the methodology of P. Brunt, Arrian: History of Alexander and India II, 448. Diodorus offers another story of the Indian Dionysus when he presents all the versions and seems to give primacy to the Indian account: iii 66.3–5, esp. iv 1.7. Diodorus held his ground against Theophrastus and other Hellenistic writers who attacked the Indian version, on whom see Fraser, Ptolemaic Alexandria IIa, 343, n. 101.

[65] i 23.8, 69.7; iv 1, 8.8; H. Volkmann, RhM 98 (1955), 354–67, E. Gabba, RSI 96 (1984), 860–62, Sartori, Athenaeum 72 (1984), 520–29.

Diodorus's understanding of progress is closely related to the cosmogony he develops in i 6–8.[66] There, he argues that primitive, hostile conditions set the stage for future development. If Diodorus had adopted the often-expressed alternative cosmogony of an initial, perfected Golden Age and a subsequent decline,[67] it would have conflicted with his notion of continued improvement through the appearance of culture heroes. Consequently, though the *Bibliotheke* is the greatest repository of utopian literature from antiquity, none of it is set in a Golden Age of the past. Following Euhemerus,[68] Diodorus frequently portrays Panchaea in the present tense, as if it were an existing island (cf. v 41.4, 42.4), like many of the others he describes. Perhaps because of its contemporary setting, the society depicted is not perfect: the Panchaeans are generally warlike (v 45.3), and soldiers are needed to protect against dangerous bands of robbers who attack farmers (v 46.1). In detailing other so-called utopias, Diodorus stresses that they are fictitious[69] or implies that they exist in the present.[70] None is portrayed as a Golden Age of antiquity, after which civilization declined. Diodorus yields to the contemporary interest in utopias,[71] but is careful to allow room for continuous progress, in the form of χρεία and benefactors.

Diodorus's stress on culture heroes was shaped by contemporary thought. Veneration for exceptional service was central to Hellenistic political and social philosophy.[72] Under the

---

[66] Cf. Havelock, *The Liberal Temper in Greek Politics*, 78.

[67] On which, most recently I. Kidd, *Posidonius. Vol. II: The Commentary* II, 962–63.

[68] v 41–46 = *FGH* 63 F 1.

[69] Iambulus's Island of the Sun (ii 55.1), which is also part of a different οἰκουμένη (ii 56); Dionysius Scytobrachion's island of Hesperia (iii 53.4–5 = *FGH* 32 F 7); and the Hyperboreans of Hecataeus (ii 47 = *FGH* 264 F 7).

[70] Nysa is described in the present tense, whereas the mythology pertaining to it is in the past tense: iii 68.4–69 = *FGH* 32 (Dionysius Scytobrachion) F 8.

[71] For the Hellenistic taste in utopias, see E. Gabba, *JRS* 71 (1981), 58–60; fuller bibliography in G. Aalders, *Political Thought in Hellenistic Times*, 64–73.

[72] M. Rostovtzeff, *SEHHW* III, 1358–59, n. 5; Oehler, *RE* 6, 978–81, for the early evidence.

newly established monarchies, benefaction became an obligation to the individual and society, as kings were expected to perform acts of goodwill and beneficence.[73] Greek cities frequently acknowledged Rome's good deeds (κοιναὶ εὐεργενίαι), too.[74] At the same time, there developed a strong association between the great benefactor and the divine. Within a generation of Alexander, his achievements were being compared with the labors of Heracles[75] and associated with the deeds of Dionysus, who became the great invader and civilizer of lands from Libya to India.[76]

Among Diodorus's sources for the first six books are several Hellenistic authors credited with the tradition of the deified mortal, especially Hecataeus of Abdera, Euhemerus, Megasthenes, and Dionysius Scytobrachion.[77] But so little of their work exists outside of the *Bibliotheke* that the integrity of their ideas apart from Diodoran intrusion cannot be established with certainty.[78] Indeed, there is substantial reason to

[73] De Romilly, *La douceur dans la pensée grecque*, 216–30; Murray, *JEA* 56 (1970), 159–60, for Ptolemaic kings; in Diodorus, see i 90.3 and cf. ii 28.7 and xxxiv 4.4 for kingly ἐπιείκεια, an attribute closely tied to εὐεργεσία.

[74] E.g., H. Volkmann, *Hermes* 82 (1954), 467; G. Bowersock, *Augustus and the Greek World*, 12–13, 150–51; L. Robert, *CRAI* (1969), 42–64; see also DS xxxi 4.1. Bowersock, *Augustus and the Greek World*, 112–21, 150–51, and C. Habicht, *Le culte des souverains dans l'empire Romaine*, Fondation Hardt, *Entretiens* 19, 61–62, discuss cults dedicated to Romans.

[75] M. van der Valk, *REG* 71 (1958), 158–59, on the *Tabula Albana (FGH* 40). On the later comparisions with Alexander, see D. Michel, *Alexander als Vorbild fur Pompeius, Caesar, und Marcus Antonius*, and D. Kienast, *Gymnasium* 76 (1969), 430–56.

[76] A. Nock, *JHS* 48 (1928), 26–30 = Nock, *Essays*, 140–44; Fraser, *Ptolemaic Alexandria* I, 342.

[77] Schwartz, *RE* 5, 670–78, is still generally convincing on the sources for books i–vi. On the redating of Dionysius Scytobrachion, see J. Rusten, *Dionysius Scytobrachion*, 85–92.

[78] E.g., Spoerri, *Späthellenistische Berichte über Welt, Kultur und Götter*, 164–211, and Thraede, *RAC* 6, 879–82, are not often followed in assigning i 11–13 to Diodorus rather than Hecataeus. But important questions remain about Diodorus's possible intrusion at i 11.1 and 13.1. Cole, *Democritus and the Sources of Greek Anthropology*, 156, n. 29, most recently argues that Diodorus himself separates the οὐράνιοι θεοί from the θεοὶ εὐεργέται, and this is

believe that Diodorus played a significant role in designing the image of culture hero often attributed to his sources.

The theme of civilizers, inventors, and city builders with their resulting deification occurs regularly in the early books of the *Bibliotheke*. Almost seventy times in the first five books and the very few fragments of book vi, Diodorus records a benefactor's gift to humanity[79] and the consequent divine election.[80] The specific description of a benefactor's deification is highly formulaic, with the precise wording being nearly unique to the *Bibliotheke*.[81] Yet it is found in every part of the work, regardless of Diodorus's current source.[82]

Now the explanation that "deities had been generals, ad-

strengthened by the comment of Tzetzes (*Chiliades* i 812–20), who states that Diodorus, like Plato and Plutarch, made that distinction himself. It is an especially compelling argument if vi 1.8 is Diodoran: most recently accepted by Fraser, *Ptolemaic Alexandria* IIa, 451, n. 816. Even among the "radicals," Schwartz, Jacoby, and Murray, there is signficant disagreement as to the extent of Diodorus's intervention in book i. See also Fraser, *Ptolemaic Alexandria* I, 497–99.

[79] Discussed generally at i 13.1; ii 25.8; iii 9.1–2; iv 1.4; v 46.3, 64.2, 66.3; vi 1.2, 2.1; individual gifts found in the *TLG* machine-readable tape, s.vv. εὐεργεσία, εὕρεσις, and ἐξευρίσκω.

[80] Osiris: i 17.2, 18.5, 20.5; Isis: i 22.2; Dionysus: ii 38.5, iii 63.4, 64.2, 70.8; Uranus: iii 56.5; Titaea: iii 57.2; Hesperus: iii 60.3; daughters of Atlas: iii 60.5; Heracles: i 24.7 and passim; Theseus: iv 62.4; Aristaeus: iv 82.5–6; Orion: iv 85.5; Halia: v 55.7; Phorbas: v 58.5; Althaemenes: v 59.4; Dactyli: v 64.6; the second generation of gods: v 66.3, 67.5; Hestia: v 68.1; Hephaestus: i 13.3 and v 74.3; Demeter: v 68.3; Zeus: v 71.6; Minos: v 79.2; Minos's sons: v 79.4; Tennes: v 83.3; the Dioscori: vi 6.1; Aeneas: vii 5.2; in general: i 2.4; iv 1.4; v 64.2.

[81] On τυχεῖν ἀθανάτων τιμῶν, see Wesseling, in Eyring, *Diodori Siculi Bibliothecae Historicae Libri* I, 325, on i 17.2, and 319, on i 13.1: Wesseling uncharacteristically cannot cite parallels in Diodorus's usual sources.

[82] A sampling: i 13.1 = *FGH* 264 (Hecataeus) F 25; ii 34.3–6 = *FGH* 688 (Ctesias) F 5 (not ii 4, 20.2 = F 1b with FF 1 c, m: Semiramis was born a god); ii 38.5 = *FGH* 715 (Megasthenes) F 42; iii 9.1–2 = Agatharchides (Schwartz, *RE* 5, 673); iii 56.5 = *FGH* 32 (Dionysius Scytobrachion) F 7; iv 8.5 = Matris of Thebes (Schwartz, *RE* 5, 676); iv 82.5 = Timaeus (Schwartz, *RE* 5, 677); v 46.2 = *FGH* 63 (Euhemerus) F 1; cf. v 35.2 = *FGH* 87 (Posidonius) F 117, on which see Chapter 4.

mirals, and kings who lived a long time ago"[83] is a classic Euhemeran sentiment, and it is an interpretation found frequently in Diodorus's sources. But the theme of lawgivers,
inventors, and the like also receiving divine election by a
grateful humanity is not found in any of Diodorus's sources
outside of what is preserved in his work. Diodorus may well
have reshaped much of the traditions he used, emphasizing
that civilizing gifts also earned mythological characters their
immortality. Some controls are available to support this theory. In drawing on Megasthenes, Diodorus employs his usual
explanation—that Dionysus in return for his numerous benefactions received divine honors from the Indians (ii 38.5). But
Arrian, using the same source, holds that as part of his benefactions Dionysus taught the Indians to worship him as the
god he already was.[84] It is possible that Diodorus refashioned
the tradition to conform to his own interpretation. And with
some degree of confidence, it can be determined that, at least
four times while following Hecataeus of Abdera, Diodorus
invents episodes involving deified culture heroes, as noted
previously. Further, when discussing who bestowed the gift
of literacy on humanity, he knows of Ephorus's version involving nondivine figures, but instead attributes the invention
to the Muses who consequently receive immortal fame from
humanity.[85] Many writers testified that the gods bestowed the
blessings of civilization on mankind, and many asserted that
the gods were originally human. But to argue that humans
were immortalized by other humans because of these civilizing gifts, instead of for being great generals or kings, was to
cross the fine line between those who wrote as euhemerizers

[83] Plut.,*Mor.* 360a = *FGH* 63 (Euhemerus) T 4e.

[84] *Ind.* 7.8 = *FGH* 715 F 12. Lactantius preserves Euhemeran material that
similarly has Zeus establish his own cults after performing benefactions: *FGH*
63 FF 23 (*Div. Inst.* i 22.21–25) and 24 (*Div. Inst.* 11.45–46). Diodorus infrequently asserts that a god established his own cult: i 86.3; iii 55.9, 65.2, 74.1;
iv 24.4.

[85] v 74.1 with v 73.1; cf. Jacoby on *FGH* 70 F 105.

and those who were heurematists.[86] Diodorus, even more than the contemporary Varro,[87] may have been among the first and the most eager to be both.

In the historical narrative, too, Diodorus emphasizes the theme of deified culture hero. He notes the deification of nearly a dozen individuals,[88] and at times his attribution of divine honors is somewhat exaggerated. The extant decrees honoring Q. Mucius Scaevola's benefactions, for example, do not mention he was deified, as Diodorus suggests.[89] Caesar is

[86] Cf. Cole, *Democritus and the Sources of Greek Anthropology*, 48–50, and esp. Thraede, *RAC* 5, 1219–21.

[87] Augustine, *De Civ. Dei* xviii 3, 6, 8, 12, 15, 16, which are fragments of *De Gente Populi Romani*; cf. H. Peter, *Historicorum Romanorum Reliquiae* II², 228–34. Yet xviii 10 suggests Varro may have treated the gods as benefactors more collectively than individually and may have cast them in a more mythological light than did Diodorus. Artapanus, a Jewish historian of the third or second century B.C., states that, because of his great benefactions to their land, Egyptian priests deemed Moses worthy of divine honors (τὸν Μώϋσον ὑπὸ τῶν ἱερέων ἰσοθέου τιμῆς καταξιωθέντα: Eusebius, *PE* ix 27.6). Although in using Hecataeus he is generally thought to be reflecting euhemerizing tendencies (e.g., *Old Testament Pseudepigraphica* II, 889–95, ed. J. Charlesworth), it is dangerous to draw that conclusion from this one example, for Egyptians traditionally deified their leaders. Moreover, to Jews and thus to Artapanus himself, Moses was obviously not considered a god. Thus Artapanus is not trying to explain how the gods began as humans.

[88] Gelon (xi 38.5–6); Hieron (xi 66.4); Diocles (xiii 35.2; xiv 18); Dion (xvi 20.6); Alexander (xvii 102.4; xviii 28.4–5); Hephaestion (xvii 115.6; on the text: E. Bickerman, *Athenaeum* 41 [1963], 81–83); Ptolemy I (xx 100.3); Demetrius (xx 102.3, as a founder); Philopoemen (xxix 18); Q. Mucius Scaevola (xxxvii 6). Cassander sought immortal fame (ἀθανάτου δόξης: xix 53.2) for reestablishing Thebes, the kind of city-building that earns Caesar Diodorus's praise. Philip's autodeification at xvi 92.5, 95.1 does not qualify. For a general discussion, see L. Taylor, *The Divinity of the Roman Emperor*, 8–34; most recently, A. Gosling, *AJP* 107 (1986), 586–89. In practice Diodorus does not differentiate among honors granted ἰσόθεοι, θεοί, and ἡρωικοί, but in theory he does distinguish between men honored as ἡρωικοί and ἰσόθεοι (i 2.4) or ἡμίθεοι (iv 1.4, 85.7), perhaps supporting the thesis of S. Price, *Rituals and Power: The Roman Imperial Cult in Asia Minor*, 32–40.

[89] Diodorus describes Scaevola as τιμῶν ἰσοθέων ἔτυχε (xxxvii 6), certainly not indicated by *OGIS*, 437–39. Diodorus suggests that Leosthenes of Athens was given heroic honors (ταφέντος ἡρωικῶς) by Hyperides (xviii 13.5). Noth-

73

the most admired of all historical figures, and Diodorus five times refers to him as a god.[90] Diodorus judges him superior to Dionysus, Heracles, and all the other heroes and dynasts for alone being able to bring Britain into the civilized world (v 21.2), and he praises Caesar for being the first since its founding by Heracles to take the Celtic city of Alesia.[91] As he did with mythological benefactors who established great cities, Diodorus eulogizes Caesar for his refounding of Corinth. He calls Caesar the greatest of all Romans and affirms that he justly received the title of *divus* on the basis of his virtues: moderation (ἐπιείκεια), noble birth, military and oratorical skills, and indifference to money. Diodorus uses phrasing reminiscent of his praise of Heracles.[92] Many historians (including Diodorus's occasional source, Megasthenes)[93] compared the feats of historical figures with those of divine char-

---

ing from the surviving *Funeral Oration* indicates that is so, unless chap. 35 is read aggressively; but given the circumstances of the funeral, Hyperides may well have honored him thus: see Bickerman, *Athenaeum* 41 (1963), 70–71. Both Diodorus and a surviving inscription (Dittenberger, *Sylloge*³, 624) describe Philopoemen's honors as ἰσόθεοι. The terms εὐεργέτης and σωτήρ were not strictly religious titles, but ranged in meaning from patron to having a close association with the godhead: R. Fears, *Princeps a Diis Electus: The Divine Election of the Emperor as a Political Concept at Rome*, 95–98, and Robert, *CRAI* (1969), 42–64. Diodorus once uses it to suggest a patron (xxxiii 1.5), but Mithridates is called θεὸς καὶ σωτήρ (xxxvii 26.1; on his autodeification, see B. McGing, *The Foreign Policy of Mithridates VI Eupator King of Pontus*, 99–102); Dion is given divine honors while still alive and also called εὐεργέτης καὶ σωτήρ (xvi 20.6; cf. xvi 11.2, Plut., *Dion* 22.4, 29.1; see C. Habicht, *Gottmenschentum und griechische Städte*², 204, n. 47), but Gelon, made divine only posthumously (xi 38.5), had bestowed upon him the same title of εὐεργέτης καὶ σωτήρ while alive (xi 26.6). Demetrius was a σωτήρ at Rhodes (xx 93.6) and Athens (xx 46.2), a status that in Plut., *Demetr.* 10.3, 13.2, borders on the divine: see K. Scott, *AJP* 49 (1928), 137–66, 217–39. Diodorus generally echoes the phrasing of Polybius v 9.9–10.

[90] i 4.7; iv 19.2; v 21.2, 25.4; xxxii 27.3.

[91] iv 19.2. Virgil also would later compare Augustus favorably with Heracles (*Aen.* vi 1061–64).

[92] xxxii 27.3; cf. on Heracles iv 8.5: both have τὴν ὑπερβολήν κτλ; τὸν αἰώνιον . . . ἔπαινον-ἀθανασίαν.

[93] *FGH* 715 F 1 = Josephus, *AJ* x 227; F 11a = Strabo xv 6.1.

acters. But the comparisons involving Caesar must be Diodorus's own interpolation. He may even have created his description of Alesia and the association between Caesar and Heracles there from his own version of Heracles' founding Sardinian Iolais.[94] Caesar is the contemporary figure Diodorus most admires. And in fact, Caesar's deification and his final plans for a great invasion of the East, have been thought to provide the inspiration for the early books of the *Bibliotheke*.[95] Now it is true that Varro, writing *De Gente Populi Romani* just after 43 B.C., lists several instances from antiquity where great kings subsequently deified; he may well have done so in order to justify Caesar's controversial apotheosis and ingratiate himself to Octavian, *divi filius*.[96] But the *Bibliotheke* had a more universalistic message. Diodorus had spent some years in Egypt, where pharaohs customarily were worshiped, both while alive and after their death (i 90.3, 95.5).

Deified conquerors were commonplace, and it forces the point to see Caesar behind his entire work. In fact, neither Sesostris of Egypt nor Ninus of Assyria, legendary figures of the early books who are thought to have been fashioned after the Dictator, is especially significant in the narrative, nor does Diodorus say they were later worshiped as gods. If Diodorus shaped Sesostris after any historical figure, it was probably Alexander the Great.[97] Even so, Sesostris does not set out to conquer the world without the wisdom and foresight of his daughter (i 53.8). Nor is Ninus presented in the *Bibliotheke* in grand terms. Although Pompeius Trogus makes him a char-

[94] v 15; J. Harmand, *Latomus* 26 (1967), 968–72; Caesar himself never associated Heracles with Alesia: cf. Rawson, *Intellectual Life*, 263, on Caesar, *BC* vii 68ff.

[95] M. Sartori, *Athenaeum* 61 (1983), 550–52, and *Athenaeum* 62 (1984), 492–536.

[96] Taylor, *CP* 29 (1934), 221–29.

[97] See Murray, *JEA* 56 (1970), 162–63. Diodorus calls the Egyptian Sesoosis, but Sesostris was popularized by Herodotus (ii 102–110) and others: see especially Wesseling, in Eyring, *Diodori Siculi Bibliothecae Historicae Libri* I, 396, on i 53.1.

acter of great accomplishments in his history,[98] Diodorus, following Ctesias, devotes only three chapters exclusively to him (ii 1–3). Ninus is then eclipsed by his wife and successor, Semiramis, who thoroughly dominates the Assyrian narrative.[99] Ninus cannot take Bactria without her help (ii 6.4), and only she is awarded divine status (ii 4.4, 20.1–2). In fact, what is especially thematic about the early books is the emphasis on female rulers.[100] Yet Diodorus certainly did not model these women after Caesar, for his ideas of what is admirable in women are quite different from his portrayal of the Roman dictator.[101] And regarding Semiramis's invasion of India, which occupies the better part of her story, Diodorus is consistently critical of her motives.[102] The invasion ends in complete failure—hardly a model derived from Caesar's planned offensive. The figure of Caesar strongly influenced the *Bibliotheke* (see Chapter 6). But it will be seen that his attributes conform to Diodorus's notion of history and not the other way around.

Beside deified characters such as Caesar, other benefactors who do not even receive divine honors are emphasized in the historical portion of the *Bibliotheke*. As part of his annalistic entries, Diodorus includes information on various intellectuals: their acmes, the years in which they produced important

---

[98] Justin 1, i 1–8: "totius Orientis populos subegit."

[99] ii 4–21 = *FGH* 688 F 1b; cf. iii 1.2: Diodorus's own words.

[100] Zarina of the Secae civilized her people, for which she was deified (ii 34.3–6 = *FGH* 688 [Ctesias F 5]). Female Scythian rulers were exceptionally brave (ii 44.1), and there is a digression on Amazons and the strength of women generally (ii 45–46). Diodorus discusses Amazons at greater length: iii 52–55 = *FGH* 32 (Dionysius Scytobrachion) F 7. For Egyptian history, women are supreme over men: i 27.2. Throughout the books involving the historical period, there are vignettes of Greek and Roman women: x 21; xii 74; xix 59.3–6, 67. Interest in female anatomy is found in xxxii 10.2–12.3, which may be Posidonian: most recently, Malitz, *Die Historien des Poseidonios*, 39. See generally: M. Casevitz, *La femme dans le monde méditerranéen I: Antiquité*, 113–35. The interest in women was well within the Hellenistic historiographical tradition; cf. Pédech, *La méthode*, 71–72.

[101] E.g., iii 55.3.

[102] ii 16.4, 18.1: the Indians in no way provoked the fight.

compositions, and, in the case of historians, the period included in their works.[103] These notations tie the process of cultural benefaction, begun in prehistory, to contemporary times. Historians are mentioned most often, because Diodorus views them as performing a special service to humanity. Now it is often thought that the references to historians and the material they cover offer a clue to Diodorus's sources. Such a connection is doubtful. Cataloging was becoming fashionable in first-century Rome,[104] and that is, in a sense, what Diodorus did by referring to other historical works. Diodorus, moreover, had spent years of research in Alexandria, possibly working in the Great Library.[105] There, one of the most important literary genres was the *pinax*: a list of books on a particular subject with brief descriptions of each work.[106] The influence of that Alexandrian genre is especially underlined by the title of Diodorus's history. His is the first narrative to be called *Bibliotheke*,[107] the same name as that given to the Library at Alexandria.[108] Diodorus intended that his work recall that great collection, whose books were listed and described by *pinakes*. In naming historians and the periods their works covered, Diodorus is cataloging and memorializing the process of history writing—but not necesssarily indicating every source he employed in composing his own *Bibliotheke*.

[103] Schwartz, *RE* 5, 668–69, lists the entries within the accepted text of the *Bibliotheke*. But there may have been others that did become part of the canon: e.g., *FGH* 71 (Zoilus) T 2 = Tzetzes, ad *Exeg.* i, 126 Herm = uncertain frag. of Diodorus no. 2.

[104] See J. Zetzel, *Latin Textual Criticism in Antiquity*, 10–26.

[105] iii 38.1, on which see Chapter 4; cf. xvii 52.6.

[106] Most recently, Fraser, *Ptolemaic Alexandria* I, 322–35, 452–53, esp. 11b, 654, n. 42.

[107] It seems probable that Diodorus referred to his work only as a *Bibliotheke*, rather than *Bibliotheke historike*: Hornblower, *Hieronymus of Cardia*, 24, n. 24. See also H. Stephanus, in Eyring, *Diodori Siculi Bibliothecae Historicae Libri Qui Supersunt, e recensione Petri Wesselingii* I, vi–vii. It means *librorum repositio*, according to Isid., *Or.* vi 3.1: *RE* 3.1, 405.

[108] Fraser, *Ptolemaic Alexandria* II 476, nn. 115 and 119.

Beside these passing references to intellectuals, allusions to men of action, striving to achieve greatness in the manner of prehistorical figures, also appear throughout the narrative. Cassander thinks that, for his benefaction (εὐεργεσία) of re-founding the city of Thebes, he will win undying glory (xix 53.2). After the *diadochos* Eumenes cleared the Pontus of pi-rates, he received praise, the noblest award for his good deed (εὐεργεσία: xx 25.2). The fame of Regulus would have been eternal, had he acted with moderation (φιλανθρωπία: xxiii 15.2). Diodorus makes the performance of a benefaction part of the normal method of creating an obligation, between in-dividuals or institutions.[109] Absolutely formulaic is his senti-ment that a benefaction (εὐεργεσία) rendered produces in re-turn (δίδωμι) gratitude (χάρις).[110] An excellent control in the narrative portion is available for an event in which there exists a papyrus fragment drawn from the same source.[111] Diodorus alone mentions benefactors (εὐεργέται) and a city's proper response to them (xx 93.6–7).

There is a direct link between Diodorus's interest in myth-ological performers of good deeds (εὐεργεσίαι) and his opin-ions about first-century international conduct. Frequently part of and even synonymous with εὐεργεσία is clement or moderate behavior: ἐπιείκεια and φιλανθρωπία.[112] The con-cepts were closely wedded in the Hellenistic period[113] and are part of Diodorus's core beliefs. Culture heroes, mythological and modern, are expected to act with ἐπιείκεια or φιλαν-

[109] E.g., ii 28.1–7; iv 71.4; v 64.1; xiv 44.4; xv 31.1; xvii 69.9; xix 53.2; xxi 20.1; xxxi 3.4, 32.1; xxxiii 17.3.

[110] i 59.4, 70.6; iv 27.4, 68.4; v 52.3; xi 71.5; xiii 27.1; xv 6.1, 11.1, 26.1; xvi 22.1; xvii 103.7; xviii 8.5; xxi 20.1; xxvii 15.3; xxxviii 3.1; xxxi 3.4; xxxiv 38.2. The formula is spelled out in different words also: e.g., x 16.3.

[111] DS xx 93–94 = *P. Berol.* 11632 = *FGH* 533 F 2; cf. Hornblower, *Hi-eronymus of Cardia*, 30–32.

[112] i 64.9; vi 1.7; xiii 27.1; xvii 16.9, 69.9; xviii 33.3; xix 53.3; xxi 21.7; xxiii 15.2; xxvii 15.1, 15.3; xxviii 3.1; xxxi 32.1.

[113] Rostovtzeff, *SEHHW* III, 1358, nn. 4, 5, and Aalders, *Political Thought in Hellenistic Times*, 22–23, for bibliography.

θρωπία.[114] Ptolemy I, who was later to receive divine honors (xx 100.3), acted ἐπιεικῶς, and consequently the gods preserved him during his greatest dangers.[115] In his invented speeches for the debate at Sicily in 413, Diodorus has a Sicilian argue that the Athenians, who performed benefactions in mythological times, ought to be rewarded by contemporary Sicilians and Spartans with ἐπιείκεια.[116] Ἐπιείκεια/φιλανθρωπία is also central to Diodorus's model for empire maintainance. Subject states will remain loyal, or display εὔνοια, if treated with moderation rather than ruled through intimidation (see Chapter 2). The same quid pro quo applies to culture heroes and in common intercourse: moral behavior produces veneration or at least a feeling of obligation. Diodorus's emphasis in the mythological books on culture heroes who later become gods anticipates the most important theme of the historical narrative—that moderation and service to humanity will be rewarded. The universalism of Diodorus's myths, finely balanced between East and West in books i–iii and iv–vi, demonstrates the universal application of his practical rule of behavior.

By imparting these lessons, history itself helps advance civilization. Diodorus's explanations for progress, χρεία and εὐεργεσία, are first introduced in the proem to book i. The opening passage declares that necessity or experience is a teacher of mankind. Experience (πεῖρα), the best type of

[114] E.g., i 55.10 (Sesostris); iii 61.4 (Zeus), 65.1 (Dionysus); iv 12.7 (Heracles), 53.1 (Jason); xi 38.1 (Gelon); xvii 73.1, 91.8 (Alexander); xxxii 27.3 (Caesar).

[115] xviii 28.6; cf. xviii 14.1, 33.3.

[116] See Chapter 4. There are striking similarities between Diodorus's description of Athens and an Amphictyonic decree of the late second century: SEG³, 704E; cf. A. Wilhelm WS 61–62 (1943–1947), 169–73, and Drews, AJP 83 (1962), 387, n. 19. Praise of Athens was also important to Lucretius (DRN vi), because of Epicurus's association with that city: Momigliano, Settimo contributo, 83–84 = On Pagans, Jews, and Christians, 37. Diodorus may have been inspired by these contemporary sentiments. On the tradition of Athenian ἐπιείκεια, famous in the time of Diodorus, see also de Romilly, La douceur dans la pensée grecque, 103–4.

knowledge (i 1.2), is frequently too painful a method of learning. History can safely transmit experience and serve as teacher (διδασκαλία: i 1.1, 1.2) for all of society: the young and old, the citizen, politician, and soldier (i 1.5). Thus civilization collectively develops through experience acquired vicariously in history. The next chapter emphasizes the contribution of individuals to progress, proclaiming that history's commemoration of good deeds encourages men to excel: to found cities, write laws, and discover the arts and sciences for the betterment of the world (i 2.1). History is a benefactor (εὐεργέτις) of all humankind (i 2.2), the prophetess of truth, and the mother-city of philosophy, spreading the fame of those deserving it with divine speech (θειοτάτῳ στόματι: i 2.3). Many men act as benefactors because they desire immortality. But human honors do not last; only history, as the guardian of good deeds, can immortalize men (i 2.4). History, then, is the benefactor (by encouraging great deeds) and the protector of benefactors; it is divine and the deifier.[117]

The work of "a small man with pretensions" is the all-too-frequently quoted judgment about this proem.[118] Though not always logical or eloquent, the first two chapters of the *Bibliotheke* resonate with important themes developed subsequently. History, as the teacher of experience and the benefactor and protector of benefactors, becomes the civilizing force espoused in i 6–8 and throughout the *Bibliotheke*. In calling history the mother-city of philosophy, Diodorus may be insisting on the subordination of philosophy, which Posidonius had argued was the great civilizer, the πρῶτος εὑρετής.[119] Diodorus viciously attacks philosophers for their immorality

[117] For history doing the bidding of the gods: cf. xxxiv/xxxv 9.

[118] Nock, *JRS* 49 (1959), 5 = Nock, *Essays* II, 860. Nock came to believe that Diodorus could himself have written the proem, rather than have plagiarized it, only after deciding that it was not of such high quality as he previously thought. See, however, the appreciations of Havelock, *The Liberal Temper in Greek Politics*, 74–75, and Pavan, *RAL* 16 (1961), 19–52, 117–50.

[119] Most recently on Sen., *Ep.* 90.5–7, and passim, is Malitz, *Die Historien des Poseidonios*, 420, and Kidd, *Posidonius. Vol. II: The Commentary* II, 960–64.

and greed,[120] and here he may be polemicizing against their august claims. For Diodorus, the honor and responsibility of aiding society rest with history, in its teaching of experience (χρεία) and its benefactions (εὐεργεσίαι). History's double strategy for advancing civilization is pursued throughout the narrative. As a provider of vicarious experience, history instructs mankind on what is morally beneficial to emulate and what to avoid. The emphasis on history's moral inspiration to society permeates the *Bibliotheke* and requires no further demonstration here.[121] But history is equally committed to extolling individual benefactors. For the mythological figures who are traditionally honored by mankind, history sings its immortal praise (iv 1.4). Even when men ignore the honors given in return for Heracles' benefactions, history celebrates his achievements (iv 8). History recalls with undying praise (τὸν αἰώνιον ἔπαινον) and serves as witness to the benefactions of Julius Caesar (xxxii 27.3) and Gelon (xi 38.6). Diodorus notes that some who received divine honors had them stripped away or were ignored later.[122] It is history's task to remember them. Of the literati mentioned throughout the *Bibliotheke*, historians are those most frequently honored. Diodorus offers a special tribute to his colleagues (and to himself: i 3) who help history in the cause of progress.

From the earliest stages of civilization to modern times, Diodorus imposes a moral philosophy on behavior. He stresses the practical benefit awarded to the barbarian and Hellene, to the great and the modest, to the individual and the ruling state if simple laws of moderate behavior and a commitment to the common good (ὠφελῆσαι τὸν κοινὸν βίον) are followed. At the very least, appropriate actions produce in others a residue of goodwill that is useful when the force of τύχη turns in opposition (on which, see Chapter 2). Although

---

[120] ii 29.5–6; ix 9; x 7.2–3.

[121] See esp. Chapter 2.

[122] Gelon, xi 38.5–7; Diocles: xiii 35.2; xiv 18; Demetrius: xx 102.3; on all of whom see Chapter 6. See also x 12, that history, rather than the inscriptions on stone, preserves men's honors.

standing with other first-century authors who believe in historical progress, Diodorus does not accept as well the explanation that the Roman civil wars signaled a fall from grace and a consequent moral decline.[123] Possibly Diodorus was more confident than his compeers; he has been described as "among the most optimistic of all our progressivists."[124] But as well, he has no interest in social decay as an explanation for human failure (see Chapter 2). And he refuses to equate the material destiny of Rome in any way with the future well-being of civilization (see Chapter 5). The inclusion of eastern myth and anthropology finds meaning within Diodorus's larger designs. His purpose in writing history is to serve as witness to the universality of certain moral values.

[123] A. Wallace-Hadrill, *Past and Present* 95 (1982), 19–36.
[124] Blundell, *The Origins of Civilization in Greek and Roman Thought*, 196.

FOUR

Aspects of History Writing

ORGANIZATIONAL and chronological markers, speeches, and polemics are essential parts of ancient historiography, and each is found in the *Bibliotheke*. In accordance with their general opinion of Diodorus, scholars customarily assume that, just as with his prologues, he had little to do with these aspects of history writing and that he drew his material, sometimes inappropriately, from the sources he followed. A closer investigation, however, indicates that Diodorus was more careful and often more original in his use of these conventions than is generally acknowledged. These findings suggest that future studies of the *Bibliotheke* will need to reexamine many assumptions about Diodorus's methods of composition.

ORGANIZATIONAL AND CHRONOLOGICAL MARKERS

Within the *Bibliotheke* there are found numerous references to other parts of the work. Although they are generally quite accurate, occasionally Diodorus incorrectly states that he has already mentioned or will mention the subject elsewhere. Scholars seize on these unfulfilled references as clues to Diodorus's sources. It is believed that the references must have existed in his original sources and that he copied them without also including the material to which they refer. Thus, they are residues of uncontaminated narrative that Diodorus preserved without understanding their implications. This, of course, assumes the worst of Diodorus—that he stupidly preserved material not pertinent to his own narrative. In fact, in every case where this is suspected, it can be shown that Diodorus was involved in the composition of these references and that he understood well their relationship to his narrative. For example, with Posidonius as his current source, Diodorus notes that somewhere in the previous books, when discussing Heracles, he had already mentioned the Pyrenees.[1] Because no reference to that mountain chain occurs earlier in the *Bibliotheke*, it is presumed that Diodorus copied it unthinkingly from Posidonius.[2] In fact, in the preceding book, when most likely following Matris of Thebes and certainly not Posidonius,[3] Diodorus recounts the deeds of Heracles in Spain (iv 17–18). Although he does not specifically mention the Pyrenees there, Diodorus later on may have been under the impression that he had.

Another example involves Diodorus's dependence on Agatharchides of Cnidus. It is easily established by a parallel excerpt in Photius that for much of book iii Diodorus quite closely follows Agatharchides. At one point Diodorus records that he had already mentioned a Red Sea voyage of Ptolemy Euergetes (iii 41.1), and in the corresponding passage Photius also remarks that the author—meaning Agatharchides—notes that he had discussed that journey earlier.[4] Because Diodorus did not in fact earlier detail Ptolemy's route along the Red Sea, it is widely assumed that he thoughtlessly copied the reference without realizing that it was irrelevant to his own narrative.[5] But at the beginning of the section where he draws on Agatharchides, he does mention Ptolemy's investigation of the lands along the coast of the Red Sea (iii 18.4). Although only a brief notation, it is sufficient to give Diodorus the benefit of

---

[1] v 35.2 = *FGH* 87 F 117 (*Anhang*).

[2] Most recently, Hornblower, *Hieronymus of Cardia*, 27–28.

[3] Schwartz, *RE* 5, 676; Jacoby, Comm. to *FGH* 39 (Matris).

[4] *Codex* 250, 84, 257a.

[5] E.g., S. Burstein, *Beiträge zur Sudanforschung* 1 (1986), 22, n. 11; Hornblower, *Hieronymus of Cardia*, 27; Walbank, *Kokalos* 14–15 (1968–1969), 491; Peremans, *Historia* 16 (1967), 434–35; and C. Dolce, *Kokalos* 6 (1960), 127.

the doubt that he understood the implication of the cross-reference in Agatharchides and employed it properly.[6]

This minor episode, which is thought to prove that Diodorus copies inappropriate material, is used to interpret another, more important passage. While again following the narrative account of Agatharchides, Diodorus declares that he draws on royal records in Alexandria and on eyewitnesses with whom he has talked (iii 38.1). Most scholars believe that Diodorus took the statement directly from Agatharchides.[7] Because Diodorus, to their minds, did not perform any independent historical research, his inclusion of someone else's claim to using royal accounts and eyewitnesses marks him as a fool or a liar.

But in this case he was neither, for there are several indications that the statement contains at least some of Diodorus's own words and that he meant what he wrote. First, part of the chapter concerns Caesar's place in the *Bibliotheke*, so Diodorus was certainly intrusive here. Second, two types of sources are mentioned: royal records (ὑπομνήματα) and eyewitnesses. Elsewhere, in a nearly parallel usage of ὑπομνήματα, Diodorus claims access to official Roman records, probably meaning that he found them within synthesized historical works.[8] It is possible that here as well Diodorus is alluding to royal material used by Agatharchides (who, as a member of the court would have easy access to such documents). Throughout book iii, Diodorus acknowledges his dependence on Agatharchides' work,[9] and here he may be referring to a type of infor-

---

[6] Similarly, at iii 31.4, Diodorus *may* be repeating Agatharchides "mechanically" (so Burstein, *Beiträge zur Sudanforschung* 1 [1986], 20), but the reference could be to Diodorus's own earlier discussion; cf. C. Rubincam, *Phoenix* 43 (1989), 58–59.

[7] Most recently, Walbank, *Kokalos* 14–15 (1968–1969), 491, and Peremans, *Historia* 16 (1967), 432–55, who does admit the possibility that Diodorus augmented Agatharchides' account with his own investigations.

[8] On i 4.4, see Chapter 5, n. 3; on ὑπομνήματα at i 4.4 and iii 38.1 suggesting official records, see McDougall, *Lexicon*, s.v.

[9] iii 11.2, 18.4, 48.4.

mation he gained from it. The claim to his interviewing eye-witnesses is even more likely Diodorus's own. The parallel Agatharchidean account preserved by Photius contains no statement on methodology. And when Photius in a different context and perhaps with a different meaning does later quote Agatharchides on the use of ὑπομνήματα, he fails to mention using eyewitnesses.[10] For his part Diodorus often boasts of being an eyewitness and of questioning eyewitnesses in Egypt,[11] with one statement particularly compelling. Diodorus earlier in book iii attributes much of his material to Agatharchides and Artemidorus, but then adds:

> Since, to bear witness ourselves, during the time of our visit to Egypt, we associated with many of its priests and conversed with not a few ambassadors from Ethiopia as well who were then in Egypt; and after inquiring carefully of them about each matter and testing the stories of the historians, we have composed our account so as to accord with the opinions on which they most fully agree. (iii 11.3; Oldfather)

This, which must be Diodorus's own creation, closely resembles the pronouncement of methodology at iii 38: the mention of written sources is followed by the claim to interviewing informants as a corrective. No one would argue that Diodorus made major changes in Agatharchides' narrative; the parallel accounts of Photius and Strabo (book xvi) prove his dependence. But there are minor differences, and Diodorus may well have discreetly supplemented Agatharchides' account with material from questioning eyewitnesses. In one instance, for example, he gives information that he specifically says differs from that in Agatharchides' version (iii 48.4). There is ample reason to give Diodorus the benefit of the doubt for the authorship of the passage on methodology at iii 38.

---

[10] Phot., *Codex* 250, 110, 460b—ὑπομνήματα there probably meaning "notes" or "memoranda."

[11] See below n. 127.

Because it is generally believed that Diodorus copied his sources uncritically and largely verbatim, many statements that contain some ambiguity are explained as Diodorus's failure to adjust the material of his sources to his own narrative. The effect of this assumption is cumulative, with the examples already discussed used in turn to support a radical interpretation of cross-references in books xix and xx. Three times Diodorus refers the reader to an earlier book of the *Bibliotheke* for a discussion that, in fact, is not found there. It is often argued that these references are drawn directly from his source, and this has helped lead to the identification of the little-known historian, Silenus, as responsible for much of Diodorus's Sicilian material.[12] But if the prejudices concerning Diodorus's methods are set aside, that theory, so far as it is based on the cross-references, becomes untenable.

At xx 57.6, Diodorus refers to his discussion in book iii of the North African town of Meschela, which the Greeks founded on their way home from the Trojan War. Since no reference to Meschela occurs in book iii, it is argued that the original discussion was in Silenus's history and that Diodorus copied it unthinkingly. There are, however, considerable difficulties with establishing the organization of Silenus's *Sicelica* so as to conform to a reference to book iii,[13] and more plausible solutions exist. The highly fragmentary book vii of the *Bibliotheke* included Greek history following the Trojan War, and Diodorus might have there mentioned the founding of Meschela. If so, emending the cross-reference in book xx from book iii to book vii would serve to complete that allusion.[14] Or, because Diodorus did include Libyan material in book iii, he may have mistakenly thought that he covered the

[12] Suggested by several scholars, especially E. Manni, most recently in *Kokalos* 16 (1970), 60–73, and *Kokalos* 16 (1970), 74–78, despite the criticisms of Walbank, *Kokalos* 14–15 (1968–1969), 487–93, and K. Meister, *Athenaeum* 48 (1970), 89–91. See also Badian, *RFIC* 96 (1968), 203–11.

[13] Walbank, *Kokalos* 14–15 (1968–1969), 489–92.

[14] Most recently discussed by Walbank, *Kokalos* 14–15 (1968–1969), 492–93.

establishment of Meschela there.[15] Either suggestion is better than assuming Diodorus copied another historian's reference to material but not the material itself.

The two other unfulfilled references—once again thought to have come from Silenus's work—occur near the beginning of book xix. There Diodorus mentions the evil Syracusans, Sostratus and Heracleides, whose earlier careers, he twice notes (xix 3.3, 10.3), were detailed in the previous book. Book xviii, however, contains no Sicilian material. Now certainly, these judgments of Sostratus must derive from a different source than Diodorus's later description of Sostratus in heroic terms (xix 71.4)—*if* they all refer to the same person. Diodorus may have copied two different characterizations without recognizing the contradiction.[16] The inclusion of inconsistent points of view is common in history writing; copying from one's source inappropriate references to earlier discussions is another matter. A different explanation is at hand.

As noted in Chapter 1, book xviii is not unique in including no material on Sicily and Italy; neither does book xvii. And just as references in the early part of book xix allude to nonexisting Sicilian material in book xviii, so too the proem of xvii falsely implies coverage of Sicily within that book (xvii 1.2). Yet, of the many scholars who argue that virtually every word of the *Bibliotheke* comes from Diodorus's sources, none would suggest that the alleged author of the prologue to xvii is the same as the source behind the unfulfilled allusions to Sicilian affairs in the early part of book xix. Thus Diodorus, within the space of little more than two books, must have copied from two different sources four allusions (when the previously cited xx 57.6 is considered) to material that he did not himself cover.

That conclusion is directly at odds with Diodoran practice elsewhere. Aside from those already discussed, all other ref-

---

[15] Rubincam, *Phoenix* 43 (1989), 43, n. 12.

[16] Similarly with Agathocles: that problem is well summarized by Kebric, *In the Shadow of Macedon*, 73–79.

erences to material in specified earlier books are completely accurate—and often Diodorus will even indicate when the referenced material is found in more than one earlier volume.[17] When all of Diodorus's references are considered, including those that refer to other discussions without naming their precise locations, his accuracy is impressive. At least eighty-five of the ninety other cross-references in the *Bibliotheke* are certainly or probably fulfilled,[18] including most where Diodorus's sources seem certain to have changed.[19] The five incompleted references admit of a reasonable explanation.[20] Although it is easy to suggest that Diodorus thoughtlessly copied from his source when the text of the original source no longer survives, the one instance in which the parallel text of a cross-reference is extant reveals Diodorus's care. He omits a Polybian reference to a discussion found earlier in that history, because Diodorus himself did not include the material in his *Bibliotheke*.[21] Moreover, comparison between Diodorus and a number of roughly contemporary Roman authors suggests that Diodorus was especially conscientious in cross-referencing his material,[22] and that his methods of doing so varied pre-

---

[17] iv 1.5–6 (to i 11.3ff.; ii 38.3–4; iii 52.3ff.); vi 1.5 (to 5.41ff.); xii 2.2 (to books xi and xii, passim); xvi 46.4 (to i 30.4–9); xviii 9.1 (to xviii 108.7ff.); drawn from Rubincam, *Phoenix* 43 (1989), 54–61. See also Neubert, *Spuren selbständiger Thätigkeit bei Diodor*, 8.

[18] Rubincam, *Phoenix* 43 (1989), 54–61.

[19] Ibid., 52, n. 27: twenty-seven out of thirty such cross-references (not including iii 41.1 and v 35.2, on which see previous discussion) are fulfilled.

[20] On iii 38.2; v 21.2, 22.1, Diodorus changed his mind as to what his work would cover without also revising some earlier promises (see Chapter 6). On xi 90.2, Rubincam, *Phoenix* 43 (1989), 56–57, suggests a completed reference might have occurred in book xxi, while K. Ziegler, *RE* 18.3, 99, posits xi 91–92; xii 8, 29. xiv 117.6 is simply an unfulfilled promise. Not included in the total of ninety are: xix 3.3, 10.3; xx 57.6 (discussed here) and iii 41.1; v 35.2 (discussed previously).

[21] DS xxxi 26.1 = Polybius xxxi 22.1–5; cf. Walbank, *Commentary* III, 494.

[22] See R. Starr, *AJP* 102 (1981), 431–37; Rubincam, *EMC/CV* 31, n.s. 6 (1987), 313–28, and *Phoenix* 43 (1989), 39–61. Comparative studies with Polybius, Dionysius of Halicarnassus, and Strabo would be especially illuminating.

dictably with the types of subject matter—mythology or narrative—with which he was currently dealing.[23]

Other organizational markers also prove his diligence. Every completely extant book, except (for no apparent reason) book v, begins and ends with accurate references to the material discussed therein,[24] and Diodorus frequently reminds the reader of the history's general chronological divisions.[25] Tempting though it is to cannibalize the *Bibliotheke* and discover important sources in the background, Diodorus's history must also be taken as a whole and judged within the context of the historiographical tradition. Herodotus, for example, made several promises to include material that he never fulfilled,[26] and the works of Plutarch contain numerous incomplete and even contradictory references, both backward and forward.[27] In comparison to other writers, Diodorus comes out quite well.

Diodorus's alleged stupidity is an unsatisfactory explanation for the unfulfilled references in the proem to xvii and the early chapters of book xix. A better answer lies in the narrative to which these references allude. All three references pertain to Sicilian and Italian events, and yet, of the ten completely extant books of the postmythological period (xi–xx), only the books to which these references apply—xvii and xviii—contain no material on Sicilian and Italian affairs (see Chapter 1). That suggests that originally these books had a more universal scope but they grew unwieldy because of coverage of Alexander and the Successors. Later, Diodorus eliminated his discussions of Sicily and Italy without also deleting his references to them. Inconsistencies abound in the *Bibliotheke*. But some

[23] Rubincam, *Phoenix* 43 (1989), 43–45.

[24] i 9.6, 98.10; ii 1.1–3, 60.3; iii 1, 74.6; iv 1.5, 85.7; xi 1.1, 92.5; xii 2.2, 84.4; xiii 1.3, 114.3; xiv 2.4, 117.9; xv 1.6, 95.4; xvi 1, 95.5; xvii 1.1–2; 118.4; xviii 1.6, 75.3; xix 1.10, 110.5; xx 2.3, 113.5; some of these are analyzed by Laqueur, *Hermes* 86 (1958), 281–85.

[25] i 4.6; xiii 1.2; xiv 2.4; xl 8; see also, e.g., xiv 2.4; xix 1.10.

[26] Jacoby, *RE* suppl. 2, 372–79.

[27] K. Ziegler, *Plutarchos von Chaironeia*, 262–63.

are better explained by the difficulties of writing—and rewriting—a large work put down in scroll form than in imagining an author who fails to change another historian's reference that is inappropriate to his own work.[28]

The assumption that Diodorus is invariably only an unthinking copyist leads to similar misunderstandings in other aspects of his organization. Diodorus drew substantially on the works of earlier historians, who would make remarks concerning contemporary conditions. Frequently scholars argue that Diodorus has taken over references that are inappropriate to his own time without adjusting the perspective. In following Hecataeus of Abdera's account throughout most of book i, Diodorus, it is claimed, copied from his source without modernizing the narrative. At three points, Diodorus gives facts that pertain to Ptolemy I, obviously the point of reference for Hecataeus, but then briefly describes how the situation stood in his own day.[29] This use of his source is somewhat lazy but is not misleading. In fact, it gives the reader two sets of data.

One case is more substantial. Diodorus records the Egyptian assertion that mortals have existed in their land for a little less than 5,000 years, down to the time he visited Egypt in the 180th Olympiad (60–56 B.C.; i 44.1). Later in the same book, in discussing Egyptian claims to cultural primacy, he reports the argument that they had been ruled by kings for 4,700 years (i 69.6). Now at the time that Hecataeus was writing, the Persians had recently completed 195 years of ruling Egypt. It has been argued that if that figure is added to the 4,700 years, the result is sufficiently close to the other figure of 5,000 that the calculations must have been performed by Hecataeus. Diodorus merely added the reference to his own time (the 180th Olympiad) without bothering to recalculate Hecataeus's origi-

---

[28] The difficulties of using the scroll form are emphasized by Starr, *AJP* 102 (1981), 431–37; for further evidence that Diodorus did not coordinate completely all his revisions, see Laqueur, *Hermes* 86 (1958), 281–85.

[29] i 31.6–8 (cf. xvii 52.4–6), 46.7, 84.8; cf. Murray, *JEA* 5 (1970), 145, n. 3.

nal figures.[30] Diodorus is elsewhere certainly guilty of arithmetical confusion, but here he is accused of wanton sloth—though unjustly. In both references to the length of human habitation in Egypt, Diodorus specifically includes not only indigenous kings but foreign ones as well: because that also covers the Persian domination, there is nothing to add to the 4,700 years. The figures themselves (just under 5,000 years and 4,700 years) are quite close, so that Diodorus has not necessarily alluded to his own time without recalculating. In several other instances also, where Diodorus is accused of copying passages inappropriate to his own time, that charge is unfounded.[31]

Diodorus's care in modernizing his account is evident in book iii, where a parallel text of his source, Agatharchides, is preserved by Photius. At one point, Agatharchides, as recounted by Photius, refers to events of his own time. Because the situation had changed by the first century, Diodorus excises that reference.[32] Again, when Agatharchides refers to himself, Diodorus changes the perspective to that of his source, at the same time updating the account by including a reference to his own time.[33] For most other references in the

---

[30] Murray, *JEA* 5 (1970), 145, n. 3.

[31] xix 78.2, referring to Chalcis in the present tense (ἔστιν) is not anachronistic (so, most recently, Hornblower, *Hieronymus of Cardia*, 28, n. 38): Diodorus does not discuss Chalcis's actual importance, but, because of its location, its potential importance. At iv 20.2, Diodorus follows Posidonius, for in the parallel account Strabo (iii 4.17) names him. Diodorus refers to the event as happening in "our day" (καθ' ἡμᾶς), a phrase not in Strabo. Posidonius, a contemporary of Diodorus, heard about the event from an eyewitness, so Diodorus is not being dishonest (so Hornblower, 28, n. 1). Perhaps similarly, xiv 31.2 and xix 72.8 (most recently, Walbank, *Kokalos* 14–15 [1968–1969], 487).

[32] DS iii 47.8 and Phot., *Codex* 250, 102, 459b. The material deleted refers to the Ptolemaic monarchy (S. Gozzoli, *Athenaeum* 56 [1978], 58–79) and not, as usually and wrongly believed, to Rome. Diodorus did not omit it out of fear of Roman censorship (so Fraser, *Ptolemaic Alexandria* iib, 785, n. 212), but because it applied only to the earlier Ptolemies (correctly, Sartori, *Athenaeum* 72 [1984], 508) and was no longer relevant. On Diodorus's attitude toward Rome, see Chapter 5.

[33] iii 18.3 with Phot., *Codex* 250, 41, 450a–b.

Bibliotheke to the time of the author, it cannot be determined whether Diodorus copied, modified, or created them himself. At times, Diodorus appears to have added material,[34] or made specific reference to contemporary events,[35] or changed the perspective of the account.[36] Thus, in the handling of material found in his sources, along with frequent confusion and many notorious doublets, there are also indications of care and precision.

SPEECHES

Perhaps the area of historiography in which Diodorus's own contribution is most evident is in the creation of speeches. It is clear, both in his theoretical discussions and in the speeches themselves, that Diodorus had specific notions of what oratory ought to contain. The prooemium of book xx (1–2) is the only extended discussion of speeches in the *Bibliotheke*. There it is assumed that the historian will either create speeches out of whole cloth or at least substantially embellish in order to display his own oratorical skills.[37] The main concern is that speeches be moderate in length and relevant to the point at

[34] i 10.6–7; on i 21.9 and 25, see Burton, *Diodorus Siculus Book I*, 95–97, 106–10; i 61.4. Μέχρι τοῦ νῦν of DS iii 18.3 is not in Phot., *Codex 250* (Agatharchides) 41, 450b. Historical references interpolated into myth, such as iv 23.2, 56.7, may well be his.

[35] E.g., i 83.8–9; ii 1.5–7, 7.2 (Jacoby, *FGH* IIc, 489–90, suggests Diodorus is responsible for ii 7.3–4, which also concerns source criticism), 17.3; iii 38.2; iv 19.2; v 15.4 (Jacoby, *FGH* IIIb Comm., 594), 21–22, 66.5; vii 5.8 (perhaps contemporary propaganda: Taylor, *The Divinity of the Roman Emperor*, 59, n. 3), 5.11; x 7.2–3 (that it is Diodorus's, cf. ii 29.5–6); xii 27.1 (cf. Casevitz, *Diodore* XII, Budé edition, xi, n. 1), 36.3; xiii 35.3 (and xvi 70.6; cf. Appendix I), 90.5; xvi 7.1 (cf. Chapter 6, p. 168); xxv 10.5; xxxii 27.

[36] On i 31.6–8, 46.7, 84.8, see n. 29; on iii 18.3, see n. 33; iv 78.1, 80; v 2.4, 3.6; xix 1.5 (descriptions of Sicily "even in our day"; cf. v 13.3); xvii 52.4–6; xxxi 10.2 (with Polybius xxix 21.9); xxxi 26.2, on which see the conclusion of Chapter 5.

[37] 1.3: λυπεῖ δ' οὐ μόνον τὸ κακῶς γραφεῖν; 2.1: ὁ μὴ τεθαρρηκότως συγκαταβαίων πρὸς τοὺς ἐν τοῖς λόγοις ἀγῶνας . . . ; 2.2, passim.

hand, for "one might justly censure those who in their histories insert over-long orations or employ frequent speeches."[38]
The authorship of this passage is constantly at issue. Ephorus is often suggested,[39] for Polybius testifies that Ephorus
considered the differences between historians and speech writers,[40] and such a distinction is also found in the proem to book
xx (1.2, 1.5). Some even interpret the prologue as an Ephoran
attack on Thucydides, inspired by Cratippus's belief that Thucydides' speeches broke the continuity of his work and so
should have no place at all in a history.[41] But the identification
with Ephorus is unlikely, for the conclusion reached in the
proem is that a history containing too many or too long
speeches will make that genre resemble a work of rhetoric.
Ephorus appears to have stood at the beginning of the very
tradition that produced these excesses in historiography. From
what is known about his style and methods, it is doubtful
whether he would have criticized the use of rhetoric in history
writing.[42] Moreover, the prologue does not attack, as had
Cratippus, the presence of all speeches in history writing, for
oratory is specifically permitted when appropriate (xx 1.2,
2.1–2).

Duris of Samos, a third-century historian, is also often
identified as the source for xx 1–2. The prooemium to xx
voices the complaint that speeches interrupt the narrative and
may discourage the reader from continuing (xx 1.1, 1.4).
Some scholars associate that thought with xx 43, where there

[38] xx 1.1 (Greer); cf. 1.3: πλεονάσαντες.

[39] Laqueur, *Hermes* 46 (1911), 206; cf. Jacoby, *FGH* IIc, 64 (to F 111);
Avenarius, *Lukians Schrift zur Geschichtsschreibung*, 107, n. 10; most recently,
O. Luschnat, *RE* suppl. 12, 1272.

[40] *FGH* 70 (Ephorus) F 111 = Polybius xii 28.8–12.

[41] *FGH* 64 (Cratippus) F 1 = Dion. Hal., *Thuc.* 16, 349. Most recently,
Luschnat, *RE* suppl. 12, 1272, with bibliography. See also the discussion in
Pritchett, *Dionysius of Halicarnassus*, 67–68. Cratippus is being more frequently identified as the author of the *Hellenica Oxyrhynchia*, a work used by
Diodorus (most recently, G. Pesely, *AHB* 2, no. 2 [1988], 31–33), though
probably with Ephorus as intermediary: Reid, "Diodorus," 59–78, and, most
recently, H. Westlake, *Phoenix* 41 (1987), 241–54.

[42] Fornara, *The Nature of History*, 148–49.

is expressed the frustration that, because simultaneous actions cannot effectively be retailed simultaneously, historical narrative fails to reflect reality (xx 43.7). This latter discussion concerning simultaneity is usually attributed to Duris, and, consequently, it is suggested that the proem to book xx is his criticism of historians for using so much rhetorical embellishment that they break the flow of the narrative.[43]

Besides the difficulties with identifying the source of xx 43,[44] that passage and the proem to book xx do not involve the same issue. The former discusses the limitations of the traditional narrative format, whereas the latter expresses fears that materials that are uninteresting or unhistorical will not attract the reader (1.1, 1.4). The concern for keeping the reader attentive was commonplace in the historical literature of Diodorus's day,[45] and he makes a similar statement himself in a slightly different context (xvi 1.2). In any case, so little of the *Bibliotheke* can with any confidence be attributed to Duris[46] that there is no compelling reason to assign him authorship of the prologue to book xx.

---

[43] Especially Fornara, *The Nature of History*, 147–51, with bibliography at 149, n. 8, to which add N. Zegers, *Wesen und Ursprung der tragischen Geschichtsschreibung*, 37ff., and Bosworth, *From Arrian to Alexander*, 94–95.

[44] That passage is nearly always attributed to Duris because of supposed similarities with his famous judgment that the narratives of Ephorus and Theopompus somehow fail in the presentation of events and so lack *mimesis* (*FGH* 76 F 1 = Phot. *Codex* 176, 121, 41a; most recently, B. Gentili and G. Cerri, *History and Biography in Ancient Thought*, 14, n. 29, with bibliography. But DS xx 43.7 argues quite differently that the narrative *can* represent the facts through *mimesis* while falling short of a true presentation. Although Pearson, *The Greek Historians of the West*, 247, suggests that the context is Timaean, a good case can be made for Diodorus himself at xx 43.7: cf. xiii 37.6 and xvi 1.1–2, with somewhat different intent but similar concerns about the disruption of the natural order (φύσις) of events. And the phenomenon of simultaneous battles, which gave rise to the discussion at xx 43, is of special interest to Diodorus: xi 24.1, 35.2, 61.7; xiii 108.4; xvi 88.3; xx 13. Polybius struggled with the same problem of simultaneous events: xxxii 11.

[45] See, e.g., Polybius ii 56.10; xii 25i.4–5; xxxvi 1.7 (on which, see Sacks, *Polybius*, 79–95); Dion. Hal., *AR* i 1.3.

[46] Cf. Kebric, *In the Shadow of Macedon*, 72–79. Jacoby identifies only the Roman material of xxi 6 (= *FGH* 76 F 56a) as certainly from Duris.

That scholars are divided on the authorship of this passage between Ephorus and Duris, who himself attacked Ephorus's methods (see n. 44), indicates the difficulty with attributing it to any source. In fact, it has recently been suggested that the proem is Diodorus's own criticism of Timaeus, who was famous in antiquity for his lengthy speeches.[47] This identification is the most likely. In the previous book, Diodorus criticizes tragic historians who describe catastrophes in too much detail (xix 8.4). Timaeus appears to be the focus of that attack, for the surrounding descriptive material concerns Agathocles' savagery, and Timaeus was notorious for his critical treatment of the tyrant.[48] Indeed, Diodorus, with arguments at least somewhat of his own making, later attacks Timaeus's treatment of Agathocles.[49] Diodorus's polemic against his source for rendering too full an account of tragic events offers a parallel to the proem to xx, which permits oratory, but not excessive amounts.

Other considerations suggest Diodorus's authorship. The proem calls for speeches in history writing, for "[one should not] allow speeches [λόγοι] to be inferior to the deeds [ἔργα]."[50] Similarly, in the introduction to book i, Diodorus states that the speeches of history writing are especially beneficial, since in the historical genre λόγοι and ἔργα exist in harmonious agreement (i 2.8). The prologue to xx emphasizes brevity in speech; and, when earlier treating the archaic period, Diodorus observes, perhaps wistfully, that the ancients kept their orations short (ix 26.3). Thus sentiments expressed in the proem appear elsewhere in the *Bibliotheke*. In addition, an important aspect of Diodoran historiography is the ethical assessments of individuals (Chapter 2). Contained within the prologue is a clear reference to such judgments (ἐγκώμια καὶ ψόγους [λόγους]: xx 1.1–2) as epideictic material, thus giving a context to the general discussion. Although book xx lacks the speeches that might require Diodorus to explain his theory

[47] L. Pearson, *AJP* 107 (1986), 368.
[48] Meister, "Die sizilische Geschichte," 139–40.
[49] xxi 17.1–3; Polybius xii 15; xv 35; see the section on polemics, below.
[50] xx 2.2 (Geer).

of λόγοι, the narrative is replete with moral characterizations of Eumenes and Agathocles.[51]

Moreover, statements on rhetoric and oratory that are found in the proem and throughout the *Bibliotheke* are more appropriate to Diodorus's time than to the fourth and third centuries when Ephorus and Duris lived. Diodorus frequently stresses the need for appropriateness in speeches.[52] In this concern, he reflects the contemporary application of rhetoric to historiography, in which τὸ πρέπον was the guiding principle of λόγοι.[53] In the prologue to xx, Diodorus justifies the inclusion of speeches, because history demands variety and should preserve things rendered cleverly; these are common requirements within Hellenistic Greek and Latin rhetoric.[54] He also mentions public and ambassadorial addresses and ethical assessments, the latter apparently as epideictic oratory—again these are standard categories in rhetorical theory.[55] In assuming that speeches are the creation of historians rather than the *ipsissima verba* of participants in the events, Diodorus urges that, if writers want to indulge extensively in producing speeches, they should compose separate pieces (καθ᾽ ἰδίαν, χωρίς) and attain fame in both rhetoric and history (ἐν ἀμφοτέραις ταῖς πραγματείαις: 1.2). The genres of history and rhetoric are distinct,[56] but if too many speeches are included in a historical work, its integrity will be threatened: history

[51] Thus resolving the contradiction suggested by Kunz, *Zur Beurteilung der Prooemien*, 71. But Polybius puts himself in a somewhat similar position at xxxvi 1 and 9–10.

[52] xiii 52.2 (cf. xiii 28.3), 92.1; xvi 32.2; xvi 88.2; xx 2.2 (a probable emendation).

[53] See K. Sacks, *Athenaeum* 64 (1986), 383–95.

[54] ποικιλία: xx 2.1; on the term, see Pritchett, *Dionysius of Halicarnassus: On Thucydides*, 141. On εὐστόχως καὶ καλῶς at xx 2.2, cf. Cic., *De Or.* ii 64; Diodorus's use in practice, see xxxiii 7.3, 7.5.

[55] δημηγορία: 1.1, 1.2; πρεσβευτικοὶ λόγοι: 1.2; ἐγκώμια καὶ ψόγοι [λόγοι]: 1.1–1.2; cf. xx 2.2 and i 2.8. Sacks, *Athenaeum* 64 (1986), 390–92, for the theory; Walbank, *Speeches in Greek Historians*, 11, n. 76 = Walbank, *Selected Papers*, 253, for their recognition by historians.

[56] τὸ γὰρ ἱστορίας γένος ἁπλοῦν ἐστι καὶ συμφυὲς αὐτῷ: 1.5. Diodorus voices hostility to forensic rhetoric at i 76.

will be subordinated to rhetoric (1.3). Aware of rhetorical theory and accepting the traditional criterion of appropriateness that history writing adapted from rhetoric, Diodorus separates the genres by arguing that their difference is largely one of degree. A similar conclusion may have been reached by the contemporary Cicero.[57]

Of the many reasons to see xx 1–2 as Diodorus's own composition, perhaps most compelling is the plea in book xx for short speeches. It fits Diodorus's larger mission, the writing of a universal history in forty volumes, a task that required a certain conciseness of detail. Polybius, also writing a forty-volume universal history, though it covered a much shorter period of time, argued as well for brevity in speeches.[58]

From what remains of the *Bibliotheke*, it appears that Diodorus held to his caveat against frequent long orations. There are found in his history only a few such set pieces,[59] but there are numerous single-sentence expressions.[60] Equally pervasive are speeches of paragraph length, in direct and indirect discourse, or in mixed form. On average, these occur about five times per book.[61] For the part of the narrative where Diodorus is following Polybius, there are controls on Diodorus's method of copying or inventing speeches. Generally Diodorus compresses the speeches found in Polybius and frequently turns *oratio recta* into *oratio obliqua*.[62] In so doing, he rarely

[57] Woodman, *Rhetoric in Classical Historiography*, 115–16, n. 149, on *Brutus* 286.

[58] xii 25i.3–9 and xxxvi 1, though he believed speeches should be the *ipsissima verba*; on which see Sacks, *Polybius*, 79–95.

[59] viii 12 (= *FGH* 106 F 12); x 34; xiii 20–32, 52–53; xiv 65–69; xxi 21; xxvii 13–18; xxxi 3.

[60] E.g., ix 25.1; xii 19.2; xiii 33.3; xv 93.2; xvii 37.6; xx 64.5; xxv 16; xxx 10.2; xxxiv/v 7.3; xxxviii/xxxix 4.3: selected to show they occur throughout his work.

[61] E.g., xi 4.3–4; xii 40.2–5; xiii 18.1–2; xiv 4.5–7; xvi 42.3–4; xvii 51.1–3; xviii 66.4–5; xix 25.6–7; xx 7.1–3; xxiii 1.4; xxvii 12.1–2; xxviii 11; xxix 8; xxxi 5; xxxiii 7; xxxvii 18; xl 1.2–3.

[62] DS xxviii 6 = Polybius xvi 34.2–7; xxviii 12 = Polybius xviii 50–51; xxix 8 = Polybius xxi 15; xxix 21 = Polybius xxiii 14; xxix 22 = Polybius

eliminates important material or makes factual mistakes.[63] Some of the compression may be due to the Constantinian excerpter of Diodorus, but it is unlikely that he intruded significantly. Where a control is available, the excerpter is shown to be a faithful copyist.[64]

The comparison between Diodorus and the Polybian original is illuminating, because so much of Polybius survives. Where Diodorus's source no longer exists, his editing of the original can only be surmised. Thus, it is supposed that Diodorus compressed or eliminated many of the speeches of Timaeus[65] and Hieronymus of Cardia.[66] The assumption makes sense: Diodorus was covering in forty books a period of time written on in several hundred books by his sources.

Diodorus's adherence to the principle of brevity is especially demonstrated with battle exhortations. Diodorus did not much care for military detail,[67] and that applies to the speeches given by generals before engagement. Ephorus was famous in antiquity for composing military harangues,[68] yet, in the books in which he employs Ephorus as his main source, Diodorus includes only three brief examples of that type of

---

xxiv 5; xxix 11 = Polybius xxi 18–24 (greatly compressed); xxx 23 = Polybius xxix 20; xxxi 15.1–2 = Polybius xxx 18; xxxii 22 = Polybius xxxviii 8.4–12 (greatly compressed); xxxii 23 = Polybius xxxviii 20.1–3 (greatly compressed). A complete list of parallel passages is in Schwartz, *RE* 5, 681.

[63] In the instances cited in n. 62, little of importance is lost. However, in DS xxxi 1 = Polybius xxvii 6, Diodorus omits that the Senate had already made up its mind; in DS xxx 5 = Polybius xxx 4, Diodorus omits the first assembly; and in DS xxix 17 = Polybius xxii 7–9, there are many blunders: the walls are completed, not dismantled; the gift of ships is rejected, not accepted. The exceptional number of mistakes may suggest outside contamination.

[64] See Chapter 5, p. 144.

[65] Pearson, *AJP* 107 (1986), 350–68, esp. 367, n. 50.

[66] Simpson, *AJP* 80 (1959), 374.

[67] See Hornblower, *Hieronymus of Cardia*, 37–38. R. Sinclair, *CQ* n.s. 16 (1966), 249–55, and C. Vial, *Diodore* xv, Budé edition, xx–xxii, show that Diodorus may have enlarged on what he found in his sources, but with descriptive formulas.

[68] *FGH* 70 T 21 = Plut., *Mor.* 803b.

speech.[69] Later, Diodorus twice notes that Alexander the Great made a speech before a battle, which he does not then detail. Other historians, however, do preserve those orations.[70] Most telling, Diodorus was probably following Timaeus at the point where the latter composed for Timoleon a harangue before the battle of the Crimisus. Although Timaeus's speech was colorful and famous in antiquity,[71] Diodorus makes but brief reference to it.[72]

In several statements on theory noted previously, Diodorus demands that speeches in historical works be not only concise, but also suitable to their circumstances (οἰκεῖοι λόγοι). In practice, Diodorus effectively applies the criterion of appropriateness. Frequently he notes that the speaker addressed an assembly or army with the apposite words. He may include some of the speech in *oratio obliqua* (e.g., xii 83.1), but usually the reference to its suitability is all that he records.[73] Elsewhere, Diodorus refuses to supply all the colorful details of a catastrophe, as do tragic historians, because the reader can conjure them in his own mind (xix 8.4). Diodorus may believe that similarly the reader can for himself expand οἰκεῖοι λόγοι. With few exceptions, speeches deemed appropriate succeed in convincing their audiences.[74] Diodorus's summation of an en-

---

[69] xi 35.2; xiii 98.1, where Diodorus indicates he is giving only a part of the original (τὸ τελευταῖον); xv 78.4.

[70] DS xvii 56.4 with Arr., *Anab.* iii 9.–10.1, though Arrian does condense it; cf. Plut., *Alex.* 33.1; and DS xvii 94.5 with Arr., *Anab.* v 25.3–26 and Curt. ix 2.12–34; on the later, Bosworth, *From Arrian to Alexander*, 123–34.

[71] *FGH* 566 FF 31a and b = Polybius xii 25.7, 26a; cf. K. Meister, *Historische Kritik bei Polybios*, 37–38.

[72] xvi 79.2; that he is following Timaeus: Jacoby, *FGH* iiib, 555; Meister, "Die sizilische Geschichte," 121.

[73] Λόγοι delivered οἰκειῶς: xi 15.4; xii 83.1; xiii 92.6, 98.1; xv 54.4, 74.5, 78.4; xvi 4.3, 18.3, 78.2; xvii 2.2, 33.1, 56.4, 74.3; xviii 30.2, 63.5; xix 81.6; xx 7.2; xxxii 6.3; πεφροντισμένως: xii 40.1; xv 78.4; xvii 15.3, 94.5; xxxvii 13.2.; ἁρμοζόντως: xi 50.7; xxiii 12.

[74] All the references in n. 73, except for xii 83.1, xvii 94.5, and xxxii 6.3: in the parallel episode, App., *Pun.* 83–85, does not comment on the appropriateness of the speech. Generals can address and rally their troops appropriately, but lose the battle: xviii 30.2 and xix 81.6.

tire speech by judging it appropriate was not original: Polybius, for example, also employed it when abbreviating speeches found in his sources.[75] Diodorus also abbreviates an oration by noting that it was spoken with moderation (φιλανθρωπία or ἐπιείκεια). A speech awarded this judgment again almost always succeeds.[76] A good illustration occurs in the Social War, when a Roman official named Domitius wins over the Italian rebels with intelligent words filled with ἐπιείκεια; earlier, the praetor Q. Servilius had angered the same Italians by treating them arrogantly (xxxvii 13.2). Moderate behavior is an important part of Diodorus's philosophical and political program (see Chapters 2 and 3), and he uses λόγοι to express it.

The most extensive oratory preserved in the Bibliotheke is the debate at Syracuse concerning the fate of the captured Athenians, in 413 (xiii 20–32). The episode departs markedly from the Thucydidean account, and there is great difficulty deciding whom Diodorus used here. Many argue for Timaeus,[77] for there are similarities between Diodorus's account and that in Plutarch, in which Timaeus is cited.[78] But the most recent defender of the Timaean origin of Diodorus's version admits that substantial differences between the accounts in Diodorus and Plutarch make that identification uncertain.[79] Others argue for Ephorus as the source, but that is largely by

[75] F. Walbank, CQ 39 (1945), 12, n. 62 = Walbank, Selected Papers, 90, n. 62.

[76] xii 67.2; xiii 96.1; xiv 70.3; xv 57.2; xvii 2.2, 4.1, 4.9; xviii 46.2; xix 9.6, 24.1; xxi 16.6; xxxvii 13.2. At xiii 20–32 (below) and xvii 5.1, words spoken in moderation fail to persuade the listener; xv 28.4 is ambiguous.

[77] Discussion in Drews, "Historiographical Objectives," 102–6 and 196–98, n. 53; and AJP 83 (1962), 386, n. 14; to which add: Jacoby, FGH 556 FF 51–56 Commentary; A. W. Gomme, A. Andrewes, and K. J. Dover, A Historical Commentary on Thucydides iv (Oxford, 1970), 461; and Meister, "Die sizilische Geschichte," 63–68, Historische Kritik bei Polybios, 38–39.

[78] DS xiii 19.5–6 and Plut., Nic. 28.3 = FGH 566 F 100b.

[79] Pearson, AJP 107 (1986), 357–58, and The Greek Historians of the West, 145–46.

process of elimination.[80] The fact is that the version in Diodorus departs in varying degrees from all known traditions. Consequently, attempts to attribute every sentiment in the speeches and surrounding narrative to a single source are doomed. A comparison between the ideas expressed in the speeches at Syracuse and others in the *Bibliotheke* indicates the extent of Diodorus's own invention and the reasons for it.

The first important speaker is Nicolaus, who urges moderation, because the Athenians had already received punishment from the gods for their arrogance (xiii 21.1). Although some scholars attribute the notion of divine compensation to the influence of Timaeus, the sentiment occurs frequently in the *Bibliotheke*, where Diodorus is following various sources.[81] Nicolaus then asks the Syracusans to be moderate amid their own good fortune (xiii 21.4–5), a philosophy also commonly found in Diodorus.[82] But Nicolaus devotes the heart of his address to describing for the Syracusans the proper method they should employ in controlling an empire, giving a paradigm that is exactly the one frequently articulated by Diodorus: that hegemons who manage their subjects through fear (φόβῳ) risk rebellion but rulers who act moderately (ἐπιεικῶς) win the loyalty of their subjects.[83] Nicolaus urges his countrymen to surpass the Athenians, not only in the feat of arms but also in kindness (φιλανθρωπία). Here he directly echoes a remark made at the beginning of the debate by Hermocrates (xiii 19.5). Because Diodorus helped shape that sen-

[80] Bibliography in Drews, *AJP* 83 (1962), 386, n. 14; to which add G. Pesely, *CP* 80 (1985), 321. Schwartz, *RE* 5, 681, thought it was either Diodorus's own creation or, because of faint echoes of Isocratean language, the work of Ephorus. Laqueur named first Ephorus (*Hermes* 46 [1911], 206) and then Timaeus (*RE* 11, 1098–99).

[81] Chapter 2, n. 73. It is not found in a Timaean fragment outside of the *Bibliotheke*.

[82] See Chapter 2.

[83] xiii 21.6–25. See Chapter 2. Neubert, *Spuren selbständiger Thätigkeit bei Diodor*, 24, also noting the Diodoran sentiment, refers to the speech by Nicolaus as "ein Hymnus auf die Philanthropie."

timent,[84] he may have done the same for Nicolaus's words.
Nicolaus concludes with the plea that prehistoric Athenians
had bestowed on humanity the gifts of wheat and law, and it
was the application of law that allowed mankind to emerge
from a savage and unjust society (xiii 26.3). Consequently, the
Athenian benefaction (εὐεργεσία) ought to be repaid with
gratitude (χάρις: xiii 27.1). This precise equation of gratitude
for benefaction occurs more than a dozen other times in the
Bibliotheke (see Chapter 3). Diodorus also previously emphasized the Athenian discovery of wheat,[85] and expressed appreciation for Athenian love of humanity.[86] Finally, the idea that
mankind was originally rough and savage but progressed
through cultural achievement is central to Diodoran thinking
(see Chapter 3). Whatever source Diodorus follows for the
events of 413, the speeches are consistent with notions articulated throughout his history.

Several speeches in different parts of the Bibliotheke contain
similar sentiments,[87] but two are especially important. A frag-

[84] It stands for what must have originally been a long speech in Timaeus.
Plutarch cites Timaeus, but has Hermocrates urge that the peace be borne
καλῶς, rather than with the φιλανθρωπία found in Diodorus (Nicias 28.3 =
FGH 566 F 100b). The difference is significant, because φιλανθρωπία is part of
Diodorus's political philosophy. The same sentiment is also found in speeches
at xxvii 14.1 and xxxi 3.2.

[85] i 29.2; v 4.6–9, 69.2, 77.4.

[86] iv 57.4; xv 63.2. The same compliments to Athens, for its introduction
of wheat and law, are offered by the contemporary, Lucretius (DNR 6.1–2).
There is also a striking similarity between Diodorus's description of Athens
and an Amphictyonic decree of the late second century: SEG³, 704E; cf. Wilhelm, WS 61–62 (1943–1947), 169–73, and Drews, AJP 83 (1962), 387, n. 19.

[87] Unnamed Syracusans urge fellow citizens to show due regard for τύχη
and νέμεσις and to spare the suppliant as an act of μεγαλοψυχία (xi 91.3). A
caution about the mutable nature of τύχη is voiced at xiii 53.2 and at xxvi 6,
which may be a fragment of a speech, as suggested by the future infinitive; cf.
Drews, "Historiographical Objectives," 181, n. 120. A brief utterance by Alexander the Great has the context of a failure to understand the changes in
τύχη and to act with ἐπιείκεια (xvii 66.5–7). The parallel in Curtius (v 2.13–
15) does not contain those sentiments; Diodorus and Curtius probably drew
indirectly on Cleitarchus: see J. Hamilton, Plutarch Alexander: A Commentary,

mentary address, which may be Cato's defense of the Rhodians of 167,[88] echoes arguments found in Nicolaus's speech: victories are lost if the conquerors become arrogant, whereas victors who treat the conquered moderately (ἐπιεικῶς) are praised by others and gain the loyalty of their subjects (xxxi 3.1–3). Moreover, the oration begins with a quotation from Pittacus, that forgiveness is better than punishment (xxxi 3.1). Pittacus plays an important role early in the *Bibliotheke*, where he is depicted as exceptionally kindly and forgiving and where he voices that aphorism (ix 12.3). Diodorus later uses the sentiment in a speech of Demetrius the Besieger (xxi 9) and employs it in the narrative to assess the motives of Demetrius (xxi 14.3). There, Diodorus shrewdly judges a historical character by his "own" words. Diodorus also uses the aphorism to describe Julius Caesar, the historical figure he most admires.[89] Diodorus's interpretation of the sentiment is consistent with his program of urging clement behavior. As with ἐπιείκεια, forgiveness (συγγνώμη) has a practical benefit: it is repaid with the loyalty of those pardoned.[90]

Most similar to the debate at Syracuse is a pair of speeches in which the Senate considered Scipio's treaty with Carthage at the end of the Second Punic War.[91] Within the surviving fragments of the first speech (xxvii 13–17), which argues for accepting the treaty, the contrast is made between winning the war with arms and yet becoming angry in victory (xxvii 14.1)—a pronouncement made twice earlier at Syracuse and in what may be the speech defending the Rhodians (xxxi 3.2;

---

lviii, n. 1; Bosworth, *From Arrian to Alexander*, 7–13. On similarities between xx 22.8–9, x 34.1, and xv 65.2–3, see the end of Chapter 5.

[88] xxxi 3–4; cf. Aulus Gellius, *NA* 6.3.

[89] xxxii 27.3. Similarly, e.g., Diodorus may have learned a saying about the false alarms of war from his source for Alexander (xvii 86.1) and then applied it himself to events in Sicily: xx 30.1, 67.4; xxi 2.3. But the phrase occurs in Thucydides (iii 30), and Diodorus could have learned it through a general education.

[90] xxi 14.3; xxxi 3.

[91] For the event, see A. Eckstein, *Senate and General: Individual Decision-making and Roman Foreign Relations, 264–194 B.C.*, 261–63.

cf. xxxi 4). Benefaction (εὐεργεσία) and kindness (ἐπιείκεια) are contrasted with the results of punishment and cruel treatment (xxvii 15.1). Εὐεργεσία and ἐπιείκεια, important terms generally to Diodorus, are paired several times in the *Bibliotheke*; in fact, nearly the exact same wording is employed in an earlier speech.[92] Fortune can shift and humble the victors (xxvii 15.2–3), especially those who do not bear their success with moderation (ἀνθρωπίνως: 17.2), another Diodoran motif. But the heart of what remains concerns the question of how to maintain an empire. Those who rule by fear become the object of hatred; those who aspire to authority should instead surpass others in ἐπιείκεια (xxvii 16). These ideas are found in Nicolaus's speech, in the defense of the Rhodians, and throughout the *Bibliotheke*.

The same episode survives completely in Appian (*Pun.* 57–61). There are some similarities in sentiment,[93] but the thrust of Appian's speech is in contrast more practical than moral: because Carthage can still defend itself, to make it desperate is unwise (*Pun.* 59; mentioned in passing by Diodorus at xxvii 17.3); and a destroyed Carthage serves no purpose, except to strengthen a potentially dangerous Masinissa (*Pun.* 61). However, the formula for empire found so often in Diodorus—the use of moderation instead of fear—is completely absent. Diodorus and Appian probably used late Roman annalistic sources here,[94] and there is no way to determine to what extent Diodorus intruded in the tradition. But as the sentiments are precisely the same as those voiced throughout the *Biblio-*

[92] xxi 21.8: Pyrrhus is mentioned at xxi 21.12; this may be a debate in Tarentum whether to ask Pyrrhus to help that city against Rome (cf. F. R. Walton, *Diodorus of Sicily* XI, Loeb edition, 39, n. 5). At other times Diodorus appears to follow Hieronymus on Pyrrhus: C. Bottin, *Revue Belge de philologie et d'histoire* 7 (1928), 1307–27; more recently discussed by Manni, *Kokalos* 16 (1970), 62, n. 5, where Silenus is also posited. For the pairings of εὐεργεσία and ἐπιείκεια, and of εὐεργεσία and φιλανθρωπία, see Chapter 3.

[93] Cf. DS xxvii 17.1–2 with App., *Pun.* 57: caution against being excessive amid good fortune and a warning that the world will despise a state that destroys a great city.

[94] Schwartz, *RE* 5, 688; Volkmann, *Hermes* 84 (1954), 466, n. 2.

theke, it is likely that he introduced much of the moral aspect of this debate.

The counterarguments that urge a rejection of the treaty survive intact in Appian (*Pun.* 62–64) but are highly fragmentary in Diodorus (xxvii 18). There is little similarity of sentiment between the two and no parallel phrasing. But striking parallels to Diodorus's speech can be found elsewhere in the *Bibliotheke*. One argument is that anyone who rids the earth of dangerous animals—such as are the Carthaginians—is to be considered a public benefactor (κοινὸς εὐεργέτης) for his good acts toward humanity (τὸν κοινὸν βίον: xxvii 18.2). The notion of an individual performing benefactions for the common good is central to Diodoran philosophy (see Chapter 3). More specifically, clearing the land of wild beasts as a necessary precondition to civilization is a belief stressed by Diodorus more than by any other known ancient writer.[95] Diodorus several times has Heracles, a local hero, perform that service as a benefaction (εὐεργεσία) to humanity.[96] The belief that barbarians,[97] including Carthaginians,[98] are beastlike is thematic to the *Bibliotheke*. The arguments, then, are well rooted in Diodoran thought and metaphor.[99] The main sentiment expressed by the speaker opposed to the treaty is that φιλανθρωπία is awarded only to those who have done no great wrong; the Carthaginians, however, have acted so brutally that they should be treated as they have treated others: "To apply to each the law that he has set for others is no more than

[95] i 8.1–2, 24.5–6; iii 25.1; see further, Chapter 3.

[96] i 24.5–8; ii 39.2; iv 17.4–5; v 76.1.

[97] E.g., i 28.7; xvii 105.3; xxi 12.6; xxxiv 4.2: examples taken from sections where Diodorus must be following disparate sources.

[98] xiii 58.2. Libyans generally: iii 49.2; and Libya full of real beasts: i 30.2; xx 40.

[99] Volkmann, *Hermes* 82 (1954), 468, argues that xxvii 18.2 might reflect pro-Roman propaganda, especially popular in Diodorus's day. Diodorus, however, makes that argument fail; on Diodorus's feelings about Rome, see Chapter 5.

just."[100] The notion is found elsewhere in the *Bibliotheke* (xiv 46.4), but the very words are used in the debate of 413 at Syracuse.[101] For the speeches already discussed, the sources Diodorus followed are no longer extant. Thus it is not possible to determine with certainty the degree to which Diodorus modified the tradition. But two other Polybian speeches used by Diodorus provide insight. In these Polybius expresses thoughts on the inconsistency of chance and the need for moderation amid good fortune. In one, Diodorus, interested more in personal morality than in political action, adds a sentiment about private affairs (τὸν ἴδιον βίον).[102] In the other, in accordance with his belief that forgiveness is more important than punishment, Diodorus emphasizes more the morality than the vengefulness of the moment.[103] Here he preserves Polybian oratory with only a moderate amount of alteration, because Polybius's ideas are largely compatible with his own. But the other speeches detailed here are found in contexts in which Ephorus, Cleitarchus, Timaeus, Hieronymus (or Silenus), Polybius, and a Roman annalist have been identified as the sources. It is too much to expect a shared philosophy among them all. Rather, the striking similarity of phrasing and argumentation within the speeches and between speeches and narrative indicates that Diodorus makes an important contribution to the λόγοι. In theory, speeches should be few and brief; in practice Diodorus is generally accurate in condensing the facts within speeches found in his sources. But when extensive oratory is to be included or when speeches are to contain moral *sententiae*, Diodorus, consistent with his statement that the historian should occasionally display his rhetorical powers

---

[100] δίκαιον γάρ ἐστιν, ὅν καθ' ἑτέρων τις νόμον ἔθηκε, τούτῳ κεχρῆσθαι: xxvii 18.1 (Walton).

[101] δικαιότατον γάρ ἐστιν ὅν καθ' ἑτέρων νόμον τις ἔθηκε, τούτῳ χρώμενον μὴ ἀγανακτεῖν: xiii 30.5.

[102] DS xxx 23 = Polybius xxix 20.

[103] DS xxxii 23 = Polybius xxxviii 20.1–3.

(xx 1.2, 2), often infuses them with his own message concerning moderate behavior.

POLEMICS

By the first century, the practice of passing judgment on earlier historians had long been established. Aside from his convention of recording the chronological limits of their works, however, Diodorus has little to say about his fellow historians. Occasionally in passing he pays compliments to the accuracy of a narrative.[104] His criticisms are more numerous, but it is usually argued that these already existed in his sources. There is some reason to believe, however, that, whatever the original source for the surrounding material, Diodorus at times helped shape and at other times invented some of these attacks. An investigation into the polemics found in the *Bibliotheke* not only will help establish Diodorus's intrusions, it will also demonstrate aspects of his research techniques.

First, there are the brief references, expressed as passing attacks on other historians. The construction "others say" recurs throughout the *Bibliotheke*.[105] In some instances it may echo what is found in his sources, perhaps as Diodorus's abbreviation of a longer polemic found there; at other times the judgment may be his own. For example, in following the account of Posidonius on tin mining in Spain, Diodorus states that other, unnamed authors wrongly suppose that tin lies about on the surface. Virtually the same words are used by Strabo, who is also here drawing on Posidonius.[106] Diodorus has not determined for himself what the other writers claimed, but simply repeats the argument found in Posidonius. That is no different than the modern habit of echoing another's opinion of a piece of research without having read it

---

[104] Thucydides and Xenophon generally (i 37.3), Agatharchides and Artemidorus (iii 11.2–3), and Timaeus (v 1.3; xiii 90.6; xxi 17.1).

[105] E.g., i 15.2, 22.2; ii 9.4, 32.1; xvii 117.5.

[106] DS v 38.4 with *FGH* 87 F 47 = Strabo iii 2.9.

oneself. But without the control of a parallel account, it is wrong to conclude that Diodorus has always copied the reference or polemic. For example, when he cites Apollodorus of Athens for the year of Euripides' death, adding that others say it happened a little earlier, it is assumed that Diodorus took the entire discussion from his source.[107] But Apollodorus composed his *Chronology* in meter, so it is doubtful whether he discussed alternative dates given by earlier writers. He completed the work near the end of the second century,[108] and it is unlikely that Diodorus would have used it through an intermediary only a half-century after its publication. Certainly, contemporaries of Diodorus had access to the original,[109] and elsewhere Diodorus claims to have followed it.[110] On the death of Euripides, Diodorus may well be responsible for comparing the information given by Apollodorus and other writers.

Indeed, Diodorus's industry is elsewhere evident. There are several instances in which Diodorus names his authorities when giving troop strengths. He frequently compares the figures in Ephorus and Timaeus, using the formula "Ephorus says x, but Timaeus y,"[111] or the reverse, with the Timaean figure first, followed by Ephorus's.[112] Twice he notes that Timaeus gives one figure, but that certain unnamed historians give another.[113] But for one calculation, he appeals to Ephorus

---

[107] xiii 103.5 = FGH 244 F 35; F. Jacoby, *Apollodors Chronik*, 33, 250–51; FGH IId, 730 (Commentary to 244 F 35).

[108] On the dating of the two editions, most recently, P. Fraser, *Ptolemaic Alexandria* I, 471, with n. 232.

[109] Atticus had a copy (Cic., *ad Att.* xii 23.2.); on Nepos and Philodemus, see Jacoby, *Apollodors Chronik*, 34–35, 57–59. The *Nachleben* is briefly discussed in *FGH* IId, 720.

[110] i 5.1; vii 8; xiii 108.1.

[111] xiii 54.5 = FGH 70 F 201, 566 F 103; xiv 54.5–6 = FGH 70 F 204, 566 F 108.

[112] xiii 60.5 = FGH 70 F 202, 566 F 104; xiii 80.5 = FGH 70 F 203, 566 F 25.

[113] xiii 109.2 = FGH 566 F 107; xx 89.5 = FGH 566 F 121.

alone;[114] for another only to Timaeus.[115] Under the assumption that Diodorus cannot do his own work, it might be thought that Diodorus received all the numbers from Timaeus, who wrote after Ephorus and whom Diodorus probably followed extensively.[116] But at one point he cites only Ephorus (see n. 114), suggesting that Diodorus compared the troop figures himself.[117] Instances where Diodorus himself appears to provide the variant tradition help support the possibility that other minor polemics are also of his own making.[118]

Some polemics in the *Bibliotheke* are more extensive. Diodorus's investigation into the problems of the origin and flooding of the Nile produces an attack on the accounts of several historians. Although concluding that he cannot reveal the origin of the Nile, for no one yet has seen it or talked with another who has, he criticizes the explanations of many historians concerning the reason for its flooding and finally gives his assent to the explanation of Agatharchides of Cnidus (i 37–41). Along with his criticisms of Timaeus, to be discussed, this detailed polemic is the most important in the *Bibliotheke*, and it is usually held that he must have taken the discussion from his main current source: either Agatharchides himself or Artemidorus, the possible transmitter of Agatharchides' discussion.[119]

Certainly, the richness of detail and clarity of thought contained in this polemic, but so infrequently found elsewhere in

[114] xiv 22.2 = *FGH* 70 F 208.

[115] xiii 85.3 = *FGH* 566 F 27.

[116] See, e.g., the discussion by Pearson, *The Greek Historians of the West*, 135–36.

[117] Cf. Meister, "Die sizilische Geschichte," 79.

[118] Examples discussed by Bosworth, *From Arrian to Alexander*, 10.

[119] To what extent Diodorus used Agatharchides or Artemidorus, and whether he used one or both, not only for i 37–41, but also for i 32–36, are thorny issues. Recent summaries are in Burton, *Diodorus Siculus Book I*, 20ff. and K. Meister, *Helikon* 13–14 (1973–1974), 454–55. Jacoby assigns all of i 32–41.9 to Agatharchides directly (*FGH* 86 F 19) on the basis of contradictions between Diodorus and Artemidorus.

the *Bibliotheke*, suggest that Diodorus drew heavily on an earlier work. But that is not to say that he depended entirely on Agatharchides or Artemidorus. For example, in the discussion of the historians who had offered an explanation as to why the Nile overflowed yearly, Herodotus is charged with inventing a solution (σχεδιάζω: i 38.12). But twice elsewhere in book i, when the source for the surrounding material is not Agatharchides but rather Hecataeus, Herodotus and Egyptian priests separately are attacked for inventing stories (σχεδιάζω).[120] Again, Diodorus repeats the charge in book ii, stating that Ctesias had proved that Herodotus is guilty of invention (σχεδιάζω).[121] Finally, Diodorus, probably on his own, also accuses Timaeus of invention (σχεδιάζω).[122] Invention was an important part of rhetorical theory, of which Diodorus appears to have been aware.[123] He approves of inventing arguments for speeches, but urges that such displays be kept to a minimum within the genre of history. Similarly, he may have felt that the invention of historical explanations was little more than excessive rhetoric. This criterion for criticism may well be Diodorus's own.

In that same discussion of the Nile, Ephorus is attacked for his explanation (i 39.11) and for his failure to observe firsthand or to question travelers who had seen the river (39.9). The polemic concludes that "under no circumstances would any man look for strict accuracy in Ephorus, when he sees that

[120] i 23.2; i 69.7 = *FGH* 264 F 25 (*Anhang*). Wesseling presents a good discussion of σχεδιάζω in Eyring, *Diodori Siculi Bibliothecae Historicae Libri* I, 425, on i 69.7. Also compare i 69.7 with iii 11.2: note the similarities with πλάσσω and ψυχαγωγία. On πλάσσω, see also v 23.4. Herodotus is also accused of preferring the sensational (θαυμάσιοι) to the real in order to amuse the reader (x 24.1). But Diodorus will himself include the παράδοξον (iii 30.2–11).

[121] ii 15.2 = *FGH* 688 F 1b.

[122] xiii 90.6; it is not in the corresponding Polybian passages on which Diodorus may have drawn (xii 7.6 and 25).

[123] On σχεδιάζω, see J. Ernesti, *Lexicon Technologiae Graecorum Rhetoricae*, s.v.; cf. s.v. εὕρεσις. On Diodorus's awareness of rhetorical theory, see the previous section on speeches.

in many matters he has paid little regard to the truth."[124] Ephorus, of course, was Diodorus's main source for Hellenic affairs, and such an attack on Ephorus's accuracy might appear hypocritical. Most scholars argue therefore that Diodorus simply copied the charge from his current source without realizing its implications.[125]

But Diodorus's independence from Ephorus concerning prehistory is demonstrable. Elsewhere he almost certainly acts on his own in dismissing Ephorus's explanation of the invention of writing.[126] Diodorus was never impressed with Ephorus's handling of legend (i 9.5) and so felt entitled to reject his traditions. The polemic regarding the Nile might only apply to Ephorus's ethnography and not his historical narrative, for the Cymaean never visited Egypt (i 39.8). In the opening proem Diodorus informs the reader of the efforts required in gathering his material. "We have visited a large portion of both Asia and Europe that we might see with our own eyes all the most important regions and as many others as possible; for many errors have been committed through ignorance of the sites" (i 4.1; Oldfather). Whatever the accuracy of his claim (see Chapter 6, n. 2), Diodorus, a writer of mostly antiquarian history, defines autopsy as the personal visitation of lands rather than the witnessing of events in progress. Diodorus is especially proud of his travels to Egypt, frequently reminding the reader of his sojourn and his access to Egyptian and Ethiopian sources.[127] His attack of Ephorus may be limited to a particular aspect of his methodology that Diodorus feels qualified to criticize.

Timaeus was the most famous historian of Sicily, and, though he may follow the narrative of his compatriot

---

[124] i 39.13 (Oldfather).

[125] Most recently, Burton, *Diodorus Siculus Book I*, 21; Meister, *Helikon* 13–14 (1973–1974), 455. That Diodorus also calls Ephorus's explanation καινοτάτη (i 39.7) is of no account; cf. Burton, *Diodorus Siculus Book I*, 22, who rightly interprets it as "the most novel," rather than "the most recent."

[126] v 74.1; cf. Jacoby's comment on *FGH* 70 F 105. See Chapter 3.

[127] E.g., i 4.1, 22.2–3, 44.1; iii 11.2–3, 38.1, xvii 52.6.

closely[128] and praise its accuracy,[129] Diodorus's intellectual independence is again evident. He first attacks Timaeus in the proem to book v, suggesting that Timaeus's own lengthy polemics against earlier historians robbed his work of effective organization. There is no reason to doubt his own authorship here.[130] Similarly, when Diodorus criticizes an unnamed writer of tragic history for giving too much detail in relating terrible events (xix 8.4), he may have Timaeus in mind. The surrounding material is attributed to that source,[131] and the passage describes the horrors committed by Agathocles, a famous Timaean *topos*. In the proem to the next book, Diodorus accuses historians of including in their works excessive numbers of overlong speeches (xx 1–2). This, it has been argued, is Diodorus's attack on Timaeus, whose oratorical excesses were famous in antiquity.[132]

But Diodorus's independence seems most obvious in his discussion of the Bull of Phalaris (xiii 90.4–7). Diodorus strongly attacks Timaeus's account, though probably misrepresenting his argument.[133] He may have been partly inspired by Polybius's attack,[134] but stories of the bull must have been popular in Sicily, and Diodorus claims to have seen it himself (xiii 90.5). As in the polemics against Herodotus and Ephorus regarding the Nile, Diodorus had an opportunity here to appeal to his own authority as an eyewitness.[135]

---

[128] That is the thesis of, among others, Meister, "Die sizilische Geschichte." But the debate continues, in particular over the question of whether Diodorus drew on the intermediary, Silenus: see n. 12.

[129] v 1.3; xiii 90.6; xxi 17.1.

[130] v 1.3; echoed at xxi 17.1. See Chapter 1.

[131] So Meister, "Die sizilische Geschichte," 139–40.

[132] Pearson, *AJP* 107 (1986), 368. Also see the previous section on speeches.

[133] Walbank, *CR* 59 (1945), 39–42; see also Walbank, *Commentary* II, 380–82. Meister, *Helikon* 13–14 (1973–1974), 455–56, argues that, when Diodorus talks about the Bull in subsequent narrative (xix 108.1 and xx 71.3), he is following Timaeus, thus disproving his own assertion that Timaeus denied its existence.

[134] Polybius xii 7.6 and xii 25.

[135] Cf. Drews, *AJP* 83 (1962), 392, n. 31, and Walbank, *CR* 59 (1945), 39–

One of Diodorus's arguments regarding the Bull of Phalaris is instructive in showing how he uses the material of his sources. Diodorus accuses Timaeus of erring intentionally, a fault that, unlike unintentional errors, should not be forgiven. This particular accusation is absent in Polybius's discussion, but, as it is a Polybian theme and one the Achaean occasionally applied to Timaeus, Diodorus may have been influenced by Polybian thought. What is most striking is that Diodorus's discussion occurs in book xiii, and Diodorus does not begin to follow Polybius's historical narrative until book xxv.[136] If Diodorus did reproduce, though somewhat inaccurately, part of Polybius's argument, it confirms that he had read through his sources, marking out material for inclusion, before composing the history.[137] In his initial research, he must have acquired historical perspectives that would be imposed throughout the *Bibliotheke*, regardless of his current source.

His lecture on the difference between errors caused by mistaken facts and those created through the historian's prejudice sets the stage for his later criticism of Timaeus and of Callias of Syracuse. Both historians are charged with biased accounts of Agathocles, but with opposite slants: Timaeus was overly harsh, whereas Callias awarded the tyrant fulsome praise.[138] Diodorus again reflects Polybius but once more uses the polemic in a different context.[139] And he employs his own arguments as well. He concedes that Timaeus is generally quite careful with the truth,[140] a statement Polybius would never

42. The attempt to attribute the treatments of Diodorus and Polybius to Silenus is just speculation; see Walbank, *Kokalos* 14–15 (1968–1969), 488.

[136] Schwartz, *RE* 5, 689.

[137] For confirming evidence of this method, see Hornblower, *Hieronymus of Cardia*, 62–63; Rubincam, *EMC/CV* 31, n.s. 6 (1987), 313–28.

[138] Timaeus: xxi 17.1–3 = *FGH* 566 F 124d; Callias xxi 17.4 = *FGH* 564 T 3, F 7.

[139] xii 15, 26b4: Walbank, *CR* 59 (1945), 41; contra, Meister, *Helikon* 13–14 (1973–1974), 456–59.

[140] [Τίμαιος] πλείστην πρόνοιαν εἶχε τῆς ἀληθείας: xxi 17.1.

make.[141] He also introduces the notion that history is best served by frankness of expression (παρρησία: 17.3), an idea that is missing in Polybius's argument and is found frequently in the *Bibliotheke*.[142] Moreover, the attack on Callias, which is not in the extant Polybian text, is effectively integrated. It is unlikely that Polybius ever did mention Callias, for he is absent from Polybius's list of historians discussed.[143] Again, as with the discussion of the Bull of Phalaris, Diodorus was probably inspired by Polybian sentiments he had read while doing his initial research. What speaks most for Diodorus's intellectual interests is that the Polybian material on which he draws comes largely from book xii, a historiographical digression without factual narrative.[144] Diodorus must have read it out of curiosity, rather than for any narrative material he could later use.

The criticisms of Timaeus strengthen the possibility that Diodorus helped fashion the attacks on Ephorus and Herodotus concerning Egyptian affairs. In censuring Timaeus on the Bull of Phalaris, Diodorus chooses a subject about which he has personal knowledge. Similarly, because Diodorus visited Egypt, when drawing on the accounts from other sources, he feels in a position to confirm or contradict them.[145] As a historian relying generally on second-hand information, when

---

[141] See, e.g., Polybius xii 10.6, 12.5–7, and 25h.2; Polybius does admit that Timaeus gave detailed chronologies and accounts (xii 10.4; cf. DS v 1.3).

[142] See Chapter 2, pp. 34–35.

[143] xii 23.8. As well, a key phrase in Diodorus's discussion also occurs in the opening proem to the *Bibliotheke* (i 2.2): history as προφῆτις τῆς ἀληθείας. Pearson, *The Greek Historians of the West*, 228–29, argues that the polemic on Timaeus is Diodorus's own, but that against Callias was borrowed from Timaeus. However, the two arguments are thematically linked, so that, if Diodorus is the author of one, he may well be the author of the other.

[144] Cf. Walbank, *CR* 59 (1945), 41.

[145] iii 11.1–3; cf. i 36.7. Diodorus's confidence in using Egyptian material is illuminated by his reference at xx 58.4 to Egyptian customs discussed at i 83.1, to Egyptian topography at xvi 46.5 discussed at i 30.6, and his inclusion of personal autopsy at i 88.8–9.

given the chance to use personal knowledge, he does so, assuming an authoritative manner.

THIS CHAPTER is not intended as a thorough evaluation of Diodorus's methodologies. In being selective, it argues that many modern interpretations ought to be reassessed and based on a closer study of the entire *Bibliotheke*. The three aspects of history writing discussed—organizational and chronological markers, speeches, and polemics—combined with the study of proems in Chapter 1 suggest that Diodorus was more involved in the composition of his history than is generally acknowledged. Themes found throughout the work are reflected in these historiographical conventions, and frequently there is evidence of care and precision in relating these conventions to the greater narrative. Certainly, serious problems do exist in the *Bibliotheke*. That fact and the assumption that Diodorus is "a mere copyist," however, frequently lead to exaggerated claims about his methods. And *that* in turn leads to *Quellenforschung* frequently based on unsound principles.

FIVE

Diodorus on Rome

FOR LONGER than any other area outside the Italian penin-
sula, Diodorus's homeland was under Roman control. Serving as an important source of grain, as well as a battlefield for
Roman armies, Sicily was protected and exploited for its fertile fields, prized and plundered for its Greek culture. During
Diodorus's lifetime, Verres shamelessly ravaged the island,
Caesar and Antony extended the franchise, and Octavian and
Sextus Pompey fought there. At the same time a series of civil
wars transformed the Roman government from oligarchy to
autocracy. No historian, not even a so-called copyist such as
Diodorus, could have ignored or remained unaffected by these
events. Diodorus may have reproduced the narratives of his
sources, but his feelings on the contemporary world must also
be reflected in the *Bibliotheke*. The present chapter studies Diodorus's general attitude toward the Empire and especially Sicily's place in it. Although Diodorus is at times ambivalent or
maddeningly contradictory, the evidence shows that he is
overall moderately critical of Rome.

Discovering Diodorus's precise views on Rome is difficult
enough. But trying to prove that Rome or any contemporary
theme is the central thread of the *Bibliotheke* is certainly bound
to fail.[1] Writing in one of the most significant periods in west-

---

[1] Rome was suggested as the unifying theme by B. Croce, *Teoria e storia
della storiografia*[6], 179; so, too, Rawson, *Intellectual Life*, 223; E. Troilo, *AIV*
(1940–1941), 24–42 (courageously anti-Nazi); and Oldfather, *Diodorus of Sicily*
I, Loeb edition, xi. Following Reinhardt, *Poseidonios*, 33ff., Laqueur, *Hermes*
86 (1958), 289, argues that i 1.3 is a Stoic sentiment transmitted through Posidonius (cf. Theiler, F 80) and employed by Diodorus to reflect the unity of
history established by Caesar. But see Nock, *JRS* 49 (1959), 5 = Nock, *Essays*
II, 859–60, and P. Hardie, *Virgil's Aeneid: Cosmos and Imperium*, 378.

ern history, embodying the essential completion of the Roman Empire and Rome's transition from republic to autocracy, Diodorus had natural organizing themes before him. These he ignored. In the early books of the *Bibliotheke*, Rome plays an insignificant role, receiving hardly a mention until the First Punic War. Besides the entries that list the annual consuls and include brief allusions to events, there is only a handful of discussions of a paragraph or more on Rome. These constitute less than three percent of the extant material of books i–xxii.[2] It was easy to find out about the origins of Rome, and there were several Greek accounts available to Diodorus.[3] But interest in the early Republic was limited; retailing that would have required greater research than Diodo-

[2] References to Rome in books vii–xx: A. Drachmann, *Diodors römische Annalen bis 302 a. Chr. samt dem Ineditum Vaticanum.* Also xxii 1.6. There are about 30 chapters on Rome, compared with nearly 700 chapters on Greece and 250 on Sicily.

[3] E. Bickerman, *CP* 47 (1952), 65–81. Diodorus draws on Fabius Pictor, among others (vii 5.4 = F 4 Peter), for the foundation of Rome (vii 4–6; viii 3–6); cf. T. Cornell, *PCPS* 21 (1975), 24–27. L. Hahn, *Rom und Römanismus in griechisch-römischen Osten*, 130–31, and Càssola, *ANRW* II 30.1, 746, argue that some of Diodorus's Latinisms may come from Pictor, but whether the Latin version was a translation of the Greek or a different work, perhaps by the grandson, N. Pictor, is unclear: B. Frier, *Libri Annales Pontificum Maximorum: The Origins of the Annalistic Tradition*, 246–52. The Greek original had long been available, even in Sicily: G. Manganaro, *PP* 29 (1974), 394–401 (= *SEG* XXVI, 1123). The extent of the Roman Empire made resources more accessible to Diodorus (i 4.3), and he claims to have obtained an accurate knowledge of the Empire "from records [ὑπομνήματα] carefully preserved among [the Romans] over a long period of time" (i 4.4; Oldfather). Although ὑπομνήματα here suggest official records (see McDougall, *Lexicon*, s.v.), Diodorus cites official material only at xl 4 (cf. Pliny, *NH* vii 97–98), so it is largely an empty claim. ὑπομνήματα cannot refer to the *annales maximi* (as argued by M. Rusconi, *CISA* 3 [1975], 105–10), for Diodorus connects their accessibility with Roman expansion. Many believe they refer to the work of Fabius Pictor (see Càssola, *ANRW* II 30.1, 746, n. 59), but it is perhaps best to understand ὑπομνήματα as official documents preserved in several historical works, now easily available because Rome had become an important center for publishing (see Chapter 6). The sources for most of the early Roman material in the *Bibliotheke* are indeterminable: Schwartz, *RE* 5, 691–97; Càssola, *ANRW* II 30.1, 728–51.

rus was willing to undertake.[4] The Sicilian's initial emphasis on Greek affairs is clear, and so with reason Jerome calls Diodorus "scriptor Graecae historiae."[5] Rome's place in the *Bibliotheke* expands substantially at the point of the First Punic War. Material was more available, as Diodorus's sources for the period after 264 B.C. became vitally interested in the Roman Empire, viewing it as the great organizing force in the Mediterranean. The First Punic War also marked the beginning of Rome's control over Diodorus's homeland; from some of Sicily's later Roman residents Diodorus himself claims to have learned Latin (i 4.4). As the *Bibliotheke* approaches contemporary times, the place of Rome grows correspondingly larger.

Praise of Rome was a long-standing tradition in Greek historiography. It is perhaps already found in the mid-third century, both in Lycophron's *Alexandra*, which notes Roman control of land and sea,[6] and in the work of Aristos of Salamis, who records Alexander the Great's compliments of Roman institutions.[7] Many first-century Greek historians who visited or resided in Rome are known to have repaid the city with laudation: Dionysius of Halicarnassus,[8] Strabo,[9] Nicolaus of Damascus,[10] Asclepiades of Athens,[11] and the panegyrist, Au-

---

[4] See E. Gabba, *Les origines de la républic romaine*, Fondation Hardt, *Entretiens* 13, 135–69.

[5] R. Helm, *Die Chronik des Hieronymus*[2], 155. The Suda refers to the *Bibliotheke* as ἱστορία Ῥωμαϊκή τε καὶ ποικίλη (1152, Adler), and Photius states πάσας τὰς ἡγεμονικὰς αὐτῆς πράξεις καὶ πάθη ἀκριβῶς ἀνελάβετο (*Codex* 70 35a, 25–26). But they were working with a text that a later author had extended seventy-four years to the death of Augustus (see Chapter 6).

[6] A. Momigliano, *JRS* 32 (1942), 53–64; but see the most recent attack on authenticity: S. West, *JHS* 104 (1984), 127–51.

[7] *FGH* 143 F 2 = Arr., *Anab.* vii 15.5; for his date: *FGH*, IIbd, 531.

[8] Discussed in the text.

[9] List of passages in Jones, *Strabo* I, Loeb edition, xviii–xix. His family was pro-Roman in the Mithridatic Wars: Rawson, *Intellectual Life*, 8, n. 25.

[10] Most recently, E. Gabba "The Historians and Augustus," in Millar and Segal, *Caesar Augustus*, 61–63.

[11] *FGH* 144 F 1 = Arr., *Anab.* vii 15.5.

lus Licinius Archias.[12] Even Timagenes, who ultimately attacked Augustus and Rome, began his career as an admirer.[13]

Diodorus's interest in Roman history in his later books was not, however, accompanied by similar affection for the imperial power, as is commonly thought.[14] Illuminating is a comparison with Polybius and Dionysius of Halicarnassus, the two Hellenistic historians whose works, besides that of Diodorus's, are still substantially preserved. They begin their studies by listing the great empires of history and conclude that the most successful was the Roman. Diodorus, who actually devotes his early books to the ancient oriental empires, in his own prologue fails to make the same comparison between the older hegemonies and Rome.[15] He mentions only that, because of Rome's control of the known world, extensive research materials were available in the imperial city (i 4.3). Polybius, in his first prologue, also describes the Roman Empire as a manifestation of divine will (τύχη).[16] When Diodorus discusses πρόνοια and history (i 1.3), he makes no such connection. Dionysius begins his *Roman Antiquities* with abundant praise, arguing that Rome achieved the greatest accomplishments and empire in history and calling its citizens "godlike men."[17] Very late in the *Bibliotheke*, in a passage

---

[12] B. Gold, *Literary Patronage in Greece and Rome*, 73–86

[13] See p. 191. See also M. Crawford, "Greek Intellectuals and the Roman Aristocracy in the First Century B.C.," in Garnsey and Whittaker, *Imperialism in the Ancient World*, 193–207.

[14] E.g., Oldfather, *Diodorus of Sicily* I, Loeb edition, x; Manganaro, *PP* 29 (1974), 399; de Romilly, *La douceur dans la pensée grecque*, 53–61; Sartori, *Athenaeum* 72 (1984), 533. Exceptions include B. Forte, *Rome and the Romans as the Greeks Saw Them*, 157–58, and Momigliano, *Settimo contributo*, 91–92 = *On Pagans, Jews, and Christians*, 45–46.

[15] Cf. Momigliano, *Settimo contributo*, 91 = *On Pagans, Jews, and Christians*, 45–46.

[16] i 4; his thoughts are complex: Walbank, *Polybius*, 157–83, and *Polybe*, Fondation Hardt, *Entretiens* 20, 1–31; P. Derow, *JRS* 69 (1979), 1–15; and Gruen, *HWCR* I, 344.

[17] *AR* i 2–3; Gabba, *RSI* 71 (1959), 365–69, and *CA* I (1982), 43–65, are essential for understanding Dionysius and the cultural partnership between Greece and Rome.

where he is probably following Posidonius, Diodorus does describe the Roman Empire as the most brilliant and greatest in memory. But that is followed immediately by a contrast between the practices of earlier Romans who had acquired the empire and the utter decadence of its contemporary citizens.[18] Finally, the contemporary philosopher Philodemus, enjoying Roman patronage, wrote that Rome and Alexandria were equally the greatest cities of his day.[19] Diodorus, who had lived in Alexandria and was then a long-time resident of Rome, twice records that many reckon Alexandria to be the first city in the world.[20]

Tendenz in Diodorus

The comparisons just outlined reveal in broad terms Diodorus's qualified attitude toward Rome. Closer analysis of the narrative confirms that Diodorus held generally hostile though often contradictory opinions of the imperial power. Before undertaking such an investigation, however, important methodological problems must be faced. Most of the Roman material in the *Bibliotheke*, located near the end of the history, survives only in fragments and is often preserved out of context. As well, there is the problem of separating Diodorus's opinion from those of his sources. Polybius recounted the history of Rome from the First Punic War, in 264, down to the Achaean War of 146. Posidonius, writing toward the middle of the first century B.C., took up the narrative where Polybius concluded. Although they are Diodorus's main sources for the middle and late Republic,[21] specific problems

---

[18] xxxvii 2.1, 3.1: on its Posidonian origin, see Chapter 2.

[19] *Philodemi Volumina Rhetorica*, ed. E. Sudhaus, II, 145 (Leipzig, 1896).

[20] I 50.7; xvii 52.5.

[21] Polybius the main source for DS xxviii–xxxii, as well as some earlier material: H. Nissen, *Kritische Untersuchungen über die Quellen der vierten und fünften Dekaden des Livius*, 110–15; Schwartz, *RE* 5, 689–90, for the parallel passages between Polybius and Diodorus. For Posidonius as the main source for xxxiii–xxxvii: Schwartz, *RE* 5, 687–90.

of source attribution abound. For example, Diodorus almost certainly departed from the Polybian text in narrating the First and Second Punic Wars. Because the Posidonian history ended before the *Bibliotheke* (see Chapter 6, p. 177), there must also be other, unknown sources that Diodorus employed for the final years. Further, Polybius and Posidonius themselves displayed ambivalence toward Rome. They admired the city-state that controlled the Mediterranean basin. Yet, observing that Rome reacted brutally against threats to its hegemony, they also raised questions about contemporary Roman practices.[22] Their ambiguities concerning Rome make it difficult to separate their *Tendenz* in the *Bibliotheke* from Diodorus's. Finally, Diodorus appears to be less precise in—or perhaps less concerned with—his own political opinions than his general notions of moral philosophy. Consequently, he may copy into the narrative sentiments with which he may not agree, and there can be a residue of material that will contradict any interpretation.

His treatment of a personal hero, Gelon, illustrates this last problem of inconsistency. Gelon's most important contact with the Greek mainland occurred when Xerxes attacked Europe, in 480. Anticipating the invasion, Athens and Sparta approached the Sicilian tyrant. Herodotus made famous one version: Gelon refused to aid the Greek cause unless he received complete control of either the land or the naval forces (vii 157–66). Diodorus summarizes that story (x 33), probably drawn through Ephorus as intermediary.[23] The preserved version may have been shortened by the Constantinian excerpter, but

---

[22] Polybius iii 4, on which see Walbank, *Polybius*, 170–71. Posidonius also covers the war in Spain, stressing that barbarians have a human side: Strasburger, *JRS* 55 (1965), 47–48. Theiler alone identifies DS xxxiii 26.2, regarding the Spanish War, as Posidonian (F 128), a statement that the Romans were brutal to those who opposed them but used ἐπιείκεια with those who obeyed them. On this and xxxiv/xxxv 23 (end) and xxx 23.2, see the discussion later in this chapter. On Polybius and Posidonius on Rome, see A. Momigliano, *Alien Wisdom: The Limits of Hellenization*, 22–49, with bibliography.

[23] Schwartz, *RE* 6, 13–14.

what remains reflects the Herodotean tradition: the attempt at alliance failed because of Gelon's desire for glory (φιλοδοξία). The next chapter contains the fragments of a debate among the Greeks about whether to accept Gelon's conditions. The argument is made that the Persian king is less demanding and more predictable than a tyrant (x 34.1, 4), and there is fear for the future once mercenaries are used to fight for Greek freedom (x 34.9). This episode is not in Herodotus, and here Diodorus was probably depending entirely on Ephorus.[24] Yet the criticism of Gelon is consistent with the picture drawn by Herodotus; it must have been part of the tradition generally espoused by mainland Greeks.

In the proem to the next book, xi, Diodorus outlines the events of the year 480: Xerxes attacks mainland Greece, and the Carthaginians, in agreement with the Persian king, simultaneously invade Sicily (xi 1.4–5).[25] The next eighteen chapters detail the battles of Thermopylae and Salamis, after which Diodorus shifts the focus to his homeland. In following another source, certainly Sicilian and quite probably Timaeus,[26] Diodorus puts Gelon's victory at Himera on the same day as the battle of Thermopylae and argues that word of his success encouraged the Greeks at Salamis.[27] Here the account is at odds with that found in Herodotus, Aristotle, and Ephorus, that the battle of Himera coincided with that of Salamis.[28] The

[24] See also Pearson, *The Greek Historians of the West*, 132–33. The source could not be Timaeus, for, according to Polybius, Timaeus's account of the debate was full of rhetorical display, while in the actual debate everyone was simply invited to help the Greeks by competing for courage and the crown of excellence (xii 26b.3 = FGH 566 F 94), sentiments quite close to those in DS x 34.6–8. As Pearson notes, Polybius could not have been following Herodotus here, so Ephorus is most likely his source also.

[25] Ephorus, however, believed that the Persian king *commanded* Carthage to attack Sicily and then the mainland: FGH 70 F 186 = Schol. Pindar *P.* i 146b.

[26] Walbank, *Commentary* II, 404; Meister, "Die sizilische Geschichte," 42–43; Pearson, *The Greek Historians of the West*, 132–40.

[27] xi 23.2, 24.1.

[28] Hdt. vii 166; Arist., *Poet.* 1459a.24–27; FGH 70 (Ephorus) F 186 = Schol. Pindar *P.* i 146b.

Sicilian bias in Diodorus's tradition is clear: the victory at Himera, moved back in time, supplies the inspiration to mainland Greeks for their own struggle at Salamis. Diodorus later recounts that Gelon intended to help the mainland once the Carthaginians were thoroughly subdued, but desisted when he heard news of the Greek success at Salamis and of Xerxes' withdrawal from Europe (26.5). This, too, contradicts the tradition preserved by Herodotus, that Gelon was unwilling to help the Greeks under any circumstances, but ready to Medize if Xerxes prevailed at Salamis.[29] The initial episode in Diodorus involving Gelon puts him in a negative light; yet the subsequent account of his victory at Himera portrays him as an inspiration to the mainland and a Greek patriot.

Diodorus must have been sympathetic to the latter image, for throughout the *Bibliotheke* there is much praise of Gelon. Some, which pertains to his military prowess and general popularity, may derive from Diodorus's main Sicilian source, Timaeus.[30] But when Gelon is extolled repeatedly for acting ἐπιεικῶς, that is Diodorus's own composition, for moderation is a central theme of his own moral program.[31] Diodorus also proclaims that history's praise for Gelon's benefactions is everlasting and is more important than the transient honors bestowed by mere mortals (xi 38.5–6). These are recurring themes in the *Bibliotheke* (see Chapter 3), and Diodorus applies the same sentiment to Julius Caesar, the other figure who shares his highest esteem (xxxii 27.3).

If Diodorus is so proud of his countryman, why does he also retain the tradition of a tyrant wrecking the Panhellenic alliance out of ambition? Obviously, despite his fierce loyalty to Gelon and Sicily, Diodorus can preserve the sentiments of a source at odds with his own view. This is an important illus-

---

[29] vii 163–64; Hdt. vii 165 is an alternate, exculpatory version—that Gelon was prevented from sending help because of the Carthaginian invasion. Diodorus never uses the tradition that Carthage and Persia are allies (xi.1.4–5) to explain Gelon's failure to give aid.

[30] xi 21.3, 22.5–6, 23.3, 25; cf. Meister, "Die sizilische Geschichte," 42–43 and esp. Polybius 12.26b.

[31] xi 26.4, 38.1, 67.2; see Chapter 2.

trative example, because, despite the fact that the subject matter was personally meaningful to him, Diodorus still does not
impose complete control on the material. It will be seen that
his inclusion of contrasting interpretations also at times holds
true in his treatment of Rome.

But contradictions such as those found in the retailing of
Gelon's story do not always indicate a change of sources. Ambiguity and ambivalence about Rome cloud the attitudes of
Polybius and Posidonius, as must surely have been the case for
any intellectual living during this tumultuous period. Diodorus spent a decade and a half writing the history, and he may
have also changed his opinions many times. These changes
cannot be charted or correlated to specific historical events. It
is enough to appreciate that contradictions might reflect his
own vacillating feelings about his contemporary world.

The clearest contradictions occur in statements that derive
from Diodorus's sources. Many of the positive sentiments
about Rome[32] and a number of criticisms[33] are attributable to

---

[32] xxviii 3, end (just wars): probably inspired by Polybius xv 20, which
suggests additional sentiments now lost. Τὴν πάτριον τῆς 'Ρώμης ἐπιείκειαν
at xxix 10 is in Diodorus's own words (cf. xl 2) but was inspired by Polybius
xxi 17.1. The Polybian original of DS xxix 31 is lost, but the sentiment appears at Polybius v 10.1; yet it is also akin to Diodorus's model for empire.
The positive descriptions of Roman behavior after the Third Macedonian War
(xxxi 6–9) and of Aemilius Paullus (xxxi 11) almost certainly derive from lost
Polybian material: DS xxxi 7.1 = Polybius xxx 19.4–7; they are directly contradictory to DS xxxii 4.5, which is demonstrably of Diodorus's own creation: see the discussion later in this chapter. DS xxxiii 28b (Scipio Aemilianus
in Egypt) may well be Polybian though the event occurred after 146 (cf. MRR
I, 480–81, Walbank, Commentary III, 630, and H. Mattingly, CQ n.s. 36
[1986], 491–95). The discussion of Roman piety at xxvi 14.2 may come from
a Roman source: Càssola, ANRW II 30.1, 763. There may be Posidonian
praise of Rome at xxxiv/xxxv 32 = F 176 (Theiler).

[33] The dishonorable actions of Roman tribunes in 149 B.C. (xxxii 7) and a
Roman consul in 148 (xxxii 18); the parallel passages in App., Pun. 101 and
110, indicate the former passages are Polybian: cf. Walbank, Commentary III,
44–46. The corruption of the Senate in 161 (xxxi 27a) has no parallel in the
extant Polybius, but the tone may be his. Corruption after the Third Macedonian War: DS xxxi 26.7 = Polybius xxxi 25.6. Diodorus makes a distinction between earlier and contemporary Roman behavior at xxx 8: δὴ τότε. No
parallel in Polybius survives, but the description of Roman diplomatic prac-

earlier authorities, especially Polybius. When Diodorus takes both positive and negative sentiments regarding Rome from Polybius and others, there is no obvious pattern; as with Gelon, he may simply have copied what he found. In these instances, the contradictory feelings may be those of his sources.

But in statements on Rome that appear to be of his own making, Diodorus adds a small amount of admiration to his generally cautious and moderate criticism. His caution may have been brought on by his surroundings: his stay in Rome, probably from the mid-50s to at least 30 B.C., coincided with a period of exceptionally violent instability there. The next chapter will show that Diodorus probably lacked patrons and political contacts, so he may have felt too much at risk to be completely candid about his host city. His moderation and the presence of some admiration also reflects his own sense of history. Diodorus's homeland had long been the target of imperialistic designs. For the past two centuries Rome had controlled Sicily, but Diodorus is fully aware that others, especially Carthage, had held the same aim.[34] Diodorus could not fault Rome too much for succeeding at what others had habitually tried to accomplish.

It is Diodorus's historical perspective that allows him to admit that, because of Roman rule, Sicily was no longer beset by the traditional tyrannies that had long plagued parts of his homeland.[35] There is a certain amount of indebtedness to Rome acknowledged here. And in the only extended praise of Rome indisputably of his own creation, Diodorus lauds Roman bravery. Yet his commendation of Roman courage is a rhetorical device intended to increase the importance of the

---

tices is so precise that it may come from Polybius. Equally impossible to determine is the origin of the statement that the Romans of old (τοὺς παλαιούς) were concerned to wage only just wars: viii 25.3; cf. viii 26; but even Roman historiography traced Rome's supposed degeneracy back to the same period (Gruen, *HWCR* I, 349), and the theme is evident in Dionysius of Halicarnassus: see Gabba *CA* I (1982), 49, with n. 24. Posidonian criticism is discussed later. On the Agatharchidean material in iii 47.8, see Chapter 4, n. 32.

[34] E.g., xi 1.4–5.

[35] xix 1.5; Diodorus's own sentiment (see Chapter 1). The perspective is more contemporary than the sources he follows for book xix.

Social War, detailed in that book.[36] Here he fails to comment on whether Rome ruled well and deserved its empire. These passages in praise of Rome may represent the only ones in the extant history that can confidently be ascribed to Diodorus.[37] There are many more extant passages in which Diodorus criticizes Rome. Some, like the expressions of praise, are passing remarks.[38] Others, however, are substantial and conform to a pattern. Diodorus's narrative of the First and Second Punic Wars, the Achaean War, and the Sicilian Slave Wars and his description of a Sicilian shrine contain pronounced or subtle sentiments of opposition historiography. They suggest a writer who, though certainly not violently hostile, is uncomfortable with the Roman success.

SICILY IN THE FIRST PUNIC WAR

What begins Diodorus's fragmentary account of the First Punic War is the attempt by the Roman consul, Appius Claudius, to make peace by negotiating with the Carthaginians and the

[36] xxxvii 1; for arguments that show it to be Diodorus's, see Chapter 1. A similar, brief, sentiment at xxxiv/xxxv 32 may be Diodorus's; but it has also been identified as Posidonian = F 176 (Theiler). DS xxxi 15 follows closely Polybius xxx 18 on Roman dealings with Prusias during and after the Third Macedonian War. When Diodorus adds that Rome desires brave enemies (xxxi 15.3), he is illuminating one of his most important principles of historiography, which he expressed at the beginning of the passage (xxxi 15.1)—that noble actions are rewarded; see Chapter 2.

[37] xxxi 3.4 is probably a speech of Cato's, where praise of Rome conforms to the principle of τὰ δέοντα.

[38] Diodorus suggests (xxxi 30), where Polybius does not (xxxii 2–3.13), that the Senate acted in a manner that was devious and intentionally obscure: σκολιὰν καὶ δυσεύρετον. The phrase may have been excised from Polybius by an excerpter (Walbank, Commentary III, 521), but generally the scribes of Constantine Porphyrogenitus did not eliminate material in the middle of a larger narrative. DS xxx 8 and xxxi 22.7 are similar passages, the origins of which are indeterminable. Diodorus criticizes Roman policy toward Celtiberian Numantia at xxxii 4.5 (see the subsequent section on the Achaean War) and xxxi 39; on the latter, see J. Richardson, Hispaniae: Spain and the Development of Roman Imperialism, 218–82 B.C., 132–34: it differs from App., Hisp. 44.180–83, in its hostile bias. On xxxi 26.2, see n. 168.

Syracusan tyrant, Hiero.[39] Although Claudius's role in the proceedings is partially obscured by a lacuna, there survives the cryptic comment, "but Claudius announced publicly [δημογορεῖν δέ] that he would not fight Hiero." It is possible that the lost μέν-clause referred to Claudian deceit proposed privately. Certainly Hiero, in his response, accuses the Romans of cynical behavior, claiming that "if, on behalf of men [i.e., the Mamertines] so utterly godless, [the Romans] should enter upon a war of such magnitude, it would be clear to all mankind that they were using pity for the imperilled as a cloak for their own advantage, and that in reality they coveted Sicily" (Walton). It is generally agreed that Diodorus is following the account of his fellow Sicilian, Philinus,[40] whom Polybius (i 14–15) identifies as being strongly anti-Roman. But even Polybius, who is generally favorable to Rome in these events, portrays the Mamertines—Italian mercenaries who had settled Messana—as utterly vile (i 7.1–5). Hiero's accusations, then, would have the ring of truth to most Greek readers. Now Diodorus had no illusions about Carthaginian intentions, as he frequently details the island's struggle against the Punic threat. Here, however, in following a source clearly hostile to Rome, Diodorus ascribes opportunism and aggression to Rome. The rest of his account is also peppered with anti-Roman and pro-Carthaginian sentiments.[41]

[39] xxiii 1.4. Diodorus and Zonaras (viii 8–9) claim that the Mamertines expelled the Carthaginian garrison only with the help of a Roman expeditionary force; Polybius (i 11.4) does not mention Roman involvement at this stage.

[40] Walbank, Commentary I, 65, and Kokalos 14–15 (1968–1969), 485–86; summary of opinions in Càssola, ANRW II 30.1, 758–59. Càssola argues for a Roman annalistic source, which would report τὰ δέοντα, despite the harshly anti-Roman sentiment. But the annalistic tradition depicted Hiero as terrified at the Roman advance (Eckstein, GRBS 26 [1985], 270, n. 15); it is doubtful if it would have portrayed him as speaking so boldly.

[41] Anti-Roman: xxiii 19 and xxiv 9.2, 12; criticism of specific individuals, the Claudii (xxiv 3) and Atilius Regulus (xxiii 12, 15.1–4), are common to Roman historiography as well: on the Regulus tradition, see Walbank, CQ 39 (1945), 5 = Walbank, Selected Papers, 82; Commentary I, 92–93. Pro-Carthaginian: xxiv 1.5 (νίκην λαμπροτέραν), 5, 9 (on which, see Walbank, CQ 39 [1945], 7 = Selected Papers, 84–85), 10, 12.1. There is also sympathy for Hiero: xxiii 18.1; xxiv 1.4. Cf. Forte, Rome and the Romans as the Greeks Saw

It has been suggested that savage treatment of his home-town by the Romans made Philinus ill-disposed to the imperial power.[42] For a similar reason Diodorus may have developed his own bias against Rome. In recording events immediately prior to the conflict, Diodorus notes that, in his war with Messana, Hiero confiscated Mamertine land and assigned it to Agyrium (xxii 13.1). Agyrium was Diodorus's hometown, and he mentions it often.[43] Hiero's gift may well be something Diodorus himself chose to stress. And it indicates that Agyrium had joined Hiero in his war against Messana,[44] a conflict that led directly to the First Punic War. Agyrium must also have been an ally of Hiero's against Rome. As Rome went to war ostensibly to defend Messana, at the end of war the Mamertines must have regained the land Hiero had given to Agyrium.

Like other Sicilians, Diodorus may have detested the Mamertines. Messana's allegiance to Italy had resulted in its having citizen status (*civitas foederata*) and special treatment. When plundering Sicily, Verres exempted only Messana from the usual obligations of supplying soldiers and grain.[45] After Octavian stripped Sicily of its recently won Roman enfranchisement, he permitted Messana its rights of complete citizenship.[46] But Romans also knew that to win the loyalty of the rest of Sicily required that they act brutally toward Messana. Sextus Pompey, when struggling to control the island during the period of the Second Triumvirate, conspicuously treated the Sicilians well and the Mamertines harshly.[47] Sextus was only following the precedent of his father, Pompeius Magnus, who, while governor of Sicily in 82/1, B.C. was known for his

---

Them, 10–11. Polybius, too, could be sympathetic toward Hiero, but his feelings toward early Roman imperialism are complex: see Eckstein, *GRBS* 26 (1985), 265–82.

[42] Walbank, *CQ* 39 (1945), 11–12 = Walbank, *Selected Papers*, 90.

[43] Chapter 6, n. 27.

[44] Cf. Walbank, *Commentary* I, 53.

[45] Cic., 2 *Verr.* iv 9.20–21; v 16.43–23.59; cf. M. Goldsberry, "Sicily and Its Cities in Hellenistic and Roman Times," 484, n. 174.

[46] Pliny, *NH* iii 8.88.

[47] On the Greeks, see Chapter 6; on the Mamertines: Dio xlviii 17.5–6.

magnanimous behavior, except for his treatment of Messana.[48] Diodorus, too, effusively praises the older Pompey's administration of Sicily as being especially moderate and virtuous (xxxviii/xxxix 20). In Diodorus's day, the two-hundred-year-old feud between Sicilians and Mamertines continued unabated. The First Punic War found Agyrium opposed to Rome; with the Roman victory came Agyrium's probable loss of Mamertine land given by Hiero. There is little wonder that Diodorus's account of that war is based on the anti-Roman tradition of Philinus.

Diodorus, in fact, may have had more of a hand in shaping that tradition than is usually suspected. For example, Hiero is said to act with moderation (φιλανθρώπως: xxiii 18.1), and criticism of the Roman general, Regulus, is also filled with Diodoran philosophy.[49] Most important, in Chapter 4 it was determined that Diodorus frequently intrudes in the speeches found in the *Bibliotheke*. Consequently, he may also have helped create Hiero's accusations against Rome. Directly preceding the speeches of Claudius and Hiero is the comment, "Sicily is the noblest (καλλίστη) of all islands, since it can contribute greatly to the growth of an empire."[50] The sentiment is consistent with the charge made by Hiero, that Rome went to war in order to conquer Sicily, for it emphasizes the importance of Sicily to aggrandizing nations. Now the perspective that Sicily can contribute greatly to an empire is that of a historian who knew of the island's eventual importance to Rome. Philinus wrote too early to have appreciated that,[51] so this judgment may be Diodorus's own. Moreover, similar de-

---

[48] Plut., *Pomp.* 10.2.

[49] Regulus completely ignored the opportunity ἀπενέγκασθαι παρὰ πᾶσιν ἀνθρώποις αἰώνιον μνήμην ἡμερότητος καὶ φιλανθρωπίας (xxiii 15.2). On immortal fame, see Chapter 3; on moderate behavior, see Chapter 2.

[50] xxiii 1 (Walton).

[51] On Philinus as a contemporary of the First Punic War, see Walbank, *CQ* 39 (1945), 4 = Walbank, *Selected Papers*, 81. In his narrative of the Athenian invasion of Sicily, Thucydides never makes the claim that the island would be a cornerstone of an empire (esp. vi 59.3, 80.4), nor does Diodorus imply that in his account of the same events. The idea may have arisen only with the Roman conquest.

scriptions of the island as exceptionally powerful or wealthy occur at least a dozen other times in the *Bibliotheke*, where Diodorus is using a variety of sources.[52] An illuminating example is the debate between Nicias and Alcibiades over the decision to invade Sicily. Nicias claims that even the Carthaginians, who were mightier than the Athenians, could not make Sicily, the largest and most powerful of islands, spearwon (δορίκτητον: xii 83.6). Although Ephorus is probably Diodorus's source for this episode,[53] that particular term of conquest became popular only after Ephorus's death and was used especially to describe the conquests of Alexander and his successors.[54] As it is found frequently in different parts of the *Bibliotheke*,[55] it is probably Diodorus who added to the debate between Nicias and Alcibiades the proud sentiments about Sicily. Similarly, it may have been Diodorus who connects the island's importance with events of the First Punic War. Although acknowledging that Carthage was not an innocent victim,[56] he appears to believe the argument expressed by Hiero that the Romans also went to war simply out of self-interest. As a result, the Roman Empire grew, while Agyrium lost Mamertine land and Sicily its freedom.

The Second Punic War

In describing the death of Hasdrubal, killed in 207 by the Romans when attempting to join Hannibal in Italy, Diodorus gives a eulogy that he says he found in his source (xxvi 24.1). Because there happens to be an encomium of Hasdrubal in Polybius (xi 2), Diodorus is thought to be following the

---

[52] iv 24.1, 30.3, 82.5, 84.1; v 1.4, 2.4–5, 69.3; xii 54.1; xii 83.6 (bis); xix 1.7: τὴν μεγίστην καὶ καλλίστην τῶν πασῶν νήσων; xxxiv/xxxv 2.26; xxxvii 2.13: τῆς εὐδαιμονεστάτης τῶν ὑπὸ τὸν ἥλιον νήσων.

[53] Meister, "Die sizilische Geschichte," 61.

[54] On its introduction, see Hornblower, *Hieronymus of Cardia*, 53.

[55] iii 55.6; iv 33.5; xvii 17.3; xviii 39.6, 43.1; xix 85.3, 105.4; xx 76.7; xxi 1.5 (bis), 2.2; xxii 1.3; xxxvii 1.4, which is certainly his own words: see Chapters 1 and 2. Also δοριάλωτος: see Neubert, *Spuren selbständiger Thätigkeit bei Diodor*, 11.

[56] E.g., xxxvii 1.4.

CHAPTER FIVE

Achaean historian.[57] The eulogies rendered by Diodorus and Polybius, however, agree in spirit but not at all in substance: Diodorus supplies, among other things, military analysis absent from Polybius's entirely preserved treatment. Indeed, for the narrative of the Italian theater of the war, Diodorus and Polybius have almost no identifiable shared material;[58] where comparisons are possible, Diodorus clearly departs from Polybius and follows traditions similar to those found in Livy.[59] There was, in fact, a variety of Roman sources upon which all three historians could draw.[60]

In another fragment, which in the complete *Bibliotheke* must have stood quite close to and indeed appears to conclude the eulogy, Diodorus states: "If Hasdrubal had enjoyed the assistance of Fortune as well, it is generally agreed that the Romans could not have carried on the struggle simultaneously against both him and Hannibal."[61] Diodorus's prediction that Carthage would have prevailed had Fortune preserved Hasdrubal stands apart from any obvious source, for no such prophecy exists in any other history of Rome. Livy (xxvii 49.4), without supplying a formal eulogy, says, as do Polybius (xi 2.10) and Diodorus, that Fortune shifted against him and that he died in a manner befitting his family. Elsewhere Livy makes it clear that Hasdrubal's death was the turning point of

[57] See Walton, *Diodorus of Sicily* XI, Loeb edition, 199, n. 3.

[58] Although Diodorus used Polybius for eastern events contemporary with the war, see Walton, *Diodorus of Sicily* XI, Loeb edition, 183, n. 3, and 202, n. 1; at least one event from the Sicilian theater is found in both DS xxvi 8 and Polybius v 88.5–8.

[59] Càssola, *ANRW*, II 30.1, 763. E.g., an anti-Hannibalic tradition at DS xxvi 11 is similar to Livy xxiii 18.10–16 and contrary to the spirit of Polybius ix 22.7–26.11; *Indibilis* in DS xxvi 22 and Livy xxix 1.20 is *Andobales* in Polybius xi 31–33.

[60] Walbank *Commentary* I, 28–29; T. Luce, *Livy: The Composition of His History*, 178–79.

[61] xxvi 24.2 (Walton). In *De Sententiis* it falls between xxvi 22 and xvii 1.2, while xxvi 24.1 in *De Virtutibus et Vitiis* comes between xxvi 23 and xxvii 1.1. For the procedure on judging how the place of fragments in the Constantinian excerpts relates to the original text, see Sacks, *Polybius*, 11–20.

the war because it enabled Rome to transfer attention from Spain to Africa (xxviii 1.1), but he does not suggest that otherwise Carthage would have won. Polybius, too, could not have agreed with Diodorus. He believed that a Roman victory was inevitable because of the superiority of its institutions (vi 51) and manly courage (vi 52.10; cf. iii 118.8–9) and specifically denies the assertion of unnamed Greeks that Fortune played so significant a role in Roman success.[62]

The judgments concerning Hasdrubal offered by Diodorus, Polybius, and Livy indicate that there was a single tradition that inspired all three. The initial version included the observation that Hasdrubal suffered because of bad luck, but Diodorus alone went on to speculate about what would have happened had Fortune remained constant. The possibility that Diodorus himself intruded is strengthened by a fragment in the previous book. What remains is the sentiment that history ought to give Hamilcar, the father of Hasdrubal, the praise he deserves (xxv 10.5). That notion pervades the *Bibliotheke*, and nearly the same syntactical arrangement concludes an earlier eulogy to Pelopidas (xv 81.4). If Diodorus composed a eulogy for Hamilcar, it is perhaps likely that he had a hand in shaping one for his son. Even more significant, following immediately upon the pronouncement that Rome could not have prevailed had Hasdrubal survived comes the warning that men must be judged for what they attempt rather than what they accomplish: men are responsible for their intentions, whereas the outcome is in the hands of Fortune (xxvi 24.2). Precisely the same sentiment with nearly the same words is found in Diodorus's eulogy to the Spartans at Thermopylae.[63] Ephorus is almost certainly the source for that episode,[64] but he died a

---

[62] i 63.9. Polybius also denies that Scipio owed his Spanish victories in the Second Punic War to Fortune, as some had argued (x 2.5, 5.8, 7.3, 9.2–3), although it was Fortune that endowed Scipio with the talents by which he succeeded (x 40.6, 40.9).

[63] xi 11.2–3; cf. Neubert, *Spuren selbständiger Thätigkeit bei Diodor*, 23.

[64] On the ultimate Isocratean origins of some of that chapter, see Chapter 2, p. 32.

century and a half before the Second Punic War. In the eulogy to Hasdrubal, Diodorus must have been responsible for the sentiment about judging intentions while attributing the results to Fortune. This points strongly to his authorship also of the speculation connecting Hasdrubal's death to the outcome of the war.

Polybius had already argued against the belief that Rome prevailed because of τύχη. Diodorus's contemporary, Dionysius of Halicarnassus, in his *Roman Antiquities* begun in 30/29 B.C. (*AR* i 7.2), went further. In criticizing that assertion, he connects the claim to critics of Rome (ii 17.3). Although it is chronologically possible, there is no way of knowing whether Dionysius had Diodorus in mind. When Dionysius makes a similar attack against historians elsewhere, these unnamed writers are said to curry favor with eastern monarchs,[65] something for which regarding Diodorus there is no evidence. Dionysius may be alluding to the historians of Mithridates VI. But the general charge that Rome owed its success to Fortune is also found in Pompeius Trogus.[66] A Gallic historian writing just after Diodorus,[67] he offered a world view that did not make Rome the center of history and was at least somewhat critical.[68] There appears to have been a contemporary, hostile tradition that attributed Rome's success largely to

[65] i 4.2–3. Accusations that Rome was founded by vagabonds were also voiced, apparently by Greek writers: *AR* i 4.2, 89.1; vii 70.1–2; cf. Gruen, *HWCR* I, 354. So, too, by Livy, but for a different purpose: Luce, *Livy*, 246.

[66] Justin, *Epitome* xliii 2.5: "Fortuna origini Romanae prospiciens"; xxx 4.16: "Macedonas Romana fortuna vicit"; cf. A. Momigliano, *Athenaeum* 12 (1934), 52 = *Terzo contributo*, 507–8.

[67] Diodorus's dates of research and writing, 60–30 B.C. (see Chapter 6), eliminate the claim (made most recently by Welles in *Diodorus of Sicily* VIII, Loeb edition, 13) that he employed Trogus as a source.

[68] On the anti-Roman tradition in Pompeius Trogus, see O. Seel, *Die Praefatio des Pompeius Trogus*, 19ff., and *Ein römische Weltgeschichte: Studien zum Text der Epitome des Iustinus und zur Historik des Pompejus Trogus*. The identification of Timagenes as Trogus's source is based on little else than the process of elimination (e.g., Fraser, *Ptolemaic Alexandria* IIa, 748). Recently, Trogus has been judged less slavishly dependent on Timagenes: for bibliography, see Malitz, *Die Historien des Poseidonios*, 56, n. 169.

τύχη.[69] Diodorus departed from his source in using that argument as an explanation for the death of Hasdrubal and Rome's victory in the Second Punic War.

Cultural resistance to Roman rule was especially strong early in the first century. The outcry may have begun in the second century, but much of the opposition literature was produced[70] or reinterpreted[71] during the wars of Mithridates VI. Mithridates' courtiers fashioned outright encomia to the king[72] or at least historical works with pronounced bias toward him.[73] Other eastern contemporaries may also have produced propaganda for the Pontic monarch in a display of solidarity against Rome.[74] But the most famous echo of hostility toward Rome that survives is found in the work of a Roman apologist. Livy, in a long passage written before 23 B.C.,[75] ridicules those who believe that Alexander, after conquering Asia, could have made a successful invasion of Italy. Livy,

[69] Cf. Cic., Rep. 2.30, on which, Walbank, Commentary I, 129–30.

[70] See McGing, The Foreign Policy of Mithridates VI, 102–4, and esp. J. Gauger, Chiron 10 (1980), 223–61, and D. Mendels, AJP 102 (1981), 330–37.

[71] Cf. A. Momigliano, "Some Preliminary Remarks on the 'Religious Opposition' to the Roman Empire," in Opposition et résistances a l'empire d'Augustus a Trajan, Fondation Hardt Entretiens, 32 106 = On Pagans, Jews, and Christians, 122, on Gauger, Chiron 10 (1980), 223–61, concerning Phlegon of Tralles (FGH 257 F 36).

[72] Aisopus: see FGH 187a T1 = Suda, s.v. Αἴσωπος.

[73] Metrodorus of Skepsis, a Mithridatic jurist who was greatly influential in the court of Mithridates (FGH 184 T 3 = Plut., Luc. 22.1–5), was known by Roman writers for his hostility toward the western power: T 6a and F 12 = Pliny, NH xxxiv 16, 34. Note, however, the Roman confusion over him and his philosopher father: FGH IIbd, 609.

[74] Teucer of Cyzicus: Jacoby FGH IIIa, 314, argues that the work had an anti-Roman bent because it was entitled Μιθριδατικαὶ πράξεις (274 T 1 = Suda, s.v.). This would also establish the bias of Heracleides of Magnesia's Μιθριδατικά: FGH 187 T 1 = Diog. Laer. v 44. Memnon of Heracleia is usually dated to the period of Hadrian, but Laqueur argued for a floruit in the time of Julius Caesar (RE 13, 1098–1102), and his suggestion is not cogently dismissed by Jacoby (FGH IIIb, 267). But though there is much local color in his account (FGH IIIb, 271, n. 33), an anti-Roman Tendenz is not apparent.

[75] ix 17–19; T. Luce TAPA 96 (1965), 227–29, for the date.

however, concedes to his opponents their argument that Alexander enjoyed better fortune than did the Romans (ix 18.9), and thus their anti-Roman polemic must have been different than that which Dionysius attacks.[76]

Among those whom Livy may have had in mind is Timagenes of Alexandria.[77] Few details about the life and work of this notorious anti-Roman writer are established with certainty.[78] After coming to Rome as a captive in 55 B.C. and then gaining his freedom, Timagenes taught rhetoric and wrote history, enjoying the patronage of influential Romans. Becoming embittered, he alienated the most powerful patron of all, Augustus, and was banished from his court. His attacks were aimed at the royal family[79] but also at the dignity of Rome. In one preserved fragment he accuses Pompey of creating trouble in Egypt in order to be called in and gain additional *gloria*.[80] Timagenes was active when Diodorus was in Rome, yet there is little chance that he influenced Diodorus: his break with Augustus probably occurred after the publication of the *Bibliotheke*.[81]

Though hostile to Rome, Diodorus did not belong to any school of anti-Roman historiography; nor did he anticipate Timagenes in an eclectic assault on Roman pride. Romans took their share of plunder in Sicily after the Second Punic War,[82] and Diodorus's hometown of Agyrium may have suf-

---

[76] *AR* ii 17.3; cf. Momigliano, *Athenaeum* 12 (1934), 52–53 = *Terzo contributo*, 507–9. Depending on one's view, the support of fortune could be a compliment instead of a criticism, as Florus, *praef.* 2.

[77] A controversial identification, made most recently by M. Sordi, *ANRW* II 30.1, 775–97, and Crawford, in Garnsey and Whittaker, *Imperialism in the Ancient World*, 193. Bowersock, *Augustus and the Greek World*, 109, n. 2, suggests Metrodorus of Scepsis; another possibility, though he is little more than a name, is Amphicrates of Athens: Schwartz, *RE* 1.2, 1903–4.

[78] Bowersock, *Augustus and the Greek World*, 109–10, 125–26.

[79] *FGH* 88 TT 2 and 3 (= Sen., *Controv.* x 5.21–22; *De Ira* iii 23.4–8).

[80] F 9 = Plut., *Pomp.* 49; also involved is Pompey's client, Theophanes, whom Timagenes may have attacked elsewhere as well: B. Gold, *AJP* 106 (1985), 321, n. 44.

[81] Bowersock, *Augustus and the Greek World*, 109–10, 125.

[82] M. Mazza, "Terra e lavoratori nella Sicilia tardo repubblicana," in

fered.[83] But by the time Diodorus wrote the *Bibliotheke*, Sicily had been part of the Roman Empire for two centuries. Other contemporary writers—such as Metrodorus of Skepsis (see n. 73) and Timagenes of Alexandria—witnessed their homelands fall under Roman control. Their reactions were fresher and generally more pronounced than were those of Diodorus, who grew up in a land that took Roman rule for granted. Diodorus held no illusion that opposition historiography could be effective. In remarking that Fortune went against Carthage at a critical moment, thereby enabling Rome to win the Second Punic War, it was enough for him to question the absolute superiority of the Roman army.

The Achaean War

In what appears to be the prologue to book xxxii, which it was argued in Chapter 2 is of his own making, Diodorus writes extensively of Roman imperialism. At one time the Romans were admired by their subjects for managing the empire with compassion and beneficence, but now "they confirmed their power by terrorism and by the destruction of the most eminent cities."[84] The casualties of the new policy were Corinth, the Macedonians (in particular Perseus), Carthage, Numantia, and the many whom the Romans terrorized. Although here calling Perseus a victim, earlier, when generally following Polybius, Diodorus condemned that king for starting the Third Macedonian War and effusively praised Rome for treating the captured monarch with clemency.[85] The con-

---

A. Giardina and A. Schiavone, *Società Romana e produzione schiavistica*, I: *L'Italia: Insediamente e forme economiche*, 22–23.

[83] G. Manganaro, *Historia* 13 (1964), 419ff.; *Helikon* 7 (1967), 217–18; and *ANRW* I.1, 444, argues that Rome stripped the town of local autonomy and attached it to another city, at least temporarily. But see Goldsberry, "Sicily and its Cities," 251–55.

[84] xxxii 4.5 (Walton).

[85] DS xxxi 8–9, inspired by Polybius xxxvi 17.13, states that Romans treated Macedonians remarkably leniently after the Third Macedonian War (there could have been a further discussion in what are now two lacunae).

tradiction occurs because in the proem to book xxxii Diodorus departs from the Polybian tradition in making his own more general point concerning Roman methods.

Within book xxxii is described Rome's destruction of Corinth during the Achaean War. In summing up the sack of Corinth, the historian clearly intrudes into the text:

> This was the city that, to the dismay of later ages, was now wiped out by her conquerors. Nor was it only at the time of her downfall that Corinth evoked great compassion from those that saw her; even in later times, when they saw the city levelled to the ground, all who looked upon her were moved to pity. . . . Nearly a hundred years later, Gaius Iulius Caesar (who for his great deeds was entitled *divus*), after viewing the site, restored the city.[86]

Diodorus notes that when Caesar visited the site, he was moved by compassion to rebuild it.

In following the narrative of Polybius on the Achaean War, Diodorus greatly exaggerates Rome's brutality and the extent to which Rome deprived Greece of its freedom:

> The Greeks, after witnessing in person the butchery and beheading of their kinsmen and friends, the capture and looting of their cities, the abusive enslavement of whole populations, after, in a word, losing both their liberty and the right to speak freely [τὴν ἐλευθερίαν καὶ τὴν παρρησίαν,] exchanged the height of prosperity for the most extreme misery. (xxxii 26.2; Walton)

Polybius's negative feelings toward Perseus are implied in the final sentence of xxv 3.1–8; cf. Plut., *Aem.* 34.1–2.

[86] xxxii 27.1 (Walton). There is minor and inconsequential contamination by the Constantinian excerpter (Chapter 6, n. 73). But the description of Caesar's deification is formulaic throughout the *Bibliotheke* (see Chapter 6, n. 100), and Diodorus also argues that Rome would have been criticized throughout the world for destroying Carthage after the Second Punic War: xxvii 17.1, on which see Chapter 4, pp. 104–7.

This is one of the strongest indictments of Roman warfare and imperial rule found in ancient literature. Nothing in the fragmentary Polybian text (xxxix 2) hints at such butchery or the suppression of Greek freedom. In what does survive, Mummius is said to have acted leniently (πρᾴως), given his extraordinary powers. If there was any brutal behavior, Polybius contends, it was due to Mummius's friends, a probable allusion to the slaying of Chalcidean cavalry (xxxix 7.4–5).

Nor do later writers who read Polybius confirm Diodorus's description. Strabo claims familiarity with Polybius's account, but notes only the latter's anger at witnessing firsthand Roman soldiers destroying valuable art objects (viii 6.23). Pausanias, too, used Polybius[87] and perhaps for this episode. The author of the *Guide to Greece* indicates that the Romans murdered or enslaved only those Corinthians who had not fled the city. Other cities that offered resistance merely had their walls torn down and their inhabitants disarmed. The Romans broke up the Greek leagues and exacted a heavy fine, but within a few years returned the money and permitted the Greeks to reconstitute their confederacies.[88] If Pausanias was hostile toward Rome,[89] he would not have minimized the extent of Roman destruction. Even so, his description is far more subdued than that of Diodorus.

Epitomizing Cassius Dio, Zonaras, like Pausanias, notes the Roman confiscation of objects d'art and the destruction of buildings. His account, however, describes even milder Roman actions. He says that the Corinthians fled the town before Mummius arrived, so that he captured a deserted city. Afterward, Mummius "both proclaimed the freedom of all the other Greeks and the enslavement of the Corinthians" (9.31). A reference to brief massacres (παραχρῆμα . . . σφαγαῖς) in Zonaras's summary may refer to Mummius's execution of

[87] C. Habicht, *Pausanias' Guide to Ancient Greece*, 97.
[88] vii 16.8–10; yet see Gruen, *HWCR* II, 525.
[89] Habicht, *Pausanias' Guide to Ancient Greece*, 119–25.

some Greek leaders[90] or the Chalcidean cavalry.[91] Even the highly creative sepulchral epigrams of the *Greek Anthology* are less expansive than Diodorus. The closest are the romanticized motif of a Corinthian mother killing her daughter and then herself rather than be enslaved by the Romans (vii 493) and the epigram by Polystratus (vii 297), which laments the unburied Corinthian dead.[92]

Diodorus's vision of the war most approximates sources on the fringes of classical historiography. Similar depictions are found in two Jewish tracts of the second century B.C. I *Maccabees* 8:9–10 describes Roman murder and mayhem during the Achaean War. Because the work is so pronouncedly anti-Greek, however, its author expresses pride and wonderment at Rome's actions. Conversely, the *Third Sibylline Oracle* was composed by Alexandrian Jews wishing to appeal to Egyptian Greeks. Accordingly, it is critical of Roman brutality.[93] Diodorus had lived in Alexandria, where he may have learned of this tradition, though Virgil in Rome knew of the *Oracle* well enough to include some of its themes in his *Fourth Eclogue*.[94] Moreover, the epitome of Pompeius Trogus, a historian generally considered somewhat critical of Rome, again echoes themes found in the *Bibliotheke*. The epitomator, Justin (xxxiv 2.1–6), records that the Corinthian soldiers, when engaging the Roman troops, were massacred under the eyes of their

---

[90] Polybius xxxix 4.3 (pagination of W. Paton, *Polybius* VI, Loeb edition).

[91] Polybius xxxix 6.5 (Loeb pagination). See Walbank *Commentary* III, 737, for the razing of the walls of Chalcis and Thebes. Cassius Dio, of course, was far more sympathetic toward Rome: see F. Millar, *A Study of Cassius Dio*, 190–92.

[92] Other ancient testimony on the Achaean War is cited by J. Wiseman, *ANRW* II 7.1, 461–62, 491–92. Recent archaeology reveals that the tradition of Corinth's complete destruction, as recorded by Diodorus and alluded to by other sources, is greatly overstated: see Wiseman, 491–96. Diodorus's contemporary, Cicero, is ambivalent about the Roman action, but uninformative: *De Off.* 1.35 and 3.46.

[93] *SibOr.* 3.520–38; the invaders of Greece are not named, but the only other possibility are Celts—not very plausible in the context.

[94] R. Nisbet and M. Hubbard, *A Commentary on Horace: Odes Book II*, 62.

families, who watched from the walls. There are traces of a tragic narrative even in the abbreviated description, as the Romans produced a mournful memory for all who observed (2.4). Afterward, all Corinthians were sold into slavery and the city destroyed as a lesson to anyone who thought about resisting Rome. All these versions are close to Diodorus's, suggesting that he added to Polybius's description an alternate tradition that emphasized Rome's brutality.

Diodorus does follow Polybius in assigning responsibility for the Achaean War not to Rome but to the victims.[95] Yet he again departs from the Polybian narrative, declaring that, as a result of the war, Greece went from great wealth to poverty. Polybius notes specifically that Greece was poor at the time of the war (xxxvi 17.5), and Diodorus himself, probably in a passage inspired by lost material in Polybius, speaks of the number of debtors.[96] Greece's sudden fall from prosperity, then, reflects Diodorus's attempt to widen the tragedy, as does his wrongheaded remark about Greek loss of political liberty and freedom of speech.[97] Finally, in what is now a highly corrupt text, Polybius apparently claims that certain Greeks displayed faithlessness and cowardice (xxxviii 3.10). Diodorus denies cowardice on the part of the soldiery, instead attributing defeat to the inexperience of the generals (xxxii 26.1). He may have been attempting to refute Polybius. The strength of his emotional response is evident when he eulogizes Caesar for his reestablishment of Corinth, pronouncing that the Dic-

[95] Polybius xxxviii 10–14.3; perhaps also in the lacunae of xxxviii 3; DS xxxii 26.2–5. For a discussion of Polybius's feelings, see E. Gruen, *JHS* 96 (1976), 46–69.

[96] xxxii 26.3. See Rostovtzeff, *SEHHW* II, 739–50.

[97] See Gruen, *HWCR* II, 523–27, and J. Larsen, "Roman Greece," in T. Frank, *An Economic Survey of Ancient Rome* IV, 306–11, who suggests that Diodorus added "rhetorical coloring." The evidence on the political settlement of Greece is ambiguous, but there is no reason to suspect a loss of παρρησία: perhaps Diodorus is attacking the Romanophilic Greeks. On the politics and economy of Greece after the Achaean War, see E. Will, *Histoire politique du monde hellénistique*[2] II, 394–400.

tator "made amends for [the] unrelenting severity [of earlier Romans]."[98]

Corinth had been a venerable Greek city—important, in fact, in the colonization and subsequent history of Sicily. But the destruction of all important cities was contrary to the civilizing spirit Diodorus espouses in the early books on mythology (see Chapter 3), and elsewhere in the historical narrative he condemns such actions (see Chapter 6). Caesar repopulated Corinth, not with Greeks of good birth, but with freedmen, Syrians, and, perhaps, even enemies of Sicily.[99] That did not matter to Diodorus, for the city's reestablishment was a symbol of human progress. As a consequence of his anger at earlier Roman actions, when following the Polybian account he adds arguments similar to those found in works critical of Rome (or, in the case of 1 *Maccabees*, one which attempted to impress the enemies of the Seleucids with Rome's destructive powers). No direct borrowing was required: the event itself was sufficiently famous and controversial to allow historians to bend their narratives to their own predilection.

THE FIRST SICILIAN SLAVE WAR

Most of what survives of books xxxiv/xxxv pertains to the First Slave War in Sicily, which began about 135 B.C.[100] Diodorus's account is rich in detail and is generally assumed to have come from Posidonius.[101] The narrative portrays Italian

---

[98] xxxii 27.3 (Walton).

[99] On the general population mix: Crinagoras, *Greek Anthology* iii 9.284. On the possible son of Q. Caecilius Niger, see M. Grant, *From Imperium to Auctoritas*, 266–68.

[100] The dating is controversial; most recently discussed by G. P. Verbrugghe, *CP* 68 (1973), 27–29. For recent bibliography on the war, see Mazza, in Giardina and Schiavone, *Società romana e produzione schiavistica* I, 468, n. 124.

[101] FF 108–10 J (*Anhang*) = FF 136 ff (Theiler); most recently, Momigliano, *Alien Wisdom*, 33–34. The attempt to distinguish different traditions preserved by Photius and by the Constantinian excerpters and so to argue that Diodorus derived some of his account from Caecilius of Calacte, is unsuccessful; so

and Roman knights as controlling much of the Sicilian farmland for raising cattle.[102] If factual, the description becomes important for understanding the extent of Roman imperialism and economic influence in the second century. The picture, however, finds no confirmation in other narrative sources, which mention neither an extensive presence of Italian *equites*[103] nor the widespread existence of ranching on the island.[104] In fact, the names of only three or four knights are known who held land in Sicily during the second century, and their specific agricultural interests are indeterminable.[105] That is hardly enough to confirm with confidence the description in Diodorus.

The attempt to validate Diodorus's narrative has led to extensive controversy.[106] But amid the debate one assumption has gone untested: whether the narrative in the *Bibliotheke* is an accurate reflection of what Posidonius wrote. The high reputation of the Stoic philosopher has always lent the account

---

F. Rizzo, "Posidonio nei frammenti Diodorei sulla prima guerra servile di Sicilia," in *Studi di storia antica offerti dagli allievi a Eugenio Manni*, 259–93. Caecilius may well have written his work on the slave wars too late for Diodorus to use: L. Pareti, *ASSO* 16–17 (1919–1920), 231–47.

[102] xxxiv/xxxv 2.1–3, 2.27, 2.31, 2.32, 2.34.

[103] T. Frank, *AJP* 66 (1935), 61–64.

[104] G. Verbrugghe, *TAPA* 103 (1972), 539–59.

[105] A. Fraschetti, "Per una prosopografia dello sfruttamento: Romani e Italici in Sicilia (212–44 a.C.)," in A. Giardina and A. Schiavone, *Società romana e produzione schiavistica, I: L'Italia: Insediamente e forme economiche*, 53–54; cf. M. Mazza, *Kokalos* 26–27 (1980–1981), 319–20, the remark by G. Clemente in Mazza, 354, and Verbrugghe, *TAPA* 103 (1972), 539–59.

[106] Mazza (*Kokalos* 26–27 [1980–1981], 292–358, and in Giardina and Schiavone, *Società romana e produzione schiavistica* I, 30–39) presents well-balanced discussions and full bibliography. T. Frank, Carcopino, Manganaro, and Verbrugghe deny the existence of great numbers of Italian latifundia on Sicily, while most scholars argue for greater Italian ownership on the island. E. Gabba, "Sulle strutture agrarie dell'Italia romana fra III e I sec. a.d.," in E. Gabba and M. Pasquinucci, *Strutture agrarie e allevamento transumante nell'Italia romana III–I sec. a.C.*, 15–73, suggests that Italians employed transhumance. Mazza, in *Società romana*, 25–27, resurrects the view that Rome turned much of Sicily into *ager publicus*, but that is impossible to determine: see Goldsberry, "Sicily and Its Cities," 303–11.

in Diodorus special credence. But it has now been shown that Diodorus can interpolate his own expressions on Roman imperialism. A reassessment of this episode, considering the possibility of such contamination, will cast a different light on the account of the Slave War.

The Diodoran text of the revolt is only partially preserved, and that by two excerpters with slightly different methods. A good control on both Photius and the Constantinian editors is available for a different episode, where both preserve Diodoran narrative for which the original Polybian account, on which Diodorus drew, also survives. A comparison of all three indicates that the Constantinian version is quite faithful to the material in Polybius, while Photius omits some important information.[107] Generally, however, the wording of the two is acceptably close.[108]

Despite gaps in the *Bibliotheke*, the main historical theme of the Slave War is clear. Posidonius was a historian who built his narrative around moralistic lessons, and his account of the First Slave War is no exception. In Diodorus is found the argument that, "in individual households [heavy-handed arrogance] paves the way for plots of slaves against masters and for terrible uprisings in concert against the state."[109] There follows directly in the fragments a description of the Sicilian, Damophilus. Extremely wealthly, but given to arrogance and decadence, his treatment of his slaves helped ignite the rebellion.[110] Athenaeus preserves a similar explanation, naming Posido-

---

[107] DS xxxi 5 = Polybius xxx 4. Photius omits the initial assembly (Polybius xxx 4.4) and Antonius's actions in the Senate (Polybius xxx 4.6).

[108] On Constantine, see Sacks, *Polybius*, 11–20; Millar, *Cassius Dio*, 1–2; P. Brunt *CQ* n.s. 30 (1980), 484; additional bibliography in Malitz, *Die Historien des Poseidonios*, 40, n. 53; on Photius, see bibliography and discussion in Malitz, *Die Historien des Poseidonios*, 40, and D. Mendels, *Byzantion* 56 (1986), 196, n. 3.

[109] xxxiv/xxxv 2.33 (Walton's translation modified). Cf. xxxiv/xxxv 2.40. The plurals τὰς πολιτικὰς δυναστείας and ταῖς πόλεσιν (bis) indicate that the notion of political arrogance is not intended to apply here to Rome, but to politicians and governments generally.

[110] xxxiv/xxxv 2.34–38; cf. 2.10.

nius as its author: "Posidonius says that the Sicilian Damophilus, on account of whom the slave war arose, was given to
decadence."¹¹¹ This confirms that Diodorus was following
Posidonius in tracing the cause of the revolt to social decay. It
also supports statements in the *Bibliotheke* that the Sicilian
Damophilus was directly responsible for the revolt.

The centrality of Sicilians in the narrative contrasts sharply,
in fact, with the emphasis scholars place on Italian involvement. In the *Bibliotheke*, the inhumanity of the Sicilians, Damophilus and his wife Megallis, is recounted with great relish
(xxxiv/v 2.10, 34–36). The leader of the rebellion, Eunus, was
owned by a Sicilian, whose decadence and stupidity are col-
orfully described (xxxiv/v 2.5–9). And the only innocent casualties specifically named are Sicilian (xxxiv/xxxv 11). Other
passages also stress Sicilian involvement. In one, the slaves, in
order to guarantee a supply of food, did not plunder store-
houses or crops in the fields. The peasantry, however, express-
ing its own resentment, looted the rich. The passage, a Constantinian excerpt and therefore probably an accurate
reflection of the original, begins: "When these many great
troubles fell upon the Sicilians [τοῖς Σικελιώταις], the common people [δημοτικὸς ὄχλος] . . ."¹¹² There is a clear suggestion here of a struggle between different classes of the same
population, rather than between conqueror and subject. And,
indeed, Damophilus's excesses are said to be responsible for
the great sufferings of his country (τῇ πατρίδι: xxxiv/xxxv
2.35), with no mention of harm to foreigners and their holdings. The emphasis on the damage to locals is borne out with
the elaboration that:

> Similar events took place throughout Asia at the same pe-
> riod, after Aristonicus laid claim to a kingdom that was
> not rightfully his, and the slaves, because of their owners'

¹¹¹ Athen. xii 542 b = *FGH* 87 F 7. For Athenaeus's methods and accuracy
in excerpting, see bibliography and discussion in Malitz, *Die Historien des Poseidonios*, 47–48.
¹¹² xxxiv/xxxv 2.48 (Walton).

maltreatment of them, joined him in his mad venture and
involved many cities in great misfortune. (xxxiv/v 2.26;
Walton)

At the time of Aristonicus's uprising, there were no important
Italian landholdings in Asia, all evidence instead pointing to
local ownership.[113] If Posidonius was using the problem in
Asia to illuminate events in Sicily ("similarly" introduces the
discussion of Asia, but it may be an interpolation by Diodorus
or the Constantinian excerpter), then he must have viewed the
revolt on the island as largely caused by and affecting the Sicilians themselves.

What of the Italian presence that occupies the attention of
scholars? The narrator contends that the Italians were the largest landowners on the island;[114] they therefore should play a
significant part in the revolt. But compared with the rich details about Sicilian involvement in the conflict, there are only
two generalized references to the Italians, and both are suspect. The first contains a notorious anachronism. When the
ill-treatment by the landowners began to drive slaves into
brigandage and the first hints of rebellion were sensed, Roman
praetors wanted to intervene. Because most of the land and
slaves were owned by Roman knights, however, the praetors
were afraid to act: Roman knights controlled the courts at
home and so might take revenge by prosecuting the governors.[115] There is a number of problems with this explanation,[116] but the most significant is the argument that what prevented justice was the equestrian control of the law courts. In

[113] See especially T. Broughton, *TAPA* 65 (1934), 209–10; also D. Magie,
Roman Rule in Asia Minor to the End of the Third Century after Christ, 151–52,
161–62; cf. Strabo xiii 14.38.

[114] xxxiv/xxxv 2.3, 2.31.

[115] xxxiv/xxxv 2.3 (Photian), 2.31 (Constantinian).

[116] Even if the praetors could not act against Romans, the historian might
have wondered why magistrates did not prosecute the Sicilian landowners and
limit abuse. Moreover, it is maintained that *most* of the landowners were Roman *equites* (2.31; cf. 2.3), clearly an exaggeration; all other references to foreigners allude generally to Italians: 2.27, 2.32, 2.34.

fact, it was not until a dozen years later, in 123 or 122 B.C., that Gaius Gracchus filled the juries with *equites*.[117] That very event is recorded later in the *Bibliotheke* in a passage usually attributed to Posidonius.[118] In order to save Posidonius from this glaring contradiction within his own narrative, it has been suggested that Diodorus employed another source for his information on the law courts during the Slave War.[119] But it is unlikely that Diodorus would take a single erroneous fact from a different account.

The other allusion to Italians serves as a clue to resolving the problem raised here. By way of introducing the Sicilian landowner, Damophilus, it is stated that he emulated the decadence of the Italians and the manner in which they treated their slaves.[120] A bit earlier the point is made more generally that the Sicilians attempted to match Italian greed and arrogance.[121] These references to Italian culpability ring of apology for the Sicilians. The narrative details local responsibility for the Slave Revolt. But here, in order to explain why Sicilians are so implicated, the author says that they are merely imitating the low morals of their Italian overlords.

Both references to Italians are troublesome. One inculpates Roman knights by misrepresenting their role in the law courts; the other shifts the blame for moral degeneracy—and hence for the cause of the revolt—from the Sicilians to the Italians. It was once long ago suggested that Diodorus himself was responsible for the passage involving the law courts,[122] and it has now been shown that Diodorus will intrude into the narrative on issues involving Roman imperialism. In this case,

---

[117] See E. Badian, *AJP* 75 (1954), 374, and *Publicans and Sinners*, 135, n. 65, and E. Gruen, *Roman Politics and the Criminal Courts*, 80–90, 293–96, who differ on details not pertinent here.

[118] xxxiv/xxxv 25.1 = *FGH* 87 F 111b (*Anhang*) = F 165 (Theiler); cf. DS xxxvii 9.

[119] Jacoby, *FGH* IIc, 207; Càssola, *ANRW* II 30.1, 768–69.

[120] xxxiv/xxxv 2.34; Constantinian.

[121] xxxiv/xxxv 2.27; Constantinian. A fragmentary reference to the Italians at 2.32 reflects material in 2.1–2 and 2.27.

[122] T. Mommsen, *Römisches Staatsrecht* (Leipzig, 1887) III, 530, 1.

the temptation may have been all the greater, for the events concerned Sicily. Diodorus on other occasions departs from Posidonius;[123] even in the narrative of the Slave Revolt there is one passage that can confidently be identified as his own.[124]

Every concrete fact of the Slave War involves Sicilians. Whereas they provide the entire foundation for the narrative, all that is told about the Romans and Italians is generality: they controlled the law courts and owned most of the land and slaves, and their low morals proved ultimately responsible for the revolt. No specific details, except for the patently false explanation about the law courts, tie them to the events. It would have been easy for Diodorus to introduce the Italians or at least to expand on Posidonius's treatment of them with little additional research.

If Diodorus did intrude, the historicity of the narrative has not been resolved. Of course, Diodorus might have invented freely, perhaps relying on later Posidonian material. Elsewhere Diodoran invention is based on descriptions of other episodes,[125] and here he would have had much to draw on. In the *Bibliotheke*, under the year 97 B.C., the *publicani* acted with impunity in Asia Minor because of their control over the law courts (xxxvii 5.1). The point is frequently recognized as Po-

---

[123] Diodorus presents a contradictory portrait of Tiberius Gracchus (xxxiv/ xxxv 5 and 33.6, 3.7; cf. A. Bernstein, *Tiberius Sempronius Gracchus: Tradition and Apostasy*, 241), which might suggest that he added his own thoughts. Strasburger, *JRS* 55 (1965), 49, incorrectly explains that Posidonius used such contradictions to show different sides of a personality. Strasburger's main example, Marius, is, in fact, portrayed as consistently becoming worse: DS xxxvii 29; cf. xxxiv/v 38. Or again, DS xxxvii 3-8 is a highly moralist view of the Social War, and is generally considered Posidonian; most recently, J. Harmatta, *AC* 7 (1971), 21-25. Yet within the discussion, chap. 4 is posed in a praise/blame formula thoroughly typical of Diodorus: see Chapter 2, and the next note.

[124] The use of history as a way of punishing or rewarding (xxxiv/xxxv 9) is fundamental to Diodorus's purpose: see Chapter 2. Posidonius's history, on the other hand, "ist kein rhetorisches ψέγειν und ἐπαινεῖν" (Jacoby, *FGH* IIc, 160).

[125] E.g., on Osiris (i 17-20), see Murray, *JEA* 56 (1970), 149-50; on Alesia (iv 19.2), see Harmand, *Latomus* 26 (1967), 968.

sidonian,[126] and there it is not anachronistic. Diodorus may have applied this explanation to his earlier narrative. Similarly, Diodorus could have used Posidonius's treatment of the Second Sicilian Slave War in blaming the Italians for the first revolt. Greedy *publicani* are at fault in the later rebellion, and Roman praetors in Sicily are either incompetent or suspected of bribe taking.[127] Italian corruption is the theme Posidonius stresses for that conflict, and Diodorus may have taken from this narrative his inspiration for blaming the Italians for the First Slave Revolt.[128]

Alternatively, any Diodoran additions might have derived from established traditions. There may have been a common local version, for Sicilian aristocrats would certainly retell the story from their point of view,[129] and throughout the *Bibliotheke* Diodorus includes in his narrative personal information about Sicily.[130] The conditions described in the narrative—that the Italians were large landowners in Sicily before the Slave War—might therefore have some truth. Florus, for example, testifies that at the time of the revolt Sicily was full of latifundia held by Roman citizens (ii 7.3). But the authority for that statement is indeterminable, and the testimony is usually not given much weight.[131] Once it is accepted that Diodorus may

[126] E.g. by Theiler (F 213) and Gruen *HWCR* I, 354, n. 199, with bibliography.

[127] DS xxxvi 3.3, 8.5, 9.1.

[128] There are various structural similarities between the First and Second Slave Revolts, but whether the two revolts fit a precise pattern is debatable: bibliography in Verbrugghe, *Historia* 24 (1975), 189, n. 4 and 191–92; yet see also his 190, n. 6.

[129] Cf. Reinhardt, *RE* 22.1, 634. Diodorus's hometown of Agyrium is near Enna, where the revolt began.

[130] E.g., iv 80, 83; xiii 90.5.

[131] Strabo (vi 2.6) notes that the Romans took what Sicilian land lay deserted and handed it over to horsekeepers, cowherders, and shepherds; later, these groups rebelled under Eunus. Mazza, in Giardina and Schiavone, *Società romana e produzione schiavistica* I, 27, and Malitz, *Die Historien des Poseidonios*, 148, n. 97, identify this as Posidonian, but not so Jacoby or Theiler (cf. Theiler II, 100). Strabo has much contemporary information on Sicily (see Appendix I) and a more recent slave war in Sicily interested him (vi 2.6); he may

be responsible for some of the material involving the Italians, it is difficult to decide how much of it could be his and how much worth it has.

Complicating any resolution of this issue is Posidonius's own method of composing narrative. Athenaeus claims that for his history Posidonius gathered material to illuminate his philosophical principles.[132] In fact, modern scholars have identified structural similarities among the Posidonian accounts of the two Sicilian slave wars, the revolt of Spartacus, and Pompey's campaign against the pirates.[133] These suggest that Posidonius had in mind a standard pattern for conflicts involving slaves, on the basis of which, after learning a few details (perhaps without even the use of autopsy),[134] he constructed his own story.

The narrative of the First Slave Revolt in the *Bibliotheke* is especially similar to the Posidonian account of Pompey and the Cilician pirates. Because patterns of characterization and story development in the two events strongly resemble one another,[135] the Posidonian material on piracy found in Plutarch, Strabo, and Appian serves as a partial control for his

---

therefore have acquired the information himself. Strabo does not detail to whom the Romans "handed over" (παρέδοσαν) the land, a phrase always suggesting a transference of control and at odds with the Diodoran account and other evidence: see V. Scramuzza, "Roman Sicily," in T. Frank, *An Economic Survey of Ancient Rome* III, 240–46, with App., *BC* i 9.

[132] Athen. iv 151e = *FGH* 87 T 12a; cf. K. Bringmann, "Geschichte und Psychologie bei Poseidonios," *Aspects de la philosophie hellénistique*, Fondation Hardt, *Entretiens*, 32, 54. The testimonium is not discussed by Jacoby, Kidd, or Malitz and barely noted by Theiler (= F 170). For a possible example of a Posidonian principle, see DS xxxiv/xxxv 30a.

[133] See Verbrugghe, *Historia* 24 (1975), 189–204, and Strasburger, *JRS* 55 (1965), 40–53.

[134] Strabo draws on his account of Sicily (vi 2.1, 2.3, 2.7, 2.11), but there is no telling whether Posidonius relied on autopsy for his description. Posidonius said that the *periplus* of Sicily was 4,400 stades (*FGH* 87 F 62 = Strabo vi 2.1). Diodorus may be correcting Posidonius when he gives the figure of 4,360 (v 2.2), though, if the text is sound, there is a miscalculation in Diodorus's later discussion.

[135] Strasburger, *JRS* 55 (1965), 43.

original, uncontaminated version of the First Slave Revolt. Unlike the Diodoran version of the Slave Revolt, in no place in Posidonius's reconstructed account of the Cilician pirates is Rome blamed. Although he notes that Rome, by establishing a thriving slave trade seventy-five years earlier, created the conditions for piracy, Posidonius attributes the recent growth to those involved locally: Mithridates and the uprooted people of the Mediterranean.[136] When narrating the First Sicilian Slave War, he might have been working from the same model.[137] He had a moral to make about the impact of slavery and domestic decadence and may not have wanted to complicate the picture with traditions involving Italians. This view strengthens the possibility that Diodorus was responsible for some or all of that material. What Diodorus might have added about the Italian presence, however, is not necessarily false. Posidonius could have simply omitted or minimized whatever was not strictly pertinent to his moral message.

The chance that Diodorus has intruded into the narrative does not, therefore, necessarily invalidate the account. Whatever Diodorus added or expanded upon could have as much worth as the Posidonian material. But it does raise more questions concerning Diodorus's fidelity to his sources. Indeed, in examining the preservation of Posidonius's account by Diodorus and other authors, a pattern emerges that further suggests Diodorus's creativity and hostility to Rome.

From the surviving fragments of Posidonius's history, outside of what is found in the *Bibliotheke*, the tradition almost uniformly emphasizes Rome's beneficial treatment of its subjects. The fragments representing this aspect of Posidonian thought are preserved in Athenaeus, Seneca, and Strabo. They argue that the weak often benefit from being ruled by the strong, who can maintain peace and bring prosperity. In that way, Posidonius justified the Roman conquest of the Mediter-

---

[136] Slave trade: Strabo xiv 5.2; direct cause: App., *Mith*. 92, 416. Pompey is praised for his great clemency toward captured pirates: Plut., *Pomp*. 28.2–4.

[137] xxxiv/xxxv 2.25–27 are especially suggestive.

ranean as a morally proper action, benefiting both conqueror and subjects. [138] In fact, only one existing Posidonian fragment outside the *Bibliotheke* is at times understood as indicating criticism of Rome. [139]

This generally sympathetic portrayal differs markedly from the judgments found in the Posidonian narrative of the *Bibliotheke*. Two themes critical of Rome have been identified. First, because Rome eliminated external threats by destroying Carthage in 146, it consequently suffered from internal decay. [140] Second, Rome could be harsh in governing the provinces, for Posidonius depicts Italian traders as viciously exploiting the peoples of Gaul and Spain. [141] In contrast to the Posidonian sentiments positively disposed toward Rome, all

[138] W. Capelle, *Klio* 25 (1932), 86–113, esp. 98–103. Strasburger, *JRS* 55 (1965), 46, and F. Walbank *JRS* 55 (1965), 14–15, rightly accept the identification of fragments from Strabo. Capelle especially stresses Sen., *Ep.* 90 (F 448 [Theiler]). Though 90.5 discusses the rule of the best only in an ideal Golden Age (so Strasburger, 47), it is intended as a law of nature with contemporary application: 90.4. Seneca follows Posidonius in generalizing that "it is part of nature that the weaker submit to the stronger" (Naturae est enim potioribus deteriora summittere). A similar sentiment is found at DS xxxiv/v 30b, which is identified as Posidonian by Theiler (F 173) but not Jacoby. It is also voiced by Dionysius of Halicarnassus (*AR* i 5.2) in referring to Roman right to rule. Thucydides may have been his inspiration, but Posidonius cannot be discounted; cf. Gabba, *RSI* 71 (1959), 365.

[139] Posidonius's bias in his description of Atheneion (Athen. v 211d–215b = *FGH* 87 F 36) is difficult to interpret, for it may be full of irony (P. Desideri, *Athenaeum* 51 [1973], 249–54) and Athenaeus may have taken it out of context (Kidd, *Posidonius. Vol. II: The Commentary* ii, 864). Irony may also be present in DS xxxiv/v 2.5–9. Desideri (3–29, 237–69) posits a Posidonian tradition hostile to Rome in App., *Mith.* 10–17 and 56–58, but see (most recently) McGing, *The Foreign Policy of Mithridates VI*, 80, n. 53.

[140] DS xxxiv/xxxv 33; xxxvii 2–5; Strasburger *JRS* 55 (1965), 47.

[141] Exploitation of provincials by Italian traders: DS v 26.3 = *FGH* 87 F 116 (*Anhang*); 36.3–4, 38.1 = F 117 (*Anhang*); rapacity of the *publicani*: xxxiv/v 25.1 = F 111b; xxxvii 5–6 is not identified as Posidonian by Jacoby, but is, e.g., by Theiler (F 213) and Gruen *HWCR* i, 354, n. 199, with bibliography. See generally Strasburger, *JRS* 55 (1965), 40–53. The belief that Posidonius focused his criticism on *equites*, while approving of the actions of the senatorial class, requires modification: see Appendix II.

of these are preserved only in Diodorus. Illuminating are the descriptions of the Spanish silver mines found in Diodorus and Strabo. Both are from Posidonius (Strabo mentions him)[142] and contain similar discussions of the Laurium mines and Archimedes' screw. But Diodorus presents a scathing picture of Italian abuse of slaves (v 36.3–4, 38.1), a subject on which Strabo is completely silent. There may, in fact, be additional criticisms of Rome, again present only in the Posidonian narrative of Diodorus. Twice while following Posidonius, Diodorus makes the charge that Rome rules not from its own strength, but because of the weakness of its subjects.[143] And the judgment that the Romans acted with brutality to those who opposed them but employed moderation (ἐπιείϰεια) with those who obeyed is twice found in contexts identified as Posidonian.[144] The appearance of ἐπιείϰεια, however, may suggest Diodoran intrusion (see Chapter 2), and the same sentiment is found at xxx 23.2, which either is drawn from Polybius[145] or is Diodorus's own. It anticipates Virgil (*Aen.* vi 853).

Within the Posidonian fragments outside of Diodorus there exists the consistent belief that Roman imperialism was useful and good, whereas the Posidonian tradition found in the *Bibliotheke* is generally hostile toward Rome.[146] This pattern of preservation probably indicates several factors at work together: a genuine ambivalence on Posidonius's part, the political biases of those who drew on his work, and Diodorus's demonstrated tendency to intrude into the narrative. Analysis of Diodorus's account of the First Sicilian Slave War reveals

[142] DS v 36–38 = *FGH* 87 F 117 (*Anhang*); Strabo iii 2.9 = F 47.

[143] xxxiv/v 33.4–6 = F 178 (Theiler) = *FGH* 87 F 112 (*Anhang*); xxxiv/v 30b = F 173 (Theiler), not in *FGH*.

[144] DS xxxiii 26.2 = F 128 (Theiler); xxxiv/xxxv 23 (end) pertains to Celtic affairs, a Posidonian specialty: on which Malitz, *Die Historien des Poseidonios*, 176.

[145] DS xxx 21.1 = Polybius xxix 20, which gives out before the material in DS xxx 23.2.

[146] Only one positive sentiment in Diodorus has been identified as Posidonian (xxxiv/xxxv 32 = F 176 [Theiler]).

anomalies and apology, suggesting that he might be responsible for at least some of the anti-Italian material there. He may have added his own criticisms or at least sharpened those expressed already by Posidonius in other episodes as well.

Aeneas in Sicily

A passage within the mythological part of the *Bibliotheke* perhaps best encapsulates Diodorus's feelings toward Rome. In describing the Sicilian shrine to Erycinian Aphrodite, Diodorus displays local pride, declaring that it is the only sanctuary in the world that has continued to flourish from the beginning of time to the present. After noting that it was established by Aphrodite's son, Eryx, Diodorus lists the visitors who subsequently paid homage. Foremost among them was Aeneas, also a son of the goddess (though by a different father), who en route to Italy anchored off Sicily and embellished the sanctuary. Diodorus relates that over the centuries the Sicanians, Carthaginians, and, in his own day, the Romans also came and contributed. The Romans were the most enthusiastic, tracing their ancestry and attributing their expansion to the goddess. All consuls, praetors, and Romans with any authority who came to the island traveled to the shrine and worshiped her. The Roman Senate even decreed special honors to the sanctuary.[147]

In this seemingly casual description there is tension. Undoubtedly, Diodorus takes pride in the importance of the Sicilian cult and the reverence it is paid by all peoples, including the Romans. But in portraying the honors that Rome bestowed on Eryx, he argues against a particular version of the

---

[147] iv 83. 83.5–7 must be Diodorus's own words. Though Meister, "Die sizilische Geschichte," 27, attributes 83.1–4 to Timaeus, Jacoby, *FGH* 566, does not; and if, as seems certain, Diodorus composed the contemporary description of the cult at Engyum a few chapters earlier (iv 80.4–6: see Chapter 6), he may well be responsible also for that at Eryx. It has been argued that Virgil, whose account of Aeneas in Sicily differs broadly from Diodorus's, followed Timaeus: T. Brown, *Virgilius* 6 (1960), 4–12.

cult. The sanctuary to Erycinian Aphrodite was a central aspect of the Roman foundation myth involving Aeneas. In an attempt to win Greek support during the Second Punic War, the Romans stressed Aeneas's landing at Sicily. A temple, inspired by that at Eryx, was set within the *pomerium*, a rare honor for a foreign cult.[148] Aeneas's Sicilian experience was emphasized during the late Republic: Cicero (2 *Verr.* iv 33.72) mentions that Aeneas founded Segesta, near Eryx, and a *denarius* of the late 60s portrays the temple of Eryx on its reverse.[149] In the Augustan Age, Aeneas's visit to Sicily became central to his story, as told by Dionysius, Livy, and especially Virgil. Dionysius and Virgil assert that Aeneas himself established the cult to Aphrodite at Eryx.[150] There were of course many authors, as Strabo (xiii 1.53) testifies, who invented legends about Aeneas's western journey in order to glorify Rome. The story illuminated the common cultural heritage of the Greeks and Romans, and helped justify the Roman conquest of Sicily, Carthage, and the Greek East.[151]

What is striking about the treatment in Diodorus is that the Aenean connection with Sicily, while acknowledged, is specifically minimized and the claim that the Trojan founded the Erycinian cult ignored. Aeneas did not remain in Sicily, but anchored off shore (προσορμισθεὶς τῇ νήσῳ) in order to pay respects at the sanctuary. The cult itself had been established much earlier by a different son of Aphrodite, Eryx, an indigenous Sicilian after whom the town and sanctuary were named.[152] Eryx himself belongs to the prehistory of the island: he fought Heracles and lived in Sicily contemporaneously with the earliest Sicanians.[153] Diodorus emphasizes the prehistoric and aboriginal status of Eryx, in contrast to his half-brother, Aeneas, who merely passed through later (ὕστερον).

[148] R. Schilling, *Kokalos* 10–11 (1964–1965), 277–78.
[149] *Coins of the Roman Republic in the British Museum* I, 473.
[150] *AR* i 53.1: Dionysius writes Elyma but intends Eryx; *Aen.* v 759–60.
[151] Most recently, Momigliano, *On Pagans, Jews, and Christians*, 278–79.
[152] iv 83.1; cf. iv 23.2.
[153] iv 23, 78; cf. v 2.4, 6.

Now Diodorus elsewhere admires Aeneas, stressing his *pietas*[154] and noting that he received divine honors (vii 5.2). Diodorus also recounts that the Julian clan descends from Aeneas,[155] an association that may have been important to Diodorus. But the historian must have felt as well that Aeneas was a good man whom history ought to praise. When Aeneas is introduced into the ancient traditions of Sicily, however, Diodorus corrects the story.[156] The ancestor of the Latins was a late-comer to Sicily and certainly not the founder of the Erycinian cult.

Diodorus was not the first Greek to deny the Roman version of Aeneas. A century earlier, Demetrius of Scepsis, a patriot of his native Troad, stressed the primacy of the story that Aeneas never went to Latium, but instead remained in Asia Minor. Having witnessed Roman incursions into his land, Demetrius rebutted the myth that connected Italy with the Greek East, implying that Romans ought to respect the true homeland of Aeneas. In standing against many contemporaries who embraced the Roman tradition, Demetrius used the Aeneas legend as part of resistance historiography.[157]

Diodorus, in making his own case against the Roman legend, even offers a coarse insult. While noting that all people who worshiped the goddess honored her shrine with dedications, he adds that Roman praetors and consuls who visited the island "laying aside the austerity of their authority . . . enter into sports and have intercourse [ὁμιλία] with women in a spirit of great gaiety, believing that only in this way will they

---

[154] vii 4; on which see N. Horsfall, *CQ* n.s. 29 (1979), 384–85.

[155] vii 5.8. Caesar himself emphasized the connection by putting Aeneas's figure on Roman coins for the first time: e.g., E. Sydenham, *The Coinage of the Roman Republic*, 458/1. The connection to Aeneas continued to be part of Caesarian and Augustan propaganda: Taylor, *The Divinity of the Roman Emperor*, 59, n. 3.

[156] By 42, Octavian was associating himself with Aeneas (Taylor, *The Divinity of the Roman Emperor*, 106), and Diodorus, hostile toward Octavian because of his attack on Sicily (see Chapter 6), may have refuted the Aenean connection with the island partly on that account.

[157] Gabba, *CISA* 4 (1976), 84–101.

ROME

make their presence there pleasing to the goddess" (83.6; Old-father's translation modified). Certainly temple prostitutes were available to anyone who came to Eryx,[158] but Diodorus connects them only with Romans, and provincial governors at that. The contrast with Strabo is illuminating: the Roman apologist mentions the temple prostitutes as being dedicated by "both Sicilians and many foreigners" (vi 2.6). Diodorus tells his story of Aeneas to defend his cultural heritage against Roman tradition and to offer a pointed barb at imperial rule.[159]

TO DRAW together some disparate strands, most of the sentiments in admiration of Rome reflect material found in Diodorus's sources rather than his own intrusion. Diodorus more obviously departs from his current source to offer criticism. In this way he inversely anticipates Cassius Dio, who echoes occasional anti-Roman sentiments yet overall is decidedly favorable toward Rome.[160] The comment about Hasdrubal's fortune indicates another aspect of Diodorus's editorializing. Like his contemporary Pompeius Trogus, he does not view Rome as destined to unify the Mediterranean. Instead, Rome is only "the factual endpoint" of his history.[161] Consequently, in contrast to Polybius and Dionysius of Halicarnassus, Diodorus does not begin his work with the succession of empires.

[158] Perhaps begun under the influence of Carthaginian worship of Astarte: E. Rawson, *Cicero: A Portrait*, 35.

[159] The seventeen Sicilians cities that formed the guard of honor at Eryx (iv 83.7) probably did not include Agyrium, as argued by E. Pais, *ASS* 13 (1888), 178ff., in connecting Cic., 2 *Verr.* v 46 with 2 *Verr.* iii 26.67. Diodorus's silence is especially telling (cf. iv 80.4–5), and Manganaro, *ANRW* I.1, 448, offers another list based on numismatic evidence. On some details of iv 83.7, see D. Kienast, *Hermes* 93 (1965), 484–86. The reluctance of the Greeks to exchange their culture for the Roman was widespread in the late Republic: see Crawford, in Garnsey and Whittaker, *Imperialism in the Ancient World*, 193–207.

[160] Gabba, in Millar and Segal, *Caesar Augustus*, 70–71.

[161] So A. Breebarrt, *Acta Historiae Neerlandica* 1 (1966), 17; cf. Momigliano, *Settimo contributo*, 91 = *On Pagans, Jews, and Christians*, 45–46, and the sensitive analysis of G. de Sanctis, *Ricerche sulla storiografia siceliota*, 84.

157

He does not wish to give the impression that the Roman achievement was part of some inevitable process in history.

On the other hand, Diodorus is a realist: the Roman Empire would not dissolve in his lifetime, and to some extent he admires its success and the stability it brought. His argument, that hegemons who cease ruling with moderation (ἐπιείκεια) and instead employ terror are destined to lose their power, may be intended as a warning to Rome (see the comments on xxxii 4 in Chapter 2). But it reflects an author who has made an accommodation with reality. Diodorus offers no alternative to an empire defended by Italian soldiers, and, in any event, by his day the historiography of opposition was clearly doomed.[162] What he argues for were more reasonable, not new, conditions.

In a passage that probably follows Ephorus, Diodorus has a Greek critic of Gelon say that he would rather live under the Persian king than the Sicilian tyrant: the Persians required gifts, but a tyrant's greed is unlimited.[163] Later, with Timaeus his likely source,[164] Diodorus has a Sicilian speaker prefer to confront Carthage rather than follow Dionysius I: Carthaginians would impose only a fixed tribute and allow for local rule according to traditional laws; the tyrant Dionysius, however, would take private property through his rapacity, sack temples, and put slaves over masters. Finally, in following perhaps Hieronymus of Cardia in recounting what may be a debate among Tarentine Greeks about whether to seek the aid of Pyrrhus against Rome, one of the participants appears to offer the same counsel.[165] Each of these speakers shrewdly argues that a foreign conqueror might govern more lightly than a fellow Greek. Perhaps with this in mind Diodorus writes that Roman rule put an end to tyranny on Sicily.[166]

---

[162] Cf. Gabba, *CA* I (1982), 62.
[163] x 34.1; on which, see the discussion earlier in this chapter.
[164] On xv 65.2–3: Meister, "Die sizilische Geschichte," 92–95.
[165] xxi 21.9–10; see Chapter 4, n. 92.
[166] xix 1.5. On Diodorus's hatred of tyranny, see ix 11.

Internal peace, however, had its price, for later, when discussing Sicilian affairs, he notes mankind's inherent desire for independence (αὐτονομία: xx 31.3). Possibly Diodorus was only following his source,[167] but it may be a personal yearning. The Rome that prevented tyranny on Sicily also brought the island great evils. Diodorus departs from the Polybian narrative to criticize in strong terms contemporary Roman greed (πλεονεξία) which, in his own day, seemed ever to increase.[168] Elsewhere he notes that exemption from imperial tribute helped the Sicilian town of Halaesa grow rich;[169] he does not say what the imposition of tribute, maladministration, and Roman civil wars did to the rest of the island. Occasionally, Diodorus intruded into the narrative with expressions of criticism toward Rome; at other times possibly he held back. Why he might have muted his attack is explored in the next chapter.

[167] Timaeus: Meister, "Die sizilische Geschichte," 150; cf. vii 12.3–4, which is thought to be from Ephorus: Schwartz, RE 5, 678; Jacoby, FGH IIc, 33.

[168] xxxi 26.2; not in Polybius xxxi 22. On the contemporary belief that Rome was rapacious: McGing, The Foreign Policy of Mithridates VI, 105–6.

[169] xiv 16.2; xxiii 4.

SIX

Diodorus in the World of
Caesar and Octavian

THE PREVIOUS chapter demonstrated that Diodorus imprinted on his history his own views of the late Republic. With his sometimes critical attitude toward Rome as a background, it is appropriate now to consider how Diodorus's experiences and his reactions to contemporary events helped shape the structure and bias of his work. After reviewing the evidence about Diodorus's life, this chapter examines the terminal date of the *Bibliotheke*. At some time while writing his history, Diodorus altered its end point so that the work concluded, not with events of 46 B.C. as originally planned, but with the year 60 B.C. The change served to eliminate Caesar's career from his work. However, Diodorus esteemed Caesar above all other contemporaries. The explanation as to why he decided to reduce Caesar's role in the history cannot be fully uncovered until other aspects of Diodorus's relationship to Rome and its rulers are investigated. Patronage and social contacts were important to Greek intellectuals in Rome. It will be suggested that Diodorus lived in isolation from Roman patrons and fellow Greeks and, consequently, may have been especially anxious about writing candidly. Another significant factor in explaining the shape of the *Bibliotheke* is the figure of Octavian, who dominated Rome during much of Diodorus's stay. As the 30s progressed, Diodorus may have reconsidered his emphasis on Julius Caesar. Outspokenly admiring of the Dictator, yet mildly hostile toward the Empire and especially its new ruler, Diodorus thought it best to eliminate contemporary history from his work. Too many people had a stake in the rendering of their past for an émigré to detail it with candor.

HIS LIFE

Almost all that is known about Diodorus comes from allusions within his work. Raised in the Sicilian town of Agyrium (i 4.4), he visited Egypt in 60/59 B.C. and may have remained there until 56.[1] Although he claims generally to have traveled throughout Asia and Europe, there is no indication that he did so.[2] The only other specific reference to a foreign journey is to Rome. It is only surmised that Diodorus went directly there from Egypt, in around 56. But the inclusion of a minor detail that must have been based on personal observation indicates that he was in the imperial city by 46 or 45,[3] when he began writing the preface to the *Bibliotheke*. He notes that he remained in Rome a long while (πλείω χρόνον: i 4.3–4). The *Bibliotheke* was published in about 30, and there is no telling how long Diodorus lived after that. If, however, he was already doing research in Egypt in 60/59 B.C., it is unlikely he survived much past the turn of the century. A grave stele found in Agyrium and bearing the name "Diodorus, son of Apollonius" is tantalizing only because so little is known about the historian.[4]

[1] By 59: i 83.8, on which see Oldfather, *Diodorus of Sicily* I, Loeb edition, vii–viii. To 56: i 44.1–4, 46.7. Allusions to his stay at iii 11.3 and xvii 52.6 reveal nothing about the date.

[2] Harmand, *Latomus* 26 (1967), 982, n. 5, and Hornblower, *Hieronymus of Cardia*, 25. It is frequently noted with scorn that Diodorus puts Nineveh on the Euphrates instead of the Tigris (ii 3.2, 7.2); in fact, he acknowledges that he never visited that city, relying on the account of Ktesias (ii 2.2, 7.1) and contemporary travelers (ii 7.2). Diodorus also admits that his account of the Red Sea is based on written records and eyewitnesses (iii 38.1). For evidence of autopsy (in Sicily, Italy, and Egypt), see Chapter 4.

[3] Casevitz, *Diodore* XII, Budé edition, xi, n. 1, on xii 26.1.

[4] *IG* XIV, 588. Early commentators identified this Diodorus with the historian (see commentary in *IG*). The name is quite common, however, as any index to *SEG* testifies. Attempts to tie another grave stele to Diodorus's con-

When Diodorus writes of his lengthy stay in Rome, he probably means that he was still there when he finished the history. Rome had recently become a center for book publishing,[5] and that would have provided an incentive for Diodorus to remain. He may have visited Sicily during the period when he was writing, for he includes a rather obscure detail about contemporary Syracuse.[6] But the island had long been an intellectual backwater[7] and suffered terrible devastations during the Pompeian wars of the 30s. That was not the environment for the writing and publication of the *Bibliotheke*.

Diodorus's work, in fact, enjoyed sufficient fame to suggest that it was no mere provincial curiosity. It was available to the Elder Pliny and Athenaeus,[8] to later legal and textual scholars,[9] and it may also have been used by Plutarch and Cassius Dio.[10] In Hadrian's time, the notoriously fraudulent Cephalion wrote a history that, as writers then noted, resembled an

---

temporary, Caecilius of Calacte, have proved amusing: discussion and bibliography in P. Fiore, *Sicilia archeologia* 34 (1977), 63–69.

[5] Cic., 2 *Phil.* 9.21; Catullus 14.17–19; cf. E. Kenney, in *CHCL* ii, 19–20. Strabo's lament (xiii 54) that poor production occurred in both Rome and Alexandria (the unquestioned leader in publishing hitherto) is the standard sort, for ancient and modern writers, and does not cast doubt on Rome's importance as a center for publishing.

[6] At xvi 70, Diodorus notes that, because Rome had enfranchised Sicily, Syracuse no longer dated by an eponymous priesthood. The passage was written after 44 but before 36, when Octavian stripped the island of citizenship rights: see Appendix 1.

[7] G. Arrighetti, "Civiltà letteraria della Sicilia antica dal II secola. a.C. al IV secolo. d.C.," in Gabba and Vallet, *La Sicilia antica* ii.2, 393–410, and Rawson, *Intellectual Life*, 36–37.

[8] *NH praef.* 25; Athen. xii 541f = DS xi 25.

[9] The *Bibliotheke* is cited by Ulpian of Ascalon, preserving ix 17; by Eustathius: e.g., *Ad Iliadem*, 4, 286 and *Ad Odysseam* 2, 324; cf. F. Vogel, *Diodori Bibliotheca Historica* ii, Teubner edition, 219–20; and by a scholiast to Homer: see A. Ludwich, *RhM* 34 (1879), 619; cf. vi 7 with vi 6.4–5.

[10] *Moralia Fragmentum Incertum*, no. 135, in *Plutarch* vii, Teubner edition, ed. G. Bernard (Leipzig, 1896); *Excerpta Planudea*, no. 37, in *Cassii Dionis Cocceiani Historiarum Romanarum Quae Supersunt* i, ed. U. Boissevain (Berlin, 1895), cxxi; cf. on Dio's use of Diodorus possibly Tzetzes, *Chiliades* 2, 148–49.

epitome of Diodorus. [11] Chroniclers relied upon the *Bibliotheke*, [12] and Diodorus's discussions of the Jews naturally made it a significant work to quote—and misquote—in arguments over the antiquity of the Judeo-Christian traditions. [13] By the later Empire, someone must have extended the *Bibliotheke* to reach at least to the death of Augustus. After paraphrasing Diodorus on the Social War and Sulla, Photius continues briefly with events from 59 to the end of Augustus's reign. [14] That material could not have been Diodorus's contribution, for within the summary is a reference to Augustus's power lasting until his death and a detailed allusion to the *illustris*, a rank not seen until the fourth century. [15] The appended material continues directly from Photius's excerpts that begin with his heading, "From the thirty-seventh and thirty-eighth books and those following." [16] Scaliger and later commentators thought Photius was responsible for the additional material. But Photius is not so inventive with other authors, and it would not be part of his purpose, which was to summarize earlier literature rather than to write history himself. It would appear that Photius found the additional narrative in his text

[11] *FGH* 93 F 1b, end; cf. Phot. *Codex* 70, 103, 35a (not in *FGH*).

[12] Perhaps as early as A.D. 15, by the author of the *Tabula Capitolina* (*IG* XIV, 1297 = *FGH* 252), but that identification is very uncertain: see J. Balcer, *HSCP* 76 (1972), 104. Africanus on DS ix 21 (in Eusebius); Porphyry, in *Fragmenta Historicorum Graecorum* III, edited by C. Müller (Paris, 1840), FF 1.1, 3.7; references to Eusebius are in *PIR*² III, 23; vi 5 is preserved by John of Antioch; vii 14 by John Malalas; xxi 1.6 by Evagrius Scholasticus; xxii 4, xxv 18, and xxxi 19.9 by Georgius Syncellus.

[13] Besides Christian chroniclers already noted, see the reshaping of Diodorus in Pseudo-Justin Martyr, *Cohortatio ad Gentiles*, in *Corpus Apologetarum Christianorum Saeculi Secundi* III, ed. J.C.T. Otto (Jena, 1879), 10b–e (which reflects first-hand knowledge of the *Bibliotheke*), 15b, 24c, 26e; cf. M. Stern, *Greek and Latin Authors on Jews and Judaism* III, 38–41. See also Joannes Philoponus, *De Opificio mundi*, 216.

[14] *Codex* 244, 393, 12a–5b.

[15] *Codex* 244, 393, 30a–33. Contra, P. Botteri, *Mélanges de archéologie et d'historie de l'école Française de Rome* 95 (1983), 665–66.

[16] Ἐκ τοῦ λζ' καὶ η' καὶ τῶν ἐφεξῆς (377a.25–28).

of the *Bibliotheke*.[17] Indeed, the Suda refers to Diodorus as "living in the time of Augustus Caesar and afterward."[18] Already in 59 B.C. Diodorus was working in Egypt and meeting foreign dignitaries,[19] so his floruit could not have lasted beyond the reign of Augustus. As did Photius, the author of the Suda must have had a text of the *Bibliotheke* that extended to the end of Augustus's reign; he then dated Diodorus's life accordingly. Moderns have viewed as empty boasting Diodorus's complaint that his uncompleted work was being published without his authorization.[20] But the impressive *Nachleben* suggests that the *Bibliotheke* did enjoy a certain popularity during his lifetime and long afterward. Given the conditions in Sicily around 30 B.C., it is more likely that Diodorus encouraged its publication in Italy.

Despite his long stay in the capital, Diodorus does not claim a close association with Romans. Through contact with them in Sicily, he had learned Latin (i 4.4), although his complete mastery of the language has been questioned.[21] Before the Antonian enfranchisement (Appendix I), many Sicilians enjoyed Roman rights individually;[22] but it is doubtful whether Diodorus was one. Had he been a recipient of citizenship, we would expect a *praenomen* and *nomen*, as well as a claim to that honor in his opening pro'em. Of particular interest is Q. Lu-

[17] In an earlier *codex*, Photius acknowledges Diodorus's terminus of 60 B.C., by paraphrasing DS i 4.7 (*Codex* 70, 35a.15–19, 33–39). But from the brief description of Diodorus and the *Bibliotheke* there, it is clear that Photius had not yet read beyond the opening prooemium.

[18] γέγονε δὲ ἐπὶ τῶν χρόνων Αὐγούστου Καίσαρος καὶ ἐπάνω (1152, Adler).

[19] On the dates, n. 1, above; on the foreign dignitaries: iii 11.

[20] xl 8; perhaps implied by i 4.6.

[21] Hahn, *Rom und Römanismus*, 130–31, gives some of his loan words; Oldfather, *Diodorus of Sicily*, I, Loeb edition, xiii–xiv, discusses some of his stumblings. A claim to learning Latin is one way of establishing legitimacy with a Greek audience: see also Dion. Hal., *AR* i 7.2.

[22] Cic., *Balb.* 9.24. Individual enfranchisements are listed by E. Badian, *Foreign Clientelae (264–70 B.C.)*, 302–8, and discussed by A. Sherwin-White, *Roman Citizenship*[2], 291–311. The evidence is skewed because of Cicero's *Verrine Orations* and his close ties with Sicily.

tatius Diodorus of Lilybaeum, whom Sulla enfranchised and Verres robbed.[23] But Lilybaeum is quite far from Agyrium, and Diodorus is a common name. Because he knew Latin and notes that he witnessed a Roman embassy in Egypt in about 59 (i 83.8–9), it is fashionable to speculate that Diodorus was actually serving on the mission, perhaps as translator.[24] But Diodorus emphasizes his special access to written materials in Rome (i 4.2–4). If he also had first-hand knowledge of Roman political practices, he should have mentioned that. And Diodorus did not just visit Egypt; he states specifically that he lived there,[25] using documents in Alexandria (iii 38.1). There is no reason to assume that he had close contact with Roman politicians while in Egypt or in Rome.

Although Diodorus notes that he came from the Sicilian town of Agyrium, that adds little information about his life. Like many Sicilian cities during the late Republic, Agyrium must have been on the decline. Lying under the modern town of Agira, it was situated on the northern ridge of the exceptionally fertile eastern plain and fed by the Chrysas River (modern Dittaino). It was also well located for commerce, being on the central route from Katana to Panormus (modern Palermo) and connected by road to Morgantina.[26] At one time, the polis may have been fairly large, for, according to Diodorus, Timoleon settled ten thousand Greek colonists there during a period when the city enjoyed exceptional wealth and notable architecture.[27] The city later figures prominently in the *Verrine Orations*. Cicero argues that Verres' ex-

---

[23] 2 *Verr.* iv 37.

[24] Sartori, *Athenaeum* 74 (1984), 535; Rawson, *Intellectual Life*, 16.

[25] κατὰ τὴν γεγενημένην ἡμῖν ἐπιδημίαν κατ᾽ Αἴγυπτον (i 83.9).

[26] DS xiv 95.2.

[27] xvi 82.5, 83.3. The ten thousand colonists may be an exaggeration: so H. Westlake, *Essays in Greek Historians*, 290. The surrounding material may come indirectly from Timaeus (so Meister, "Die sizilische Geschichte," 120–29), but the discussion about Agyrium is so detailed that it is likely Diodorus's own observation. Diodorus is proud of Sicily's fertility generally: iv 24.1, 82.5, 84.1; v 2.4–5, 69.3. For a discussion of the fourth-century bronzes produced in Agyrium, see S. Garraffo, *AIIN* 23–24 (1976–1977), 9–50.

tortion and heavy taxation impoverished the wealthy farming town,[28] driving numerous owners off land that subsequently lay untilled.[29] Because the speeches were never delivered, however, Cicero may have felt free to exaggerate the current wealth of Agyrium and, consequently, the damage caused by his opponent.[30] Agyrium's coinage, in fact, offers a different picture. Sicilian municipalities were permitted to issue bronze coins after the Roman conquest in 212 B.C.,[31] but only one specimen of the Agyrium issue has been identified.[32] Again, during the civil wars of the mid-first century, important Sicilian towns produced Roman coins reflecting various allegiances; none has been found from Agyrium.[33] Although the ancient site has not been systematically excavated, there is some reason to believe that little of importance will be discovered.[34] When Diodorus speaks of Agyrium's great buildings, he refers to the fourth century and makes no reference to contemporary conditions (xvi 83.3). If there were reason to boast

[28] 2 *Verr.* iii 27.67.

[29] E.g., Cicero, 2 *Verr.* 3.18.47, 3.31.73, 3.51.120–21.

[30] Most recently, S. Calderone, *Kokalos* 12–13 (1976–1977), 372–73; G. Manganaro, *ANRW* I.1, 449–50; S. Stone III, *AJA* 87 (1983), 12.

[31] M. Crawford, *Coinage and Money under the Roman Republic*, 103–5.

[32] E. Gàbrici, *La monetazione del bronzo nella Sicilia antica*, 120, no. 8 = S. Consolo Langher, *Contributo alla storia della antica moneta bronzea in Sicilia*, 216, no. 40. Even before Roman rule, Agyrian coins are never plentiful: see, e.g., Gàbrici; also *British Museum Catalogue Sicily*, 25–26; *McClean Collection* I, 247–48; *Weber Collection* I, 255–56; Consolo Langher, 193. After Agyrium's liberation, in 339/8, the subsequent small emission of Agyrian coinage could be explained either by Timoleon's grant to Agyrium of Syracusan citizenship (as many would read DS xvi 82.4: e.g., Westlake, *Essays*, 291) or by Agyrium's copying of the Syracusan type (so R. Talbert, *Timoleon and the Revival of Greek Sicily*, 188).

[33] Cf. Grant, *From Imperium to Auctoritas.*

[34] The Hellenistic necropolis has been identified, but no finds have been reported: G. Fiorentini, *Kokalos* 26–27 (1980–1981), 600; note the pessimism of L. Polacco, "La posizione del teatro di Siracusa nel quardo dell'architettura teatrale Greca in Sicilia," in ΑΠΑΡΧΑΙ: *Nuove ricerche a studi sulla Magna Grecia e la Sicilia in onore di Paolo Enrica Arias* II, 438. Some remains from the third century A.D. are described by G. Scibona, *ASM* 32 (1981), 333–59.

of his hometown, Diodorus's failure to do so would be highly uncharacteristic. Strabo does not even mention the city in his description of Sicily, written perhaps between 20 and 10 B.C.[35] Although Agyrium may not have been prominent in his own day, Diodorus himself must have been prosperous.[36] He traveled to Egypt, meeting priests and ambassadors (iii 11.3), and spent a large part of his life in Rome. Unlike similar Greek émigrés in the capital, he probably did not earn his living by tutoring. His criticism of the middle class suggests wealth (i 74.7), though he was not so hostile to democracy as he is usually portrayed. To Diodorus, that system can at times work well,[37] and he praises the actions of a democracy where a parallel account drawn from the same tradition does not.[38] It is rather that in democracies erratic and easily swayed masses facilitate the rise of demagogues.[39] Both his travels and his political sentiments suggest he enjoyed independent wealth.

References to how he composed the *Bibliotheke* establish a few more points in Diodorus's biography. He says that the work was thirty years in the making (i 4.1). Because an event

[35] vi 2.1–9; on the date: Stone, *AJP* 87 (1983), 19, n. 65.

[36] Cf. B. Farrington, *Diodorus Siculus Universal Historian*, 5; Rawson, *Intellectual Life*, 92.

[37] xii 11.3; cf. xi 68.5–6.

[38] Cf. xx 93.6–7 with P. *Berol.*, 11632 = *FGH* 533 F 2.

[39] E.g., xv 58.1; xix 5–10; xxv 8; esp. xix 1.1–8; or they show poor judgment (xiii 95.1); and specific groups and excesses ruin a democracy (i 74.7, 76; xv 40). Sartori, *Athenaeum* 72 (1984), 492–536, sees Diodorus as supporting monarchy in the early books. But the echo at v 42.1 is too faint to prove Diodorus imposed it on Euhemerus, and Diodorus preserves the tradition in Agatharchides of opposition to the Ptolemaic monarchy (Gozzoli, *Athenaeum* 56 [1978], 58–79): DS iii 12–14 = Phot., *Codex* 250, 23–29, 447b; 39.5–9 = Phot. 82–83, 456b–457a; 48.7 = Phot. 102, 459a–b. Moreover, Diodorus (ii 38.6) has democracy developing naturally out of monarchy, whereas Arrian, probably following Megasthenes more closely here than did Diodorus (Stein, *RE* 15.1, 254), describes the Indians only as becoming ἐλευθέρους (*Ind.* x 8 = *FGH* 715 F 16). Diodorus also has Zeus replace impiety on earth with democracy (v 71.2), and assumes that independence creates political equality (xx 79.3).

he witnessed in Egypt can be dated to 59, he must have begun his research by then.⁴⁰ The latest event mentioned in the extant *Bibliotheke* is Octavian's expulsion of Greeks from Tauromenium and their replacement by a Roman *colonia* (xvi 7.1). Diodorus offers no date for that event. But Appian notes that, in his struggle with Sextus Pompeius in 36, Octavian found himself barred from Tauromenium as he searched for a safe port (*BC* v 109). Cassius Dio adds that certain unnamed Sicilian towns were punished by Octavian for refusing to surrender during the actions of 36 (xlix 12.5). Thus Octavian probably took vengeance on Tauromenium soon after 36 by colonizing the town.⁴¹ The thirty years of research and writing, then, must have spanned approximately 60 to 30 B.C. Diodorus may have lived comfortably and worked at a leisurely pace despite his claim to having undergone trouble and danger in writing his history (i 4.1).

The evidence suggests that Diodorus spent a great deal of time in Rome, perhaps coming as early as 56, but certainly being there by 46, and apparently remaining until the completion of his work in around 30. Although he was probably wealthy, there is no indication that Diodorus knew Roman politicians or had entrée to Roman society. More about Diodorus's life and work can be surmised from the terminal dates of the *Bibliotheke*.

⁴⁰ See n. 1, above. The thirty years must refer to both the research and writing: see Sartori, *Athenaeum* 61 (1983), 549, against G. Zecchini, *RIL* 112 (1978), 19, and Burton, *Diodorus Siculus Book I*, 42–44.

⁴¹ Most recently, M. Reinhold, *From Republic to Principate: An Historical Commentary on Cassius Dio's "Roman History" Books 49–52 (36–29 B.C.)*, 32, with bibliography. Cassius Dio (liv 7.1) later specifies that Augustus resettled most of Sicily and established Roman colonies in 21, and some use that to date the Roman colony at Tauromenium (bibliography in Reinhold). But G. Manganaro, "La provincia romana," in E. Gabba and G. Vallet, *La Sicilia antica* II.2, 451, offers epigraphical evidence that the colony at Tauromenium was established immediately after the Sicilian War. Further, Diodorus claims that the work took thirty years, and it is known that he was doing research in Egypt by 59; cf. C. Rubincam, *AJA* 89 (1985), 521–22.

THE TERMINAL DATES

In the introduction to book i, Diodorus makes clear that he will begin with the prehistoric, or mythological period,[42] but his statements on where he intends to conclude are conflicting. In one passage (i 4.7), he promises to bring his work down to the year 60. That, in fact, is his actual stopping point: though book xl is highly fragmentary, Photius indicates that Pompey's conquest of Judea in 63 occurs midway through that final book.[43] The number of years included in any given book of the *Bibliotheke* generally decreases as Diodorus approaches his own time, with the earliest completely extant book of the historical period, xi, covering thirty years and the latest, xx, encompassing a mere nine.[44] Books xxi to xxxix average a little more than twelve years each. Book xl contains events at least as far back as 69,[45] and the last datable fragment concerns the Catilinarian conspiracy of 63 (xl 5). It could not have gone much beyond 60.

Despite the certainty of where he actually stopped, in the opening prooemium Diodorus gives two substantially different terminal dates. At one point he declares unambiguously that he will conclude with the year 60, establishing that date by reference to Olympic festival, Athenian archon, and the beginning of the Gallic War (i 4.7). A few sentences later, however, he announces that his work will end with the 730th year after the first Olympic Festival (i 5.1). Because he uses the traditional date of 776 for the latter (cf. also vii 5.1, 8), he intends

---

[42] i 3.2, 4.6, 5.1; iv 1.1–4; xl 8.

[43] περὶ τὸ μέσον: *Codex* 244, 380a.7. Whether Photius meant the chronological or quantitative midpoint cannot be determined.

[44] Cf. Laqueur, *Hermes* 46 (1911), 337.

[45] xl 1a–b. Episodes of 71 B.C. involving the Cilician pirates (xl 1) may only be background for Pompey's subsequent dealings with them. If Diodorus was using an episodic, rather than an annalistic arrangement, he may still have been following Posidonius. On Posidonius's use of summary, see E. Gabba, "Posidonio, Marcello, e la Sicilia," in ΑΠΑΡΧΑΙ: *Nuove ricerchea studi sulla Magna Grecia e la Sicilia antica in onore di Paolo Enrica Arias* II, 611–14.

CHAPTER SIX

to end with the year 46. He then attaches the beginning (ἀρχή) of the Gallic War to that date, and concludes by working his chronology from the end of the Trojan War, 1,138 years before the end of his book, or again, 46.[46]

The confusion admits of no easy resolution. Appeal to a copyist's error will not do, because Diodorus works his calculations for the year 46 twice in the passage, counting down from the first Olympic festival and from the sack of Troy, arriving at the same conclusion each time.[47] Some have argued that, in equating the beginning of the Gallic War with 46, Diodorus or his source simply had the wrong date for that conflict.[48] This solution too fails, for elsewhere in the prooemium Diodorus gives the correct date for the beginning of that war, calculated by Olympiads (i 4.7). And, no matter how sloppy Diodorus might at times be, it is unthinkable that he could make such a gross error involving a contemporary event. Diodorus's statement that he intends to cover events to 46 cannot be explained away. In fact, in the early books Diodorus promises to include discussions of Caesar's invasion of Britain in its chronologically appropriate position.[49] Among contemporary historians Diodorus was especially precise with such anticipatory references.[50] He must have intended to treat Caesar's campaign near the end of his work.

The contradictions in the proem suggest that Diodorus at some point changed his mind as to when he would end the *Bibliotheke*, but failed to correct his text completely. He states explicitly that the part of the first prologue involving the terminal dates was written after he had finished his history,[51] and

[46] On the date of the end of the Trojan War: xiii 1.2; xix 1.10.

[47] Cf. C. Wachsmuth, *Ueber das Geschichtswerk des sikelioten Diodors* 1, 5.

[48] Schwartz, *RE* 5, 665; cf. Burton, *Diodorus Siculus Book I*, 40–42, generally. More radical emendations by Scaliger and others clearly do not work: see Wesseling in Eyring, *Diodori Siculi Bibliothecae Historicae Libri*, 1, 303–6.

[49] v 22.1 and esp. v 21.2: ἐν τοῖς οἰκείοις χρόνοις, a phrase used throughout: see Rubincam, *Phoenix* 43 (1989), 41, n. 7, and 50, n. 23; cf. iii 38.2.

[50] Rubincam, *Phoenix* 43 (1989), 39–61, and Chapter 4.

[51] i 4.6: Ἐπεὶ δ' ἡ μὲν ὑπόθεσις ἔχει τέλος. . . . Cf. R. Syme, *Sallust*, 219:

the aorist and perfect tenses confirm it. It appears that Diodorus initially intended to end the history in 46, but later decided to conclude with the beginning the Gallic War, in 60.[52] When revising the prooemium, he forgot to recalculate his figures relative to the First Olympiad, as well as to remove promises to discuss Caesar's campaigns.[53] The initial terminal date of 46 B.C. was probably also the year in which Diodorus began writing the work. That appears to be confirmed by references to Julius Caesar. Each time he mentions Caesar, save one, Diodorus notes his apotheosis.

These references are formulaic and differ substantially from Diodorus's usual phrase concerning deification; they reflect his special understanding of that particular event. The formula describing Caesar's divine election occurs three times in books iv and v and in sections of the *Bibliotheke* written or revised later.[54] In book iii (38.3–4), however, Diodorus refers to Caesar without mentioning his deification, suggesting that book iii was composed before that event. The consecration of Caesar's cult occurred on January 1, 42,[55] and that is taken as the terminus ante quem for book iii.[56] It is, however, impossible to be so precise, for in popular sentiment Caesar was being called a god from the day of his funeral in 44.[57] But it confirms the general picture of Diodorus beginning to write the *Bib-*

"A preface is often the latest portion of the work to be composed, or at least revised."

[52] On that date for the outbreak of war: see M. Gelzer, *Caesar: Politician and Statesman*, 84–85, and below n. 78.

[53] Laqueur, *Hermes* 86 (1958), 285–90, complicates his otherwise fine analysis by arguing tortuously for three different terminal dates, the last of which was unfulfilled.

[54] iv 19.2; v 21.2, 25.4. i 4.7 is clearly added after the *Bibliotheke* was completed; xxxii 27.1–3 was written in the late 30s.

[55] App., *BC* ii 148; Dio xlvii 18.3–6; cf. S. Weinstock, *Divus Julius*, 386.

[56] F. Vogel, "Die Veroffentlichung von Diodors Geschichtswerk," in *Verhandlungen der einundvierzigsten Versammlung Deutscher Philologen und Schulmänner in München*, 228–36, and generally followed: most recently, e.g., Zecchini, *RIL* 112 (1978), 19; Sartori, *Athenaeum* 72 (1984), 529.

[57] Weinstock, *Divus Julius*, 346–86.

liotheke around 46. Thus Diodorus probably devoted several years to research only, perhaps from 60 to 46. He then fixed 46 as his terminal date—not an insignificant year to a contemporary—and spent the following fifteen years composing the history. The *Bibliotheke* should not require three decades of continuous and arduous labor. But the timetable presented best fits the allusions in the text.[58]

CAESAR IN THE *Bibliotheke*

The initial terminal date of 46 probably marked the point at which Diodorus stopped his research and began writing. There was much to recommend it, for in that year Caesar celebrated his extraordinary triple triumph for victories against the Pompeians, and the world appeared to be at peace. When Caesar's assassination and the subsequent instability of the empire made that date seem inconclusive, Diodorus was offered an opportunity. He could have extended his *Bibliotheke* a mere two years, to 44, giving the work a more certain terminus. In the part of the prologue written after the *Bibliotheke* was finished, Diodorus divides his work into three periods: that before the Trojan War, from the War at Troy to the death of Alexander, and thence to the Roman invasion of Gaul which resulted in Caesar's magnificent victories (i 4.6–7). It would seem that Diodorus made the two man-gods, Alexander and Caesar, his signposts. If Diodorus had wanted to adjust his end point because of the assassination, nothing could have been more natural than to include Caesar's demise, allowing the reader to understand that, as in the case of Alexander, his *diadochoi* also would rend the world and its unity.[59] But ending with the year 60 produces a notable vacuum in the *Bibliotheke*. Along with Gelon, Caesar was Diodorus's greatest hero, and the new terminus served to eliminate most of his

[58] Cf. the analysis of Rubincam, *EMC/CV* 31, n.s. 6 (1987), 324–26.

[59] Diodorus produced an especially positive account of Alexander in book xvii (Drews, *AJP* 83 [1962], 391–92) and used Alexander frequently as a chronological marker: Walton, *Diodorus of Sicily* xii, Loeb edition, p. 335.

career from the history. Moreover, in the opening proem Diodorus argued that his work was superior to that of his predecessors because it alone brought events down to his own day (i 3.2–6); moving the terminus back 14 years weakened his claim. Other, more important considerations must have attracted Diodorus to the earlier date of 60, and it is necessary to examine more closely the chronology of composition.

At the end of his work, Diodorus disavows certain unspecified books of the *Bibliotheke* that were pirated and published before he had completed his revisions.[60] Now in Jerome's version of Eusebius's *Chronicle* is found the entry that in 49 B.C. Diodorus Siculus, a writer of Greek history, achieved fame.[61] A floruit in 49, however, makes little sense for a historian who apparently had no public persona and published his *Bibliotheke* around 30. And Diodorus is sufficiently boastful in the opening prooemium that he would have mentioned an earlier history, had he written one. The testimonium in Jerome is usually explained by assuming that in 49 there appeared the pirated material from the *Bibliotheke* to which Diodorus alludes. Consequently, his floruit was somehow associated with its appearance.[62] That explanation, however, faces serious objections. If Diodorus devoted his early years to research and began writing earnestly in the mid-40s, how much was worth pirating in 49? And how would Eusebius or Jerome, if the entry be his, have been able to date the unauthorized version so precisely?

Jerome's entry is itself troublesome and can be eliminated; that in turn casts light on Diodorus's revision of his terminal

---

[60] xl 8; perhaps implied by i 4.6. Evidence of an initial draft may be found in one family of manuscripts: see Murray, *JEA* 56 (1970), 170.

[61] "Diodorus Siculus Graecae scriptor historiae clarus habetur": R. Helm, *Eusebius Werke: Siebenter band: Die Chronik des Hieronymus*[2], 155.

[62] E.g., *Diodorus of Sicily* I, Oldfather, Loeb edition, vii, n. 1; most recently by Zecchini *RIL* 112 (1978), 19. Sartori, *Athenaeum* 61 (1983), 549, and *Athenaeum* 62 (1984), 530, suggests that Diodorus published the part covering Greek events first, in 49; hence Jerome's reference to Diodorus as "Graecae scriptor historiae." But then, what right would Diodorus have to complain about editions published before he had finished correcting them (xl 8)?

date. There are two versions of Eusebius's *Chronicle* extant:
Jerome's Latin edition and an anonymous Armenian translation. Neither is an exact reproduction of what Eusebius
wrote; each contains omissions, additions, and reorganized
material.[63] The Armenian version lacks most of the floruits
detailed by Jerome, including that of Diodorus. Jerome lists
the floruits of only four Greek historians: those of Herodotus,
Thucydides, Xenophon, and Diodorus. The first three are expected and, along with the other giants of the classical experience, must have been in the original Eusebian text. The reference to Diodorus stands out as the only mention of a
Hellenistic historian. Jerome himself supplied the floruits for
Roman writers of the first centuries[64] and probably added the
reference to Diodorus as well.[65] But what source could Jerome
have used to date Diodorus so precisely? There is a better explanation than the appearance of an earlier, pirated edition of
the *Bibliotheke*.

In the Armenian version is a table of authors that describes
Diodorus's work as a synopsis of history in forty volumes "up
to" Julius Caesar.[66] If the list was part of Eusebius's original
edition, there is an answer for Diodorus's strange floruit. Eusebius, who used Diodorus extensively in the *Chronicle* and
Praeparatio Evangelica, stated in his table of authors that the *Bibliotheke* went "up to" Julius Caesar, intending 60/59. Jerome,
however, for whom there is no reason to suspect that he read
Diodorus himself, might think Eusebius's phrase referred to
the year 49. His ascribing Diodorus's floruit to the same year
as the history supposedly ended would conform to practice:
Eusebius had placed Thucydides' floruit, for example, in

[63] The long, fierce debate over which version has primacy has now quieted:
see D. S. Wallace-Hadrill, *JTS* 106 (1955), 248–53.

[64] A. Wallace-Hadrill, *Suetonius: The Scholar and His Caesars*, 50–59.

[65] Cf. Helm, *Die Chronik des Hieronymus*[2], commentary.

[66] J. Karst, *Eusebius Werke: Fünfter Band: Die Chronik aus dem armenischen
Übersetzt*, 125, translates the Armenian as "bis auf." On the table of authors:
Schwartz, *RE* 6, 1378; cf. A. Mosshammer, *The Chronicle of Eusebius and
Greek Chronographic Tradition*, 140.

430,[67] close enough to the beginning of the war he chronicled to suggest how that date originated.

If Jerome's testimony is eliminated, there is no way of knowing what parts of the *Bibliotheke* were pirated or when. In fact, what is most important is the inference drawn from Diodorus's claim that the unauthorized parts were published before he completed the revisions. Although mistakes and unrevised material are glaringly evident even to the casual reader, Diodorus believes that the final version of the *Bibliotheke* was completed, at least to his own satisfaction (cf. i 4.6). He gives no indication that, in a sudden haste to finish, he changed the terminal date from 46 to 60 simply because he grew tired and wanted to draw the work to a close.[68]

On the contrary, there is evidence that Diodorus had decided on the new terminal date at least a few years in advance of when he finished working. In book xxxii, after describing the Roman sack of Corinth of 146, Diodorus mentions that much later the city was restored by Julius Caesar and offers an extended eulogy of the Dictator (xxxii 27.3). This discussion of Caesar is markedly different from all other such references in the *Bibliotheke*. In the mythological section, Diodorus simply notes that events related to those that he is currently narrating involve Caesar and will be covered later.[69] Here, however, he elaborates on Caesar's personal qualities, many of which have nothing to do with the issue at hand. The surviving version, edited and preserved by the Constantinian excerpter, contains redundancy and awkward transition, which suggests that the original was even longer.[70] Diodorus is offering here a general character assessment of Caesar similar to those found so often in the *Bibliotheke* following the death of an individual.

The placement of Caesar's eulogy is surprising. By 44, the

---

[67] Helm, *Die Chronik des Hieronymus*[2], 115

[68] So Oldfather, *Diodorus of Sicily* I, Loeb edition, xix; Zecchini, *RIL* 112 (1978), 20; and Rubincam, *EMC/CV* 31, n.s. 6 (1987), 326.

[69] iii 38.2; v 21.2, 22.1.

[70] Cf. Walton, *Diodorus of Sicily* XI, Loeb edition, 443, n. 2.

colony at Corinth was thriving.[71] Although precisely when Caesar planned it is uncertain,[72] in the *Bibliotheke* Caesar was moved to found the colony when he actually visited the site (θεασάμενος τὴν Κόρινθον); that could not have been after 47. Diodorus confirms this by putting Caesar's decision at a little less (σχεδόν) than a century after Corinth's destruction in 146.[73] Thus Corinth's rebirth fell within the initial scope of the *Bibliotheke*. Had Diodorus still intended to go down to the year 46, there would have been the proper opportunity to elaborate on it. Instead, his extensive praise of Caesar, far beyond what the single deed at Corinth demanded, suggests that, by the time he began writing book xxxii, he had already decided to abbreviate the *Bibliotheke* and used the refounding of Corinth for the ethical assessment of the politician he most admired. Of course it is possible that Diodorus inserted the judgment after he finished the *Bibliotheke*. But Caesar must have been mentioned in what became the final book of the history (at least for his role in the Catilinarian conspiracy). Had Diodorus decided abruptly to stop writing with the year 60, it would have been more natural to connect the assessment with the later events than to introduce it in a context recounted eight books earlier. The praise of Caesar suggests that by the time he was writing book xxxii, in about 34 or 33,[74] Diodorus had decided on a *Bibliotheke* of lesser extent than he had originally announced.

---

[71] Coins from that year: Grant, *From Imperium to Auctoritas*, 266. It is impossible to tell whether the colony was consecrated before the Ides of March.

[72] Z. Yavetz, *Julius Caesar and His Public Image*, 137–50, discusses dates between 49 and 45; on the evidence: *RE* suppl. 4, 1033.

[73] Although the Constantinian excerpter modified the very beginning of the sentence to create the time frame of his own day (κατὰ τοὺς τῆς παλαιᾶς ἡλικίας καιρούς; cf. Walton, *Diodorus of Sicily* XI, Loeb edition, 443, n. 1), there is no reason to suspect the phrase concerning the century hiatus is also contaminated.

[74] Books vary in length, in the nature of the material, and in the requirements of narrative. But as he wrote the forty books from ca. 46 to ca. 30 B.C., Diodorus produced on average two and a third books a year.

Other considerations confirm this conclusion. For the better part of his treatment of the late Republic Diodorus employed Posidonius's history. The precise number and nature of Posidonius's historical works, as well as their possible terminal dates, are unclear. But whether Posidonius's coverage ended in the mid-80s or went through Pompey's eastern campaign in 63,[75] it is evident that, by changing the terminal date of his own work to 60, Diodorus did not simply quit at the point when his main source ran out. If Posidonius's work did extend to 63, as appears likely,[76] Diodorus's revised terminus of 60 represents an especially conscious decision to stop just at the edge of the Caesarian period. Diodorus, in fact, leaves no doubt that the work ends precisely before Caesar's first consulship.[77] He says that his history will extend to the beginning of the Gallic War, which the Romans undertook and in the course of which as commander Caesar conquered the Celts and invaded Britain (i 4.7). He then rightly assigns the initiation of hostilities to the year 60,[78] indicating that he ends his history in the year before Caesar rose to prominence.

In accounting for Diodorus's new terminal date, attention has been drawn to Asinius Pollio's influential history. That work covered a period slightly beyond Diodorus's original

---

[75] The various terminal dates for Posidonius's work(s) are discussed by Càssola, *ANRW* II.30, 764, n. 104. In support of Jacoby's date of the mid-80s, add Malitz, *Die Historien des Poseidonios*, 32.

[76] Strasburger, *JRS* 55 (1965), 42–44.

[77] Cf. Zecchini, *RIL* 112 (1978), 12–15.

[78] i 4.7: τούτου δ' αἱ πρῶται πράξεις ἐπετελέσθησαν Ὀλυμπιάδος τῆς ἑκατοστῆς καὶ ὀγδοηκοστῇ κατὰ τὸ πρῶτον ἔτος ἐπ' ἄρχοντος Ἀθήνησιν Ἡρώδου. Holzapfel (see ap. crit. of Teubner edition, vol. I, ed. F. Vogel) suggested τρίτον for πρῶτον in order to bring the end of the *Bibliotheke* down to Caesar's involvement in Gaul in 58. The year of Herodes' archonship, however, is solidly fixed at 60/59: J. Kirchner, *RhM* 53 (1898), 389–90. Though technically correct (Gelzer, *Caesar*, 84–85), the insistence that the Gallic War began before Caesar's command may reflect Caesarian and Augustan propaganda, which attempted to shift the focus of the war from Caesar's questionable attacks on the Helvetii in 58: Zecchini, *RIL* 112 (1978), 12–15; cf. Sartori, *Athenaeum* 61 (1983), 547, n. 5, and 549.

plan, going down to Philippi in 42, or beyond.[79] It is argued that Diodorus eliminated the final part of the *Bibliotheke* because of possible competition from Pollio.[80] But Pollio published later than did Diodorus;[81] and, in any case, the appearance of a Latin history would hardly have been a deterrent to a Greek work. There were competing narratives for every period Diodorus wrote about, and Pollio's was not the only one covering the Caesarian period: both while the Dictator was alive and after his assassination, numerous Latin accounts of every bias were produced.[82] Indeed, Pollio, unlike Diodorus, was somewhat circumspect in his feelings about Caesar.[83] Surely there was room on the market for Diodorus's account as well.

Soon after the fall of the Republic, Romans looked back and identified the year 60, which witnessed the beginnings of the so-called First Triumvirate, as an essential stage in the Republic's demise.[84] Pollio chose that year for the start of his history, for, as Horace claimed, that was the beginning of the civil unrest. Others followed in assigning it significance.[85] The

[79] See the well-tempered discussion by E. Gabba, *Appiani bellorum civilium liber quintus*, xxxvii–xli, and the doubts of E. Badian, *CR* n.s. 8 (1958), 161–62.

[80] P. Burde, "Untersuchungen zur antiken Universalgeschichtsschreibung," 90–91.

[81] Pollio's work is celebrated by Horace in *Ode* 2.1, now generally dated to 30–23. Horace appears to be indicating that the history is quite fresh, indeed perhaps still incomplete: see G. Zecchini, *ANRW* II 30.2, 1281–86; Nisbet and Hubbard, *Commentary on Horace: Odes II*, 9–10.

[82] M. Schanz and C. Hosius, *Geschichte der römischen Literatur*⁴ I, 349–51; most recently, Rawson, *Intellectual Life*, 111 and 229.

[83] Cf. Nisbet and Hubbard *Commentary on Horace: Odes II*, 9; Gabba, *Appiano e la storia delle guerre civili*, 119ff.; Suet., *Iul.* 56.4, records that Pollio criticized Caesar's memoirs for its historical inaccuracies.

[84] E. Gruen, *The Last Generation of the Roman Republic*, 90.

[85] *Odes* 2.1.1. R. Syme, *The Roman Revolution*, 8 with nn. 3 and 4. Gabba, *Appiano e la storia delle guerre civile*, argues that Pollio prefaced his narrative with a summary of Roman history going back to the Gracchi. The decision by Pollio to start in 60 misled subsequent historians into thinking that the

decision to change a terminal date from 46 to 60 could not have been arbitrary: Diodorus wanted to eliminate much of Caesar's career and the fall of the Republic from his narrative. To understand Diodorus's motives requires an appreciation of Caesar's role in the *Bibliotheke* and Diodorus's place within Roman society.

Although Diodorus excised the most important part of Caesar's life from his narrative, allusions to his later achievements are included in the first few books of the *Bibliotheke*. There the dominant theme is the many mythological and prehistorical figures who displayed clemency (ἐπιείκεια) and aided the world with their gifts of law and culture; consequently, they were worshiped as gods by humanity. Heracles and Dionysus are especially prominent, but Diodorus details the accomplishments of numerous others who were later venerated (see Chapter 3). Within the mythological material of books i–vi, the only figure from the modern period whose deification is mentioned is Julius Caesar. Diodorus compares him to mythohistorical individuals similarly venerated, noting that the Celtic city of Alesia was founded by Heracles and remained unconquered until Caesar's siege there (iv 19). Further, Caesar's invasion of Britain was a feat that neither Heracles nor Dionysus had accomplished.[86] A comparison with Heracles, greatly honored at Agyrium,[87] was Diodorus's highest compliment. No other historical character is so esteemed in the early books; even Alexander the Great is introduced into the narrative to show the *limitations* of his conquests.[88] Then in book xxxii, Diodorus portrays Caesar as a founder of cities

---

"First Triumvirate" was formalized in that year, instead of 59: R. Hanslik, *RhM* 98 (1955); see also Gruen, *Last Generation*, 88–90, and Nisbet and Hubbard, *Horace: Odes Book II*, 12. Diodorus's terminus was probably based on the date of the initial agreement of Pompey and Caesar, in 60.

[86] v 21.2; cf. iii 38.2.

[87] DS iv 24.1–6; *Catalogue of Greek Coins in the British Museum: Sicily*, 25–26.

[88] i 55.3; ii 37.3; the reference at iii 47.9 is neutral.

and a lawgiver, as a possessor of humanistic traits such as ἐπιείκεια (*clementia*), and thus as one justly called a god. Despite
avoiding a narrative of Caesar's accomplishments, Diodorus
is able to extol the Dictator in the earlier books of the *Bibliotheke*.[89]

It is, in fact, Diodorus's treatment of deification generally
and Caesar's specifically in the early books that offers insight
into his decision to abridge his work. In the prologue to book
i, Diodorus explains that one obvious purpose of history is
that the praise of great benefactors to humanity might induce
others to follow in their paths. The example he uses is Heracles, who, for his great deeds, was immortalized and given
divine honors (i 2.1–5). In the proem to book iv Diodorus
restates his purpose. Myths describe the great benefactors
who are worshiped by subsequent generations. Moreover, in
every instance, "the voice of history" (ὁ τῆς ἱστορίας λόγος)
sings their praise (iv 1.4–6).

Central to Diodorus's work is the idea that by praising noble deeds of the past the historian spurs on readers to similar
accomplishments (see Chapter 2). In fact, history's own eulogy is more effective and longer lasting than posthumous divine honors. Diodorus asserts that even after being deified
Heracles was disparaged; therefore, it is up to history to reveal
his greatness.[90] Within the historical part of the *Bibliotheke*,
Diodorus notes that some who were once deified have lost
that honor. Diocles of Syracuse was considered a hero and
given a temple, but within ten years his shrine was torn down
to make way for city walls.[91] Demetrius the Besieger, for his
benefactions to the people of Sicyon, was worshiped as a
founder, but "time, . . . whose continuity has been broken by

---

[89] Besides that in xxxii, there are also references to Caesar as god at i 4.7; iv
19.2; and v 25.4; and an allusion to him at v 20.2: cf. Suet., *Iul.* 7.1.

[90] i 2.4–5; iv 8.5. On the questionable status of Heracles' divinity, see
S. Price, *Rituals and Power: The Roman Imperial Cult in Asia Minor*, 33, n. 33.

[91] xiii 35.2; xiv 18. It is not important whether Diodorus confuses this Diocles with the legendary lawgiver: on which, see G. de Sanctis, *SIFC* 11 (1903)
= *Scritti minori* I, 31–42.

changes of conditions, has invalidated these honors."[92] Most notable in this group is Gelon, the man whom, along with Caesar, Diodorus admires most. Gelon was honored as a hero, but his monument was torn down by the Carthaginians and his towers destroyed by a jealous Agathocles. No matter, remarks Diodorus, for history serves as a remembrance of Gelon's deeds and provides his immortality (xi 38.5–7). Diodorus bears witness to how frequently divine honors were accorded in the Hellenistic Age (see Chapter 3, n. 88). The civil wars at Rome brought about a civil war in the Heavens, with generals appealing to gods as patrons and benefactors. From Sulla to Octavian, Roman politicians claimed the support of godheads as an instrument of propaganda, and victors laid claim to the gods of the vanquished.[93] Save for Octavian, few others who claimed divinity or the special protection of the gods survived.[94] Diodorus himself records that a promagistrate of Asia, Q. Mucius Scaevola, received divine honors from the people of his province,[95] yet was later slaughtered by the younger Marius.[96] Virtually all major politicians at the end of the Republic vied for divine honors, either by direct claim to a godhead or by having grateful communities

[92] xx 102.3 (Geer). See also x 10.2 on Pythagoras. At x 12 honors increase with time, because they are history's honors, not those written on stone—certainly an echo of Thuc. ii 43.3.

[93] E.g., Octavian assumed the support of Neptune, the former protector of Sextus Pompeius: see Gosling, *AJP* 107 (1986), 586–89, and J. Evans, *ANSMN* 32 (1987), 111–12. Pompey had actually claimed the title of son of Neptune: P. Hill, *Numismatica e antichità classiche: Quaderni ticinesi* 4 (1975), 172 and 186.

[94] E.g., Pompey and the elder Marius (Pliny, *NH* vii 95; xxxiii 150; cf. Nock, *JHS* 48 [1928], 30, n. 48 = Nock, *Essays*, 144. n. 48), Caesar (Servius on Virgil, *Ecl.* v 29), and Antony (Fraser, *Ptolemaic Alexandria* i, 205, with notes) all associated themselves with Dionysus.

[95] xxxvii 6: τιμῶν ἰσοθέων ἔτυχε; Diodorus's standard phrase for complete deification: cf., e.g., i 90.2. For a comparison with *OGIS*, 437–39, see Chapter 3. The date and nature of Scaevola's promagistracy are in doubt; see E. Badian, *Athenaeum* 34 (1956), 104–23, who places it in 94; contra *MRR* ii suppl., 42.

[96] xxxviii/xxxix 17; cf. xxxvii 29.5.

respond to a benefaction.⁹⁷ Diodorus's statement on how, over time, the people of Sicyon ceased to honor Demetrius suggests that for Diodorus such acts could be fleeting gestures. Most of all, it is Caesar with whom Diodorus is concerned. Although honored as a god by the Greeks as early as 48,⁹⁸ that was not enough to safeguard his life; nor, the past had shown, could posthumous honors even assure his immortality. With divine status counting for little, Diodorus qualifies his references to Caesar's deification. Throughout the *Bibliotheke*, in almost every passage involving the act of apotheosis, he says that the individual *received* divine honors: τιμῶν ἰσοθέων ἔτυχε or a similar construction.⁹⁹ Remarkably, in each of the five instances in which Caesar's deification is alluded to, Diodorus states precisely that he has been *called* a god.¹⁰⁰ It is found in the opening prooemium, in the early books, and in a very late book. It is so formulaic and consistently different from that used for the dozens of other apotheoses that Diodorus must have intended the distinction. Only once elsewhere does Diodorus describe an individual as being "called" a god, instead of being "honored" as one. Darius I of Persia so fairly ruled Egypt that only him of all pharaohs did the Egyptians address (προσαγορεύεσθαι) as a god while alive.¹⁰¹ Only five chapters earlier, however, Diodorus writes that the Egyptians custom-

---

⁹⁷ Nock, *JHS* 48 (1928), 30–37 = Nock, *Essays*, 144–52; most recently Gosling, *AJP* 107 (1986), 586–89.

⁹⁸ A. Raubitschek, *JRS* 44 (1954), 65–75.

⁹⁹ i 2.4, 17.2, 22.2, 24.7; ii 38.5, etc.: on the "mythological characters," see Chapter 3, n. 80. xi 38.5, 66.4, etc.: on the "historical characters," see Chapter 3, n. 88. The τυγχάνω formula itself is particularly Diodoran: see Chapter 3, n. 81.

¹⁰⁰ ὁ διὰ τὰς πράξεις προσαγορευθεὶς θεός (i 4.7); τοῦ διὰ τὸ μέγεθος τῶν πράξεων θεοῦ προσαγορευθέντος (iv 19.2); ὁ διὰ τὰς πράξεις ἐπονομασθεὶς θεός (v 21.2); ὁ κληθεὶς θεός (v 25.4); ὁ διὰ τὰς πράξεις ὀνομανθεὶς θεός (xxxii 27.3).

¹⁰¹ i 95.5; Diodorus's intrusion: most recently, Murray, *JEA* 56 (1970), 149, n. 1.

arily worshiped all their living kings as gods.[102] Diodorus must mean that Darius was the only Persian whom the Egyptians wished so to esteem. After Alexander's conquest, it is unlikely that Egyptians would recall with special honors the memory of the Persian monarch. Diodorus may, then, be qualifying Darius's status, as well as suggesting transient honors.

Diodorus venerated Caesar, so he implies no criticism in making the distinction concerning his deification. Indeed, in the eulogy in book xxxii, Diodorus argues that by his native character and his accomplishments Caesar was elected justly (δικαίως: xxxii 27.3). But as well, Caesar merits something else, which offers a clue to Diodorus's treatment of the Dictator: "It is therefore just that this man and his high standard of conduct should receive our full approval and that we should by our history accord him enduring praise for his generosity" (Walton). The same sentiment is repeated later in the chapter, and it is clear that history's lasting praise of Caesar (τὸν αἰώνιον ἔπαινον) is to Diodorus a more transcendent honor. Diodorus makes the same argument on behalf of his other favorite, Gelon, stating that history proved a better preserver of his immortality than the fleeting honors bestowed by mortals (xi 38.5–7).

While Diodorus was writing, threats to Caesar's immortality were already arising—from Caesar's enemies and friends. The Epicurean philosopher, Philodemus, influenced many Romans of republican sentiment. He spoke out against the "new gods," having in mind Caesar's recent election.[103] From the other side, Octavian began claiming association with the godhead through Caesar's divinity. Diodorus had reason to abhor Caesar's nephew; consequently, he must have felt that Octavian's proximity to divine status cheapened Caesar's own

---

[102] i 90.3, a passage following logically from material thought to be Diodorus's: contra, Murray, *JEA* 56 (1970), 148 n. 4.

[103] On νέοι θεοί in *Peri Theon* iii 10, see Momigliano, *JRS* 31 (1941), 157.

183

deification. Caesar's deification is qualified because Diodorus anticipates that it will not last.

Tensions within the *Bibliotheke* begin to converge. At some point and probably by 34 or 33, despite his sincere affection for Caesar, Diodorus decided to exclude from his work a formal treatment of Caesar's life, along with the fall of the Republic. He was content instead to emphasize tangentially in the early books the true immortality that history, rather than contemporaries, can bestow upon Caesar. The decisions to eliminate most of Caesar's accomplishments from the *Bibliotheke* and yet to emphasize his immortality through history appear contradictory. But contemporary forces influenced the composition of Diodorus's work. In the previous chapter it was shown that Diodorus is ambivalent about the Roman Empire; the remainder of this chapter discusses how, while writing the *Bibliotheke*, Diodorus may have been isolated in the imperial capital and hostile toward its ruler, Octavian. Writing of the fall of the Republic in a manner sometimes unflattering to participants could prove dangerous to the Greek émigré. And retailing the deeds of Caesar would require great subtlety and tact in an age when the legacy of *Divus Iulius* was so controversial. Social and political considerations played their parts in shaping the *Bibliotheke*. It will be profitable to explore conditions that might have influenced Diodorus to change the terminal date of the *Bibliotheke*.

INTELLECTUAL AND SOCIAL PRESSURES

Diodorus's long stay in the imperial city began after his visit to Egypt. He probably came to Rome around 56 and remained there at least to 30. Diodorus may have been independently wealthy: he voices a dislike of the masses and lived in Egypt as long as four years, apparently as a tourist; he makes no mention of teaching or of any sort of work to sustain him while writing his history. Tutoring in rhetoric, a common means of employment for emigrant Greeks, seems an unlikely occupation for Diodorus, whose work is conspicuously lacking in rhetorical embellishment.[104] Despite his appreciation of certain Roman political figures, especially Caesar and Pompey, there is no reason to suspect that he made their acquaintance. He dedicates his work to no friend or patron and not once in the extant *Bibliotheke* indicates a personal familiarity with any public figure. Diodorus may have lived as an outsider in Rome—secure enough to write his history without otherwise working, but lacking the social and political contacts that wealth often brings.

By the time Diodorus arrived in Rome, educated Greeks had long been prized as teachers and intellectuals.[105] But especially since the Mithridatic Wars, as Rome grew more receptive to eastern ideas, they were appreciated for their scholarly writings in rhetoric, grammar, poetry, and history.[106] *Graecia capta*, as it was to be termed, virtually monopolized certain professions at Rome.[107] Although many intellectuals were brought there as slaves,[108] others were drawn to the capital of their own accord, during times of war and peace.[109]

[104] Palm, *Über Sprache und Stil*, 110; Hornblower, *Hieronymus of Cardia*, 272, n. 10; and F. Lasserre, "Prose grecque classicisante," *Le classicisme à Rome aux 1ers siècles avant et après J.C.*, Fondation Hardt, *Entretiens* 25, 153–63. On the speeches in the *Bibliotheke*, see Chapter 4.

[105] Evidence collected by M. Beard, *JRS* 76 (1986), 37–38; add Plut., *Aem.* 6.5.

[106] T. Wiseman, *Clio's Cosmetics: Three Studies in Greco-Roman Literature*, 154–55; M. Crawford, in Garnsey and Whittaker, *Imperialism in the Ancient World*. For Roman opposition to Greek ideas, see most recently, E. Jenkinson, *ANRW* I.3, 711–13.

[107] Most *grammatici* were emancipated slaves: Suet., *Gram.* 3.4; cf. Rawson, *Intellectual Life*, 68–76.

[108] Examples in Rawson, *Intellectual Life*, 69–70. Because of Suetonius's *De Grammaticis*, knowledge of grammarians is disproportionate (Rawson, 68), but Philodemus hints that many philosophers also came as slaves: *Philodemi Volumina Rhetorica* II, ed. E. Sudhaus, 145. For example: Cornelius Epicadus (Suet., *Gram.* 12), Aetius Philologus (Rawson, *Intellectual Life*, 8), and probably the parents of Theodorus of Gadara (Bowersock, *Augustus and the Greek World*, 35).

[109] E.g., Asclepiades of Bithynia (E. Rawson, *CQ* n.s. 32 [1982], 358–70), Philodemus, and Strabo (Bowersock, *Augustus and the Greek World*, 126–27). The resolution of civil strife at Actium brought a fresh wave of Greeks from

Greek intellectuals enjoyed a privileged status, it having become fashionable for important Romans to include Greeks in their inner circles.[110]

Whether emancipated slaves or freemen, most of these Greeks had Roman patrons who offered support and social contacts.[111] The evidence is overwhelming that the Greek intelligentsia was closely associated with the Roman upper class.[112] Freed slaves could look to their previous owners as patrons[113] or develop new sponsors,[114] and those who had come voluntarily to Rome sought out or were drawn to important Romans.[115] Grammarians and rhetoricians needed so-

---

the East (Bowersock, *Augustus and the Greek World*, 122–23), most notably Dionysius of Halicarnassus who arrived in 30 B.C. For a fuller (though incomplete) list of foreign intellectuals in Rome, see A. Hillscher, *Jahrbücher für classische Philologie*, Suppl. 18 (1982), 355–444. Rawson, *Intellectual Life*, 3–18 and passim, fleshes out the list.

[110] On the Greek group around L. Licinius Lucullus, see Crawford, in Garnsey and Whittaker, *Imperialism in the Ancient World*, 205; on Pompey's entourage, see W. Anderson, *Pompey, His Friends and the Literature of the First Century B.C.*, 35–40, 54–56; Crawford, 203–4; Gold, *AJP* 106 (1985), 312–27. On the group around Caesar, Rawson, *Intellectual Life*, 17. G. Julius Polyaenus of Sardis, author of a three-volume work on Parthia (*FGH* 196) in 38 B.C., may have been in Rome because of Caesar: Jacoby, *FGH* II 2b, 622.

[111] T. Wiseman, "*Pete nobiles amicos*: Poets and Patrons in Late Republican Rome," in Gold, *Literary and Artistic Patronage*, 31–34. See R. Saller, *Personal Patronage under the Early Empire*, 41–65, for the nature and material aspects of patronage provided by the emperor in the early Principate.

[112] Most recently Rawson, *Intellectual Life*, 100–14, and Gold, *Literary and Artistic Patronage*. It would not matter much if Romans failed to embrace Greek philosophy, as argued by H. Jocelyn, *Bulletin of the John Rylands Library* 59 (1977), 323–66. The dynamics of Roman patronage of *Roman* writers still need investigation: see E. Badian, *CP* 80 (1985), 341–57.

[113] E.g., L. Cornelius Epicadus, who remained close to Sulla's family: Suet., *Gram.* 5, 8, 12; cf. Rawson, *Intellectual Life*, 72.

[114] E.g., Parthenius had Cornelius Gallus, first prefect of Egypt, as his patron and knew Cinna and Virgil; see W. Clausen, *GRBS* 5 (1964), 181–96.

[115] Asclepiades addressed at least one of his early medical works to a Roman (Cael. Aurel., *Morb. Chron.* 2.110; cf. Rawson, *Intellectual Life*, 60); Philodemus had Piso: see esp. *Anth. Pal.* 11.44, where Philodemus hopes for favors from him; cf. G. Williams, "Phases of Political Patronage of Literature in Rome," in Gold, *Literary and Artistic Patronage*, 10. Some philosophers were

cial connections to attract students. The rhetorical writings of Dionysius of Halicarnassus contain specific dedications and indicate direct social access to important Romans.[116] In the prologue to his *Roman Antiquities*, Dionysius announces his hope that the work will benefit the godlike Romans (ἰσόθεοι), from whom he received much support (i 6.4–5). He claims that he was helped in gathering information for the history by his personal acquaintance with knowledgeable Romans (i 7.3). Similar sentiments pointing proudly to contact with Romans are found in Strabo's *Geography*,[117] and are known to have been present in many works no longer extant.[118] The exception proves the rule: Nicolaus of Damascus, who had easy access to the most powerful men in the early Principate, was criticized for maintaining a philosophical distance from Roman society.[119]

Besides the support of the ruling class, Greeks living in Rome had each other. Dionysius, because most of his work is extant, supplies the best evidence,[120] and Strabo also refers to a great number of contemporary literati.[121] Although these

wealthy and less dependent on patronage and social contacts than grammarians and rhetoricians (Rawson, *Intellectual Life*, 79–83). Posidonius, for example, wrote a monograph for Pompey but denied Cicero's request.

[116] On his dedication to Q. Aelius Tubero, father of the consul of 11 B.C., and other Roman contacts, see Bowersock, *Augustus and the Greek World*, 130; S. Bonner, *The Literary Treatises of Dionysius of Halicarnassus*, 4–5; R. Ogilvie, *A Commentary on Livy Books 1–5*, 16–17.

[117] Bowersock, *Augustus and the Greek World*, 128–29. The powerful Aelius Gallus was Strabo's most notable contact.

[118] For the dozens of Greek dedications to Roman patrons and friends, see Rawson, *Intellectual Life*, 54–65.

[119] *FGH* 90 F 138.

[120] Many of the Greeks to whom he refers in his writings are not identifiable: see W. Roberts, *CR* 14 (1900), 439–42. Dionysius counts as a close friend Caecilius of Calacte, (*Pomp.* 777), who in turn knew Apollodorus of Pergamum (Quint. ix 1.12), Timagenes of Alexandria (*FGH* 183 T2b = Suda, s.v, Τιμαγένες), and possibly Theodorus of Gadara: Roberts, *CR* 14 (1900), 440–41; G. Kennedy, *Art of Rhetoric in the Roman World: 300 B.C.–A.D. 300*, 364.

[121] Strabo knows well the poet Diodorus Zonas of Sardis (xiii 4.9) and al-

complex groupings occur in the early Principate, there is abundant evidence of casual contact among the Greeks in Rome throughout the late republican period.[122] In the professions of grammar, rhetoric, and philosophy, such connections naturally arose through schools of thought and teacher-disciple relationships.

For their livelihood, historians were particularly dependent on teaching other disciplines or on patronage. Performing no obvious service in writing history, they occupied an anomalous place within the intelligentsia.[123] Especially revealing is a list from the mid-second century B.C. of the intellectual professions in Alexandria: seven groups are named followed by the entry, ἄλλων πολλῶν τεχνιτῶν; that presumably includes historians.[124] Juvenal bears witness that followers of Clio went begging unless they were willing to sell their wares to a wealthy patron.[125]

Diodorus, disclosing nothing about his relations with fellow émigrés and unmentioned by contemporaries,[126] is the only historian of all those in Rome during the late Republic or the Augustan period not known to be part of the professional teaching circle or to be well connected socially. Especially among his compatriots in Rome, Diodorus stands out. The depressed condition of Diodorus's homeland helps explain the paucity of Sicilian intellectuals in the late Republic.[127] But their frequent bilinguality and the long and close relations between Sicily and Rome afforded those few Sicilians entrée to

---

ludes to Dionysius of Halicarnassus (xiv 2.16), Nicolaus of Damascus (xv 1.72), Crinagoras of Mytilene (xiii 2.3), and Theophanes (xiii 2.3). It is uncertain whether he knew Posidonius: Strabo, *Geography* vii, frag. 60 (H. Jones), with *Strabo* III, Loeb edition, 383, n. 6 = Athen. xiv 657 f.

[122] See Rawson, *Intellectual Life*, 66–83, and passim.

[123] Cf. A. Momigliano, *The American Scholar* 47 (1978), 194 = *Sesto contributo*, 363.

[124] Andron of Alexandria (*FGH* 246 F 1), who takes it from Menecles of Barca (*FGH* 270 F 9) = Athen. iv 184 bc.

[125] *Sat.* 7.5–7; cf. 98–105.

[126] The earliest reference is Pliny, *NH praef.* 25.

[127] See n. 7.

the intellectual community in Rome.[128] During the last stages of the Republic, besides Diodorus only two other Sicilians have been identified as living and working in the capital. Caecilius of Calacte, a rhetorician of substantial repute, was part of a prominent intellectual circle.[129] The other, Sextus Clodius, also a rhetorician, was generously rewarded with confiscated property for his close association with the triumvir, Mark Antony.[130] Their names suggest they enjoyed Roman citizenship and perhaps the patronage of other important families.[131]

In contrast to the intellectual and social connections of Caecilius and Clodius, there are passing remarks in the *Bibliotheke* reflecting an author ill at ease in that society. Diodorus criticizes forensic orators, depicting them as sophists,[132] and several times attacks contemporary philosophers, accusing them of superficiality, moral laziness, and mercenary objectives.[133] Such attitudes would not endear him to the intellectual class at Rome, or to its patrons. Diodorus does imply having access to Roman sources, but that may be through the purchase of books rather than by entrance into the private libraries of Roman nobles.[134] Perhaps having enough money to sustain him

---

[128] Clodius (Suet., *Rhet.* 5), Caecilius (*Suda*, s.v., Κεκίλιος), and Diodorus (i 4.4) all knew Latin.

[129] On his social contacts, see Roberts, *CR* 14 (1900), 439–42; *RE* 3.1, 1174–75. The evidence for his dates is contradictory, although he may be older than Dionysius of Halicarnassus: see *RE* suppl. 7, 1106, and Bowersock, *Augustus and the Greek World*, 35, n. 5, contra *RE* 3, 1175.

[130] Cic., 2 *Phil.* 17.42–43. See further Brzoska, *RE* 4.1, 66–67, who, however, confuses him with Sextus Cloelius: D. Shackleton Bailey, *Cicero's Letters to Atticus* I, 376. See further, Appendix I.

[131] See Badian, *Foreign Clientelae*, 302–4, on Sextus Clodius; but Badian, 257, offers a cautionary note on assuming enfranchisement from Roman names.

[132] i 76; perhaps implied in ix 26.3.

[133] ii 29.5–6; ix 9; x 7.2–3.

[134] On i 4.2–4, as perhaps suggesting the personal acquisition of books, see Chapter 5, n. 3. The first public library was established by Asinius Pollio only in 39 (A. Marshall, *Phoenix* 30 [1976], 261); previously scholars depended on access to private holdings: see Marshall, 252–61, and Rawson, *Intellectual Life*, 40–42.

and feeling a certain alienation from his Roman masters and their Greek followers, he lived apart from society.[135]

Diodorus's views on the Empire also separated him from others in the Capital. Émigrés and guests were generally well disposed toward Rome. The two other Greek authors of the period whose works survive, Dionysius and Strabo, wrote appreciatively of the Roman Empire,[136] and other Greeks of the late Republic expressly attempted to flatter their hosts.[137] The spirit of adulation, if not affection, toward Rome was almost universal.

In the late 30s, however, as Diodorus neared completion of the *Bibliotheke*, Greek intellectuals were forced to choose not between Rome and its enemies, but between two Roman leaders. Soon afterward, the conflict came to be understood as a war between East and West.[138] In the East, Antony paraded as a Greek[139] and had already taken at least one Sicilian into his entourage.[140] Octavian held power in Italy, and many émigrés there were drawn to him—or switched allegiance in time.[141] Some simply stayed out of sight and survived.[142] It was not a time for an opinionated Greek writer to be without patrons or influential friends.

---

[135] Cf. Rawson, *Intellectual Life*, 92.

[136] Though their messages were complex: see Gabba, *CA* 1 (1982), 43–65.

[137] Rawson, *Intellectual Life*, 55. See also the sensitive comment by Murray, *JRS* 74 (1984), 236.

[138] Virgil, *Aen.* 8.685–86.; Florus 2.21; Philo, *Legatio ad Gaium* 144; *SibOr.* 3.350–80; cf. *Old Testament Pseudepigraphia* I, ed. J. C. Charlesworth, 358.

[139] He especially encouraged the cult of Dionysus: see n. 94.

[140] On Sextus Clodius, see previous discussion. For Antony's benefactions in the East, see R. Syme, *The Roman Revolution*, 262; most recently, L. Robert, "Inscriptions," in *Laodicée du Lycos: Le nymphée (campagnes 1961–63)*, 307–9.

[141] Syme, *The Roman Revolution*, 262, lists several; also Timagenes (*FGH* 88 T2) and possibly Theodorus of Gadara (Bowersock, *Augustus and the Greek World*, 35–36) and Nicolaus of Damascus (Bowersock, 135).

[142] For Greeks who came to Rome only after Actium, see Bowersock *Augustus and the Greek World*, 123; so too the Spanish Seneca the Elder and Porcius Latro: Rawson, *Intellectual Life*, 317. Several of the *grammatici* practiced the noninvolvement of Epicureanism and survived in Rome: Rawson, *Intellectual Life*, 317.

Diodorus was not harshly critical of Rome. He admired some of its leaders and understood the inevitability of imperialism. But there is a tone of provincial pride running through the *Bibliotheke*,[143] and Diodorus's moral imperatives demanded condemnation of certain behaviors, as Rome abandoned the practice of moderate rule. Living in the capital, Diodorus may have thought himself more outspoken than the fragments of his work make him appear.

Other critics displayed caution. Timagenes is the best-known example of a foreign intellectual who composed attacks on Rome. Yet, when Augustus banished him from court for anti-Roman sentiments, Timagenes burned an earlier work written in praise of the princeps.[144] He had begun his career by paying due respect to his host. Nor was he foolhardy, for he could still rely on powerful friends: expelled from Augustus's household, he sought refuge with the venerable Asinius Pollio. And Pompeius Trogus, who refused to put Rome in the center of his historical work, could claim through his family two generations of outstanding contacts within the Roman aristocracy.[145] Those who were outspoken were also well protected.

DIODORUS IN THE WORLD OF OCTAVIAN

While Diodorus may have been isolated in Rome, conditions in his mother country tested his restraint. Sicily was the major battleground during the First Punic War and by degrees became a Roman province. Required to pay a yearly tithe and harbor and pasture taxes during the late Republic,[146] Sicily also suffered from bloody slave revolts, uneven administration,[147] and finally the excesses of Verres. In the First Punic War, Rome had acted brutally toward the Sicilian town of

---

[143] Cf. Schwartz, *RE* 5, 663.

[144] Bowersock, *Augustus and the Greek World*, 125.

[145] Seel, *Eine römische Weltgeschichte*, 88–93.

[146] Sources collected and discussed by Goldsberry, "Sicily and Its Cities," 315–27.

[147] Cic., 2 *Verr.* ii 8–9.155.

Agrigentum, the home of the historian, Philinus. That may account for Philinus's strongly anti-Roman bias.[148] Diodorus grew up during the rule of Verres, but Octavian's war for the island in the 30s and its subsequent punishment were particularly devastating. A similar anti-Roman bias on Diodorus's part would be understandable.

In the *Bellum Siculum*, the island apparently was quick to embrace Sextus Pompeius. In return, he acted moderately,[149] and offered full Roman citizenship (Appendix I). Octavian's subsequent actions of revenge confirm Pompeius's popularity. Controlling the island with some forty-four legions,[150] Octavian imposed an indemnity of sixteen hundred talents, seized tracts of land for himself and his friends, and punished towns that had resisted.[151] Archaeology reveals that Morgantina, close by Diodorus's Agyrium, was destroyed in about 35, perhaps a calculated act by Octavian.[152] Strabo, describing a few decades later what had been Morgantina, confirms the evidence of the spade: πόλις δ' ἦν αὕτη, νῦν δ' οὐκ ἔστιν (vi 2.4). He notes that the central plain of Sicily, the Catania, on the fringe of which stood Agyrium, was practically depopulated (vi 2.6).

Near the end of his life, Caesar had proposed at the very least *Latinitas* for Sicily; Antony later claimed that Caesar had intended to offer the island the right to vote as well. When Pompey took control, he implemented the enfranchisement, an obviously popular move with Sicilians. After what he had done to the island, Octavian could not have competed for cli-

---

[148] Walbank, CQ 39 (1945), 11–12 = Walbank, *Selected Papers*, 90.

[149] Cassius Dio xlviii 17.4–6; cf. xlviii 17.2 on the the first time Pompey controlled the island. Velleius ii 73.3 says that Pompey supported his army by plunder, but his bias is clear (cf. Scramuzza, in *An Economic Survey of Ancient Rome* III, 251), as is that of Strabo at vi 2.4 (cf. Appendix I).

[150] App., *BC* v 127; cf. Orosius vi 18.33; including Lepidus's troops after they deserted.

[151] Indemnity: App., *BC* v 29; plundering: Dio xlix 12.5; on the personal holdings of Octavian and Agrippa: Hor., *Ep.* i 12; Plut. *Ant.*, 55.1; discussion of all literature by Goldsberry, "Sicily and Its Cities," 560, n. 139.

[152] Cf. Stone, *AJA* 87 (1983), 16–19.

ents there, and he was generally reluctant to extend the franchise outside of Italy.[153] As a result, Sicilians, save for the Mamertines, lost all their newly acquired rights.[154] Agyrium naturally shared the fate of the rest of Sicily.[155] With the surrender of citizenship came the reinstatement of taxation.[156] Sicily's economic and cultural status during the early Principate was substantially diminished.[157]

Octavian's victory cost the island dearly but released Italy from the fears of grain shortages and piracy.[158] Wishing to cover his own military deficiencies (this time Agrippa had saved him),[159] Octavian claimed that his triumph in Sicily had brought the civil war to a close.[160] He was nearly right. After defeating Pompeius, he stripped Marcus Lepidus of his army and power, while the other triumvir, Antony, suffered an embarrassing failure in Parthia. The ascendant Octavian used his victory to increase his popularity within Italy,[161] and a grateful and obedient Rome offered him his greatest honors to date. Cornelius Severus celebrated the new Caesar in an epic nar-

---

[153] Suet., *Aug.* 40.

[154] Most recently M. Finley, *A History of Sicily*, 148–52, and Stone, *AJA* 87 (1983). See Appendix I for further discussion.

[155] Pliny, *NH* iii 8.91.

[156] J. Carcopino, *La loi de Hiéron et les Romains*, 288–89, Scramuzza, in *An Economic Survey of Ancient Rome* III, 344, and Goldsberry, "Sicily and Its Cities," 520–21, argue that Antony's citizenship included immunity to the previous taxation, which, through Caesar's reforms, may have been the *stipendarium* (below, n. 184). (On the stipulation regarding grain in the pact of 39 [App., *BC* v 72; Dio xlviii 36.6; Plut., *Ant.* 32.2], see Carcopino, 287; cf. Goldsberry, 520.) Augustus must have reinstituted the *stipendarium* on Sicily, as indicated by Pliny, *NH* iii 8.88–91.

[157] See the trenchant remarks on Octavian's damaging influence by F. Vittinghoff, *Römische Kolonisation und Bürgerrechtspolitik unter Caesar und Augustus*, 123.

[158] App., *BC* v 67 and 74.

[159] E. Gabba, *HSCP* 75 (1971), 158–59. Octavian admitted this: Suet., *Aug.* 25.3.

[160] App., *BC* v 130. Later, after Actium, he called Pompey a mere pirate and harborer of slaves: *Res Gestae* 25.1.

[161] Dio xlix 15; App., *BC* v 130; Syme, *The Roman Revolution*, 233–34.

rative, *Bellum Siculum*,[162] and Virgil hailed him as a god,[163] a title formalized in many cities.[164] His image, cast in gold, was placed in the Forum, and a day of public thanksgiving was declared, to be observed henceforth.[165] Octavian himself wrote a poem, the *Sicilia*,[166] and promoted his victory on coins, both soon after the event and again two decades later.[167] Diodorus frequently boasted of his native land (see n. 27). Whether in Rome or in Sicily at the time, the brutal treatment of his mother country and the accompanying celebrations in Rome could not have made the historian well disposed to Octavian or the imperial city.

Because the *Bibliotheke* ended with the year 60, there may have been little in the work that pertained to the future autocrat. Even if Diodorus had been tempted to voice his opinion, fear may have interceded as he witnessed Octavian's proscriptions and brutal suppressions. The only preserved reference to Octavian involves Sicilian affairs. Early in the history, Diodorus discusses Tauromenium, a polis long-honored by Rome for its loyalty and one of only three Sicilian towns to which Rome offered a separate treaty.[168] Diodorus notes that, as a consequence of his war with Pompeius, Octavian expelled the Greeks from that city of great renown (ἀξιόλογον ἀξίωμα) and established there a Roman colony (xvi 7.1). He states it matter-of-factly and renders no judgment. But Diodorus did not hesitate to criticize similar Roman actions of a much earlier period. He suggests that Rome would have been censured by humanity at the end of the Second Punic War had it destroyed

---

[162] Quint. x 1.89.

[163] *Ecl.* i 6–8. The *Eclogues* were published by 35 (G. Bowersock, *HSCP* 75 [1971], 73–80), and *Ecl.* i should be dated to about then: L. Wilkinson, in *CHCL* II, 313–15; a better interpretation than 41, suggested by J. Santero, *Athenaeum* 61 (1983), 113–15.

[164] App., *BC* v 131.

[165] Sources in Taylor, *The Divinity of the Roman Emperor*, 134, n. 73.

[166] Suet., *Aug.* 85.2.

[167] Taylor, *The Divinity of the Roman Emperor*, 132.

[168] Cic., 2 *Verr.* ii 66.160, iii 6.13, v 19.49–50, v 22.56; App., *Sic.* 5.

Carthage, "the most distinguished city of all,"[169] and he later attacks Rome for destroying Corinth, Carthage, and Numantia, "cities of great prominence."[170] An implied criticism of Octavian for expelling Sicilians from Tauromenium, "a city of great renown," would not have been just his usual chauvinism. Diodorus saw great cities as products of the civilizing force of humanity, a theme pervading the *Bibliotheke* (see Chapter 3).

In book xxxii, written perhaps a few years after Octavian's conquest of Sicily, Diodorus praises Julius Caesar for rebuilding Corinth (xxxii 27). Earlier Romans had committed acts of cruelty, but Caesar's gesture earned him divine status justly (δικαίως), for he won it on the basis of his own character (ἀπὸ τῆς περὶ αὐτὸν ἀρετῆς). Of the dozens of apotheoses Diodorus describes, this is the only one where he judges the worthiness of the recipient, here emphasizing that Caesar gained his honors himself. There may be an implied contrast with Octavian, whose wealth, power, and name rested largely on the glory of Caesar. Octavian assumed the title *divi filius* in 42,[171] and by 38 was known by the inflated name of *Imperator Caesar divi filius*.[172] Diodorus may be signaling criticism of Octavian by emphasizing that Caesar was only "called" a god, as noted previously. For he indicates, as he did throughout the *Bibliotheke* and specifically with Caesar (xxxii 27.3), that only history's honors, and not those of mankind, are lasting and meaningful. By so doing, he affirms Caesar's accomplishments, as celebrated in history, without recognizing Octavian's claim to a formal association with them. No matter what title Octavian took in connection with his great-uncle, history alone would judge his worth. And, by stressing how Caesar

---

[169] πόλις ἐπισημοτάτη πασῶν: xxvii 17.1, on which see Chapter 4, pp. 104–7.

[170] τῶν ἐπιφανεστάτως πόλεων: xxxii 4.5; cf. on Corinth xxxii 27.1.

[171] Taylor, *The Divinity of the Roman Emperor*, 106; it is found on coins at least by the early 30s: Grant, *From Imperium to Auctoritas*, 47–50. On the name, see Weinstock, *Divus Julius* 399, n. 12.

[172] R. Syme, *Historia* 7 (1958), 181.

CHAPTER SIX

rebuilt a Greek city in contrast to earlier Romans who destroyed one, Diodorus may be offering a comparison with the
actions of Octavian. A portrait of Pompeius Magnus may have a similar intent.
Near the end of the *Bibliotheke* Diodorus praises the young
man who served as governor of Sicily in 82/1: "[Pompey] rendered his decisions with such unerring skill and such incor-
ruptibility that no one could hope to surpass him. . . . He
lived during his stay on the island with such austerity and so-
briety that the Sicilians were astounded, and marvelled at the
young man's display of character."[173] Diodorus here may be
following the account of Posidonius, a known admirer of
Magnus. But Pompey's Sicilian accomplishments were famous,[174] and, as a native, Diodorus probably wrote out of
personal belief. Diodorus fashioned this description of the
elder Pompey after Octavian had defeated his son and ravaged
Sicily. Sextus Pompey used coinage to remind Sicilians of his
father,[175] and Diodorus may well be suggesting a comparison
between the fair dealings in Sicily of the Pompeii, father and
son, and the actions of Octavian.

Another passage also carries the possibility of criticism.
Diodorus notes that the shrine of Mother Rhea at Engyum was
celebrated in his time throughout Sicily and held in special esteem at Agyrium. Votives of gold and silver were still being
offered (iv 80.4–5), but the precinct had recently lost its sizable
property holdings: "for up until now the goddess possessed
three thousand head of sacred cattle and vast holdings of land
so that they were the recipients of great revenues."[176] What
caused the loss of such great wealth? Verres had earlier re-

[173] ἀρετή: xxxviii/xxxix 20 (Walton).
[174] Cic., 2 *Verr.* iii 16.42; *Leg. Man.* 9.30, 20.61; Plut., *Pomp.* 10.2.
[175] E. Sydenham, *The Coinage of the Roman Republic,* 210–11.
[176] iv 80.6 (Oldfather's translation with modifications). Oldfather translates
βραχὺ γὰρ πρὸ ἡμῶν as "only a short time before our day." But in its only other
use (i 3.1), it means up to the point at which Diodorus is writing: compare it
with τὰς . . . πράξεις . . . τῶν καθ' αὐτοὺς καιρῶν (3.2) and τῶν . . . πράξεων
. . . μέχρι τοῦ καθ' ἡμᾶς βίον (3.3).

196

moved dedications from the shrine.[177] But the passage indicates a more recent event, and the permanent loss of temple land suggests instead the work of Octavian, who claimed parts of the island for himself and Agrippa (see n. 151). Diodorus's discretion would be understandable: it might be dangerous to accuse the *divi filius* of impiety. Perhaps the best Diodorus could do, when following the narrative of Polybius for events of the second century, was to say what Polybius did not: "we cannot properly judge the freedom of the ancients from avarice by the dishonest greed of present-day Romans. For in our lifetime (ἐπὶ καθ᾽ ἡμᾶς βίου) this people has, it appears, acquired a strong tendency to want more and more."[178] Julius Caesar and Pompey were the dominant Roman figures throughout much of Diodorus's adult life, and the historian praises them specifically for their lack of avarice.[179] Diodorus may have had most in mind someone he chose not to mention.

Diodorus praises Julius Caesar and Gnaeus Pompeius, both of whom treated Sicily favorably. Pompey's kindness is preserved in Diodorus's work, as discussed previously. Caesar's actions occurred in the period after the terminus of the *Bibliotheke*, but Cicero testifies to his benefactions. Even before Caesar proposed *Latinitas* for the entire island, many Sicilians were being granted full citizenship in the Dictator's name.[180] But Caesar must have done more, for Cicero, ever one to brag about his own patronage of provincials, admits that Caesar had done many other things for Sicily.[181] One way in which Caesar may have helped Sicily involves taxation. Collection of the tithe by tax farmers had produced serious corruption and suffering wherever it was imposed.[182] For the province of

---

[177] 2 *Verr.* iv 44.97–98; cf. v 72.186; on the town: iii 43.103.

[178] xxxvi 26.2 (Walton). Not in the parallel Polybius xxxi 22.

[179] Caesar: xxxvii 27.3; Pompey: xxxviii/xxxix 20.

[180] *Ad Fam.* xiii 36.1.

[181] "Multa illis [Siculis] Caesar, neque me invito, etsi Latinitas erat non ferenda": *ad Att.* xiv 12.1.

[182] Although in Sicily, alone among the provinces, the *decumani* were ap-

Asia, it is known that Caesar changed the method of taxation from the tithe to the *stipendium*, a fixed payment collected by the cities themselves.[183] Possibly Caesar had done the same for Sicily.[184]

If Diodorus's sympathies were affected by the way contemporary Roman politicians treated his homeland, he would naturally be hostile toward Octavian. But it would not be easy for a Greek émigré to attack the political and military leader of his host city. In the Principate, after the *Bibliotheke* was already published, Octavian displayed an interest in managing public opinion.[185] But even in the triumviral period, Octavian revealed himself capable of proscription and revenge, and he acted to suppress criticism. After the victory in the Sicilian War, Octavian published his own version of his actions throughout the troubled times, destroying the accounts of others.[186] Octavian's behavior and his enormous power would give pause to any historian not well disposed to Rome or its leader.

---

pointed locally, *publicani* were still responsible for the harbor and grazing taxes: G. Rickman, *The Corn Supply of Ancient Rome*, 39–40.

[183] Dio xlii 6.3; cf. App., *BC* v 4. Most recently, T. Drew-Bear, *BCH* 96 (1972), 471.

[184] The suggestion is frequently made, most recently by Rickman, *The Corn Supply of Ancient Rome*, 60.

[185] Senatorial transactions became private (Suet., *Aug.* 36); books were removed from library shelves (Suet., *Iul.* 56; a date of the mid-20s depends on when the chief librarian, Pompeius Macer, resigned his position, and there are serious problems with the chronology: *RE* 21.2, 2276–77); Augustus hinted that he might close the Palatine library (sometime after 20 B.C.: Hor., *Ep.* i 3.15–20); sacred prophecies were burned (Suet., *Aug.* 31.1); Antony's papers were selectively destroyed (in 29 B.C.: Dio lii 42.8); evidence was fabricated in 29 to deny M. Licinius Crassus his right to celebrate the *spolia opima* (Luce, *TAPA* 96 [1965], 215); Augustus viewed with disfavor anyone writing about him frivolously (Suet., *Aug.* 89.3); authors were punished for writing libelous pamphlets and their works burned (R. Syme, *The Augustan Aristocracy*, 410–12, for evidence and redating). For a different view, K. Raaflaub and L. Samons II, in K. Raaflaub and M. Toher, *Between Republic and Empire: Interpretations of Augustus and His Princeps*.

[186] App., *BC* v 130, 132.

There was not just Octavian to fear. Diodorus clearly admired the young Pompeius Magnus, but he avoided treating him as triumvir and enemy of Caesar when he altered the terminal date for the *Bibliotheke*.[187] Caution perhaps intervened, as many Pompeians and Liberators, admitted to the courts of the triumvirs, might find offense with a history recalling their roles in the recent civil wars.[188] Enemies can later reconcile and friends can have a falling out. Those dangers always exist for one writing contemporary history, but never more so than in the period of the Second Triumvirate.

The careers of a few *consulares* and *nobiles* illustrate the elasticity of Roman political loyalties during the period of upheaval.[189] Ap. Claudius Pulcher, though working for the older Pompey in 50,[190] was awarded the consulship in 38[191] and joined Octavian in defeating Sextus Pompey in Sicily.[192] M. Valerius Messalla Corvinus, who had associated with Caesar's assassins and had been proscribed by the triumvirs, was subsequently courted by both Antony and Octavian; he later held the consulship (31 B.C.) and enjoyed a distinguished career as orator and politician under Octavian.[193] L. Munatius

[187] Posidonius perhaps inspired some of the pro-Pompeian material, but the description at the beginning of xxxviii/xxxix 9 may be Diodorus's own attempt at a general eulogy after realizing that, with the *Bibliotheke* now ending before 48 B.C., Pompey would be denied a final ethical assessment. Diodorus may have begun his research in 60 under the inspiration of Pompey's achievements, but, by the time he began writing in 46, Caesar had become his focus: Rubincam, *EMC/CV* 31, n.s. 6 (1987), 327.

[188] Cf. Syme, *HSCP* 64 (1959), 58–59 = *Roman Papers*, 435–36.

[189] The evidence is scattered and tenuous, because many perished during the Civil War: Syme, *The Roman Revolution*, 236–44; the families reemerged in the 20s: Syme, *The Augustan Aristocracy*.

[190] Münzer, *RE* 3, 2853–54 (Claudius 298). He was the nephew of the homonymous consul of 54, a devoted follower of Magnus. They were related by marriage and Pulcher governed Greece on his behalf in 49 and 48: Münzer, *RE* 3, 2850 (Claudius 297); *MRR* II, 261, 276.

[191] *MRR* II, 390

[192] Syme, *The Roman Revolution*, 237. He may have been with Antony in 43: *MRR* II suppl., 16.

[193] Syme, *The Augustan Aristocracy*, 200–7.

Plancus, who had served Julius Caesar loyally, had extensive dealings with the tyrannicides. He subsequently shifted to Antony and then, in time, to Octavian.[194] "Dubia, id est sua fide," Velleius (ii 63.3) said of him. Cn. Domitius Ahenobarbus, proscribed in 43 but surviving to serve as admiral of the fleet for the Liberators, had similar fortunes, attaching himself first to Antony and then to Octavian a few days before Actium.[195] These and many other *nobiles* who fit the pattern[196] would be concerned about their place in a history extending to 46. And, with the rupture between Antony and Octavian ever widening, how was Diodorus to treat Antony, for whose safety Caesar ostensibly began the Civil War?[197] In short, how would a historian living in Rome without obvious political contacts or patronage treat history that refused to settle?[198]

In a later era, the Younger Pliny agonized about turning to contemporary history:

Considering now what period of history I am to treat . . . shall it be recent times which no one has handled? I shall receive small thanks and give serious offence, for besides the fact that there is much more to censure than to praise in the serious vice of the present day, such praise as one gives, however generous, is considered grudging, and however restrained one's blame is said to be excessive.[199]

---

[194] *RE* 16.1, 545–51.

[195] Syme, *The Augustan Aristocracy*, 156. He had been married to Antony's daughter.

[196] E.g., Paullus Aemilius Lepidus (Syme, *The Augustan Aristocracy*, 109), L. Calpurnius Bibulus and C. Furius (Syme, *The Augustan Aristocracy*, 206–7), L. Gellius Poplicola (Syme, *The Roman Revolution*, 296–97), and L. Scribonius Libo (*RE* 2A.1, 881–85).

[197] This was one of Caesar's explanations for his march on Rome, expressed in his *Civil Wars*, and emphasized by Cicero (2 *Phil.* 22, 55; cf. Plut., *Ant.* 6.1). Antony made himself out to be Caesar's heir, even after the will was read: Florus ii 15.1; also Cic., *ad Fam.* xii 3.1; 2 *Phil.* 29; he was also the *Flamen Iulialis* of Caesar's cult: Dio xliv 6.4; Cic., 2 *Phil.* 110; Weinstock, *Divus Julius*, 305–8.

[198] Hor., *Odes* ii 1.7–8, on Pollio's work.

[199] *Letters* v 8.12–14 (Radice's translation).

Pliny's concerns are especially apt for Diodorus, a writer who stressed moral judgments and παρρησία. A few years after Diodorus finished, Horace greeted the new history by Asinus Pollio, but worried that the narrative would reach as far as 42. That, the poet declared, seemed full of risk.[200] Other contemporary historians understood the problem; they avoided discussing the period or else used appropriate hindsight.[201] Titus Labienus, orator and historian, would later declare that the best defense against a civil war was in forgetting it.[202] He was not, however, cautious enough. Later, his works were ordered burned by the Augustan Senate and he committed suicide.

BY THE mid-30s, Diodorus's situation had changed markedly since he had begun writing the *Bibliotheke* in 46. Caesar, who had initiated the process of enfranchising Sicily, was dead; gone too was political stability. Diodorus might have been placed in a tenuous situation. If he remained in Italy, he probably was without extensive patronage from Roman nobles or support from fellow Greeks. His history was not an overt attack on the Empire, but Diodorus was sufficiently troubled

[200] *Odes* ii 1.6. On the history's terminus and the date of the poem, see pp. 177–78.

[201] Dionysius of Halicarnassus mentions no Roman after Sulla, and, though promising to discuss the Julii (*AR* i 70.4), fails to do so: they might, however, be in a lost book: cf. E. Ramage, *Historia* 34 (1985), 234–35. Strabo had nothing to fear. The only surviving fragment of his history (probably written in the 20s: Bowersock, *Augustus and the Greek World*, 126–28) that concerns the Second Triumvirate casts Antony in a bad light (F 18), and the *Geography* leaves no doubt: e.g., xii 3.14; xiii 1.3; xvii 1.9; xvii 1.11. Livy withheld publication of the books on contemporary history (43–9 B.C.) until Augustus's death: Syme, *HSCP* 64 (1959), 58 = *Roman Papers* I, 434. The young Claudius was dissuaded from writing of his grandfather, Antony (Suet., *Claud.* 41.2). Tacitus (*Ann.* i 1.2) suggests that at the beginning of Augustus's reign there were still practicing historians of discrimination, but, besides Pollio, it is difficult to name any: see F. Goodyear, *The Annals of Tacitus: Books 1–6* I, 95. Note also the concerns of Ammianus Marcellinus, 26.1.1. On the use of Imperial censorship in the writing of history, see Momigliano, *The American Scholar* 47 (1978), 200–1 = *Sesto contributo*, 371–72.

[202] Sen., *Controv.* x 3.5.

that he might have felt the need to keep to himself. Diodorus had some knowledge of Sicily in the 30s; if he had returned there, the pressures followed. The war for Sicily ended in 36, but the island continued to suffer. Cities were destroyed, replaced by Roman colonies. Octavian himself returned in 35 (Dio xlix 34.1), perhaps to oversee confiscations and reorganization. Probably then he acted to deprive Sicily of Roman citizenship (Appendix I). In 32, Sicily had to take an oath of allegiance to Octavian in anticipation of his final struggle with Antony.[203] Wherever Diodorus resided, he was affected.

Much of the reconstruction is speculative. Diodorus offers little information about his personal life, and none is known from any other source. But to be sure, he altered the terminal date of his work from 46 to 60 B.C., and that latter year is too significant to be arbitrary. Various conditions during this period could have influenced Diodorus's decision: the need for patronage and social contacts, which Diodorus is not known to have had; the unsettled politics that would have to be included in a history reaching to 46; and the fear that struck many historians, especially those who might consider their work as being critical of Rome and its leaders. Diodorus composed most of *Bibliotheke* during the period of the Second Triumvirate, and its shape and structure must be judged in that light. Eastern Greek historians were generally well disposed to Octavian. Like most other provincials, they had little to lose from the change of government and much to gain by Octavian's favor.[204] Diodorus, however, had witnessed Octavian's devastation and disenfranchisement of his homeland. If he could not bring himself to praise the new autocrat, he would need at least to be discreet. The *Bibliotheke* is not sufficiently hostile to mark its author as an enemy of Rome engaged in writing resistance literature. But the closer the history came to the present, the more trouble it invited. The fall of the Republic was still being played out in the 30s, and actors in that

---

[203] *Res Gestae* 25.2.
[204] Cf. Raaflaub and Samons, *Between Republic and Empire.*

bloody drama were still very much on stage. Although he had the highest esteem for Julius Caesar, apparently by the mid-30s Diodorus chose generally to limit his admiration for the Dictator to the early narrative and to excise entirely the civil wars from his history.

CONCLUSIONS

THE SUGGESTION was once made that Arnaldo Momigliano devote himself to a commentary on Diodorus. In a earlier age, the same challenge could have been put to Eduard Meyer. The *Bibliotheke* encompasses a broader expanse of time and locale than any history surviving from antiquity, and only such great polymaths might control its diverse material. Until a commentary on a grand scale is undertaken, more modest scholars must examine individual aspects of Diodorus's work.

The present study is part of that tradition. During the nineteenth century, the impression grew that Diodorus remained quite loyal to the narratives he followed. Behind the *Bibliotheke* stood important sources, which, it was thought, with proper method could be identified and appreciated in their own right. The major changes Diodorus made when transmitting these texts were for the worse: repetition of the same events given by different sources, mistakes in chronology, arbitrary abbreviation of the traditions he employed. The assumption that Diodorus was "a mere copyist"—a phrase that scholars uncritically repeat with amazing frequency—is conjoined with the belief that whatever Diodorus might have himself written is hardly worth studying: thus, the now-famous description of the opening proem as the work of "a small man with pretensions" is habitually appealed to as a sufficient analysis. Only in the past two decades have a few scholars methodically questioned the assumptions of nineteenth-century *Quellenforschung*.[1] I have attempted to argue the case more fully, to show that Diodorus is responsible for much of the subjective material in the *Bibliotheke* and that the thoughts he expresses are representative of late Hellenistic times. Be-

---

[1] They are indicated in the Introduction, n. 5.

cause so little of Greek prose is preserved from that period, Diodorus's opinions take on special significance. The book examines three aspects of Diodorus's originality. Chapters 1 and 4 discuss common literary conventions found in the *Bibliotheke*. Although his material is usually ascribed to the sources he follows, there is strong reason to believe that Diodorus intruded substantially. Indeed, for someone who read as much history as Diodorus must have in order to create the *Bibliotheke*, how would he not have gained knowledge of the various historiographical conventions in vogue? Chapters 2 and 3 cover Diodorus's general control and infusion into the narrative of thoughts on morality, fortune, philanthropy, universalism, and human progress. The themes are sufficiently consistent and mutually supportive throughout the breadth of the *Bibliotheke* to suggest that they must have been independent of the sources Diodorus is said to have used. The final part of the book deals with the practical world. Diodorus was a Greek living in Rome. Other historians in the same circumstance are frequently scrutinized for their political feelings. Diodorus has largely escaped such an investigation, because, it has been felt, he was merely echoing the opinions of his sources. Once that assumption is put aside, individual notions about the empire emerge that illuminate the obscure tradition of opposition historiography and help explain the shape and structure of his work.

Without patrons or recourse to political action, Diodorus constructs the *Bibliotheke* around a program for moral living. Again and again, he judges individuals and nations by how benevolently they act while enjoying good fortune and awards special praise to benefactors, mythological and historical, who contributed civilizing gifts in the arts and sciences and in politics. Broadly moralistic and nonpragmatic, the *Bibliotheke* was composed by an author who has survived the devastations of the imperial capital and his own mother country, who is moderately ill disposed toward Rome and the manner in which Rome imposes its will, and who now is taking stock of what is important in advancing civilization.

Until the time when a complete commentary on Diodorus is produced, narrower works will have inherent flaws. For example, the present study ought to have behind it a complete and systematic discussion of *Quellenforschung*, for none exists. It is beyond the scope of this book to examine closely the degree to which Diodorus depended on Hecataeus of Abdera throughout book i. Certainly, there are specific passages that Diodorus himself authored. But because Diodorus also visited Egypt and boasted of his autopsy, he may have contributed more to the narrative than is usually believed. From chapter 69 onward, the discussion of Egyptian ethnography is full of comparisons to Greek customs, with the Egyptian practices generally judged the superior. This is not the obvious method or political sympathies of the court historian, Hecataeus. Rather, the universalism is consistent with Diodorus's feelings, as discussed in Chapter 3, and the methodology of comparing Greek and barbarian customs is evident throughout the following books, where Hecataeus is no longer his source.[2] The belief that Diodorus could not have substantially intruded is based on assumptions that are not, as this book attempts to show, on firm ground. A thorough study of book i, within the context of larger issues of *Quellenforschung* and based on the possibility that Diodorus may have influenced its contents significantly, would be of great help in understanding Diodorus's notions of universalism and human progress.

The *Bibliotheke* is the largest Greek history to survive from antiquity. As a result, whatever its quality, in historical research it may be the most frequently cited ancient source. Conversely, there are few extensive studies devoted to the overall composition of the *Bibliotheke*. The severe judgment that Diodorus is "a mere copyist" may deter such investigations. The present work leaves much unexplored, but possibly it has raised significant questions that will encourage a fresh look at the *Bibliotheke*.

---

[2] E.g., ii 29.5-6, 31.6, 38.2; iii 33.3, 45.2.

APPENDIX ONE

Sicilian Enfranchisement

CAESAR initially granted Sicily rights *sine suffragio*, but, soon after the assassination and because of a bribe (according to Cicero), Antony claimed that the Dictator had intended complete citizenship for the island (Cic., *Ad Att.* xiv 12.1; see Vittinghoff, *Römische Kolonisation und Bürgerrechtspolitik unter Caesar und Augustus*, 71). Antony had an unscrupulous Sicilian in his entourage, Sextus Clodius (Cic., 2 *Phil.* 17.42–43): perhaps he was the middleman in the fraud? After Sextus Pompeius took the island in late 43, it was to his benefit to extend the full franchise.

Other evidence verifies that picture. The Sicilian city of Tauromenium yields two inscriptions from the period when the town enjoyed Roman rights—that is, some time after 44 B.C. Yet for the seventh Roman month, the name *Quinctilis* is used, suggesting Pompey's rule, for he would have resisted renaming the month in honor of the dead Dictator: H. Willers, *RhM* 60 (1905), 329–37; G. Manganaro, *Cronache di archeologia e di storia dell' arte* 3 (1964), 53–55; cf. Goldsberry, "Sicily and Its Cities," 501–2; accepted by Crawford, *Coinage and Money*, 115, n. 16, without discussion. Another inscription, from Lilybaeum, similarly suggests that the Sicilians enjoyed the Roman franchise during Pompey's control over the island: O. Cuntz, *Klio* 6 (1906), 474.

Coins, too, tend to confirm the process of enfranchisment under Pompey, though, as is common with numismatics, the evidence is less precise. Grant, *From Imperium to Auctoritas*, 189–94, examines a series of Sicilian coins that commemorate the refounding of Sicilian towns as Roman municipalities. These can be dated to the period of Pompey's rule, 43–36.

Against Grant's identification of specimens bearing the legend *HISPANORUM*, however, see K. Erim, *AJA* 68 (1958), 79–90; L. Breglia, *AIIN* 5–6 (1958–1959), 338–42.

Most of the literary evidence is easily reconciled with the archaeological record. The agreement at Misenum of 39, between Antony, Octavian, and Pompey, guaranteed that slaves in Pompey's army would be freed upon discharge and that free men in his army would receive the same privileges as the discharged veterans of Octavian and Antony (App., *BC* v 72; cf. Dio xlviii 36.3–6). Certainly, if slaves were to receive their freedom, Sicilians whose loyalty Pompey also needed would have had to have guaranteed their own special privileges—that is, complete Roman citizenship. Some sources suggest that Pompey put estate slaves, usually kept in chain gangs, or *ergastula*, into the army (Florus ii 4.1–2; [Aurelius Victor], *De Vir. Ill.* 84.2), and after his victory Octavian returned the slaves to their masters (*Res Gestae* 25.1; App., *BC* v 131). Given Pompey's general popularity with Sicilians, it may be that he conscripted the slaves of Italian landowners only. This possibility is strengthened by the fact that Octavian, though dealing harshly with Sicily for its loyalty to Pompey, did try to return the slaves to their owners.

Diodorus testifies that the Sicilians received complete Roman rights (τῶν γὰρ Ῥωμαίων μεταδόντων τοῖς Σικελιώταις τῆς πολιτείας: xvi 70.6; cf. xiii 35.3; on the phrase, see also xxxii 4.4, argued in Chapter 1 that it is Diodoran) and that as a consequence a Syracusan priesthood was no longer used for eponymous dating (xvi 70.6). Because he notes that the priesthood had been established in 343/2 and had been used for dating for *over* (πλείω) three hundred years, the enfranchisement was being instituted during Sextus Pompeius's rule. Because Octavian stripped Sicily of its citizen status in 36, however, references to the enfranchisement found in Diodorus must have been anachronistic when the *Bibliotheke* was later published (xiii 35.3; xvi 70.6). Diodorus entered them as asides unconnected to his larger historical discussions and might not have remembered to delete them when historical circumstances changed. For a defense of Diodorus's accuracy at the time he wrote the statements, see Vittinghoff, *Römische Kolonisation und Bürgerrechtspolitik unter Caesar und Augustus*, 119, n. 2.

Strabo, completing his *Geography* near the end of Augustus's reign (Syme, *The Augustan Aristocracy*, 370), took a decidedly favorable view toward the Princeps (see Chapter 6, n. 201). Consequently his description of Sicily (written perhaps in 20–10 B.C.: Stone, *AJP* 87 [1983], 19, n. 65) is highly biased. He mentions Tauromenium (vi 2.3), without noting Octavian's resettlement as indicated by Diodorus (xvi 7.1); he records that Morgantina was unpopulated, but fails to give the reason (vi 2.4), the destruction of which appears to have been revealed by archaeology (Stone, *AJA* 87 [1983], 16–19); he explains Octavian's colonization of Syracuse in 21 (date: Dio LIV 7.1) as a restoration after Sextus Pompeius harmed (κακώσαντος) both other towns and Syracuse (vi 2.4, 270), though in fact Dio (xlviii 17.6) indicates that Syracuse had gone over to Pompey readily; he writes that Octavian restored (ἀνέλαβεν) Catana (vi 2.4, 272), yet earlier (vi 2.3, 268) he notes that Octavian sent Roman colonists there, confirmed by Pliny (*NH* iii 89). Other intentional oversights may be suspected: he calls Tyndaris a city and juxtaposes it to Panormus, which had become a Roman colony (vi 2.5, 272); yet Tyndaris was also colonized by Octavian (*RE* 7A.2 1781–82), for it resisted Agrippa in the Pompeian war (App., *BC* v 109). It had been celebrated in republican times for exceptional loyalty to Rome: Cicero, 2 *Verr.* v 46.124. A complete list of Sicilian colonies is found in Vittinghoff, *Römische Kolonisation und Bürgerrechtspolitik unter Caesar und Augustus*, 120–21.

Later in the first century A.D., Pliny (*NH* iii 8. 91) lists for the island's interior only three towns with *Latinitas* and one with the complete franchise, Messana. When Octavian broke the treaty regarding the slaves in 36 (App., *BC* v 131), he probably deprived Sicily of her recently bestowed privileges (see Chapter 6, pp. 192–93). A few scholars, from Mommsen (*CIL* x, p. 713) to Sherwin-White, *Roman Citizenship*², 365,

n. 1, think Pliny's list reflects the status of Sicily before the Pompeian enfranchisement. Although several anachronisms do occur in Pliny's catalogue, there is abundant evidence that the list generally reflects the time of Augustus: Ziegler, *RE* 2A.2, 2508–9.

APPENDIX TWO

Posidonius on Italian Knights

POSIDONIUS is generally held to have had an antiequestrian bias: e.g., Jacoby, *FGH* IIc, 159; Strasburger, *JRS* 55 (1956), 41, n. 17; and Càssola, *ANRW* II 30.1, 765. The issue, however, is not so simple, and once again (see Chapter 5) all the evidence for Posidonius's criticisms of the knights is preserved by Diodorus alone. The passages discussed in Chapter 5 for the exploitation of provincials (v 26.3 = *FGH* 87 F 116 [*Anhang*]; v 36.3–4, 38.1 = *FGH* 87 F 117 [*Anhang*]) and the rapacity of the *publicani* (xxxiv/v 25.1 = *FGH* 87 F 111b; xxxvii 5–6 = F 213 [Theiler]) include no direct condemnation of the equestrian class per se. (On the Spanish mines [v 26, 36] specifically, see Richardson, *JRS* 66 [1976], 140–47, and *Hispaniae: Spain and the Development of Roman Imperialism, 218–82 B.C.*, 163.) Posidonius's only discussion of *equites* as a class occurs when he criticizes Gaius Gracchus for taking the courts away from the Senate and handing them over to the *equites*, thereby making "the inferior element in the state supreme over their betters [τὸ χεῖρον τῆς πολιτείας τοῦ κρείττονος κύριον ἐποίησε]; by disrupting the existing harmony [σύμπνοια] of senate and knights, he rendered the common people hostile towards both" (xxxiv/xxxv 25.1; Walton). Posidonius is not condemning the knights; he is just commenting on their status relative to the nobles (cf. DS xxxvii 22 on the Italians). The final phrase indicates an association of the two groups, and there had been a "breathing together" (σύμπνοια—contra P. Botteri and M. Raskolnikoff, "Diodore, Caius Gracchus et la démocratie," in Cl. Nicolet, *Democratia et aristokratia*, 62–64, who suggest that the knights are here associated with the people). The criticism is aimed at Gaius Gracchus, who upset

211

the natural order of things, thereby providing the masses with a dangerous example of social and constitutional change. On the other side, at least one Roman *eques* is awarded Posidonius's highest praise for his service abroad (xxxvii 8.2–3) and is included in the essay on contemporary Romans who displayed traditional values (xxxvii 4 and 7). Moreover, Posidonius can be criticial of individual Roman nobles for their running of the state and empire (e.g., DS xxxiii 2; xxxvi 3.3, 8.5, 9.1; especially xxxviii/xxxix 8 and 11).

BIBLIOGRAPHY

Texts and Editions

Diodore de Sicile: Bibliothèque historique. Budé edition. By several authors, under the direction of F. Chamoux. Paris, 1972–.

Diodori Bibliotheca Historica. Teubner edition. 6 vols. Edited by F. Vogel and K. T. Fisher based on the text of I. Bekker and L. Dindorf. Stuttart, 1964–1969.

Diodorus of Sicily. Loeb edition. 12 vols. Edited by C. H. Oldfather, R. M. Geer, F. R. Walton, C. L. Sherman, and C. B. Welles. Cambridge, Mass., 1933–1967.

Thesaurus Linguae Graecae. Machine-readable tape under the direction of T. F. Brunner: books 1–20 based on the Teubner edition, fragments of 21–40 and the *fragmenta sedis incertae* based on the Loeb edition, vols. 11 and 12, edited by F. R. Walton.

Wesseling, P. [text and commentary, 1746]. In N. Eyring, *Diodori Siculi Bibliothecae Historicae Libri Qui Supersunt, e recensione Petri Wesselingii, etc.* 11 vols. Amsterdam, 1793.

Works Cited

Aalders, G.J.P. *Political Thought in Hellenistic Times*. Amsterdam, 1975.

Africa, T. "Ephorus and Oxyrhynchus Papyrus 1610." *AJP* 83 (1962), 86–89.

Anderson, W. S. *Pompey, His Friends, and the Literature of the First Century, B.C.* Berkeley, 1963.

Arrighetti, G. "Civiltà letteraria della Sicilia antica dal II secola. a.C. al IV secolo d.C." In *La Sicilia antica* II.2, edited by E. Gabba and G. Vallet, 393–410. Naples, 1980.

Avenarius, G. *Lukians Schrift zur Geschichtsschreibung*. Meisenheim am Glan, 1956.

Badian, E. "*Lex Acilia Repetundarum*." *AJP* 75 (1954), 374–84.

———. "Q. Mucius Scaevola and the Province of Asia." *Athenaeum* 34 (1956), 104–23.

———. *Foreign Clientelae (264–70 B.C.)*. Oxford, 1958.

Badian, E. Review of *Appiano e la storia delle guerre civili* by E. Gabba. *CR* n.s. 8 (1958), 159–62.

———. Review of *Filino-Polibio, Sileno-Diodoro*, by V. La Bua. *RFIC* 96 (1968), 203–11.

———. *Publicans and Sinners*. Ithaca, 1972.

———. "*Nobiles amici*: Art and Literature in an Aristocratic Society." *CP* 80 (1985), 341–57.

Balcer, J. M. "The Date of *Herodotus* IV.1: Darius' Scythian Invasion." *HSCP* 76 (1972), 99–132.

Barber, G. L. *The Historian Ephorus*. Cambridge, 1935.

Beard, M. "Cicero and Divination: The Formation of a Latin Discourse." *JRS* 76 (1986), 33–46.

Bernstein, A. H. *Tiberius Sempronius Gracchus: Tradition and Apostasy*. Ithaca, 1978.

Bickerman, E. "Origines Gentium." *CP* 47 (1952), 65–81.

———. "Sur un passage d'Hypéride, *Epitaphios*, col. VIII." *Athenaeum* 41 (1963), 70–85.

Blundell, S. *The Origins of Civilization in Greek and Roman Thought*. London, 1986.

Bonner, S. *The Literary Treatises of Dionysius of Halicarnassus*. Cambridge, 1939.

Bosworth, A. *From Arrian to Alexander: Studies in Historical Interpretation*. Oxford, 1988.

Botteri, P. "Arbitraire d'un éditeur et extraits disparus: Photius, 244, Diodore de Sicile." *Mélanges d' archéologie et d'historie de l'École Française de Rome* 95 (1983), 665–76.

Botteri, P., and M. Raskolnikoff. "Diodore, Caius Gracchus et la démocratie." I *Demokratia et aristokratia: A propos de Caius Gracchus: Mots grecs et réalités romaines*, edited by Cl. Nicolet, 59–101. Paris, 1983.

Bottin, C. "Les sources de Diodore de Sicile (pour l'histoire de Pyrhus, des successeurs d'Alexandre le Grand et d'Agathocle)." *Revue Belge de philologie et d'histoire* 7 (1928), 1307–27.

Bowersock, G. W. *Augustus and the Greek World*. Oxford, 1965.

———. "A Date in the *Eighth Eclogue*." *HSCP* 75 (1971), 73–80.

Braund, D. C. "Three Hellenistic Personages: Amynander, Prusias II, Daphidas." *CQ* n.s. 32 (1982), 350–57.

Breebarrt, A. "Weltgeschichte as Thema der antiken Geschichtsschreibung." *Acta Historiae Neerlandica* 1 (1966), 1–21.

Breglia, L. "Morgantina: Studi e problemi." *AIIN* 5–6 (1958/1959), 336–44.

Bringmann, K. "Geschichte und Psychologie bei Poseidonios." In *Aspects de la philosophie hellénistique*, Fondation Hardt, *Entretiens* 32, 29–66. Geneva, 1986.

Broughton, T.R.S. "Roman Landholding in Asia Minor." *TAPA* 65 (1934), 207–39.

———. *The Magistrates of the Roman Republic.* 3 vols. Cleveland, 1951–1986.

Brown, T. S. "Timaeus and the Aeneid." *Virgilius* 6 (1960), 4–12.

Brunt, P. A. "On Historical Fragments and Epitomes." *CQ* n.s. 30 (1980), 477–94.

———. *Arrian: History of Alexander and India.* 2 vols. Cambridge, 1983.

Burde, P. "Untersuchungen zur antiken Universalgeschichtsschreibung." Diss., Munich, 1974.

Burstein, S. "The Ethiopian War of Ptolemy V: An Historical Myth?" *Beiträge zur Sudanforschung* 1 (1986), 17–23.

Burton, A. *Diodorus Siculus Book I: A Commentary.* Leiden, 1972.

Busolt, G. "Diodors Verhältniss zum Stoicismus." *Neue Jahrbücher für Philologie und Paedagogik* 140 (1889), 297–315.

———. "Quellenkritische Beiträge zur Geschichte der römischen Revolutionszeit." *Neue Jahrbücher für Philologie und Paedagogik* 141 (1890), 321–49, 405–38.

Calderone, S. "Storia della Sicilia romana." *Kokalos* 12–13 (1976/1977), 363–80.

Cambridge History of Classical Literature, II: Latin Liberature. Edited by E. J. Kenney and W. V. Clausen. Cambridge, 1982.

Capelle W. "Griechische Ethik und römischer Imperialismus." *Klio* 25 (1932), 86–113.

Carcopino, J. *La loi de Heïron et les Romains.* Paris, 1919.

Casevitz, M. "La femme dans l'oeuvre de Diodore de Sicile." In *La femme dans le monde méditerranéen I, Antiquité*, edited by A.-M. Vérilhac, 113–35. Lyon, 1985.

Càssola, F. "Diodoro e la storia romana." In *ANRW* II 30.1, edited by H. Temporini and W. Haase, New York, 1982. 724–73.

Catalogue of the Greek Coins in the British Museum: Sicily. London, 1876.

Catalogue of the McClean Collection of Greek Coins (Fitzwilliam Museum). Edited by S. W. Grosse. Cambridge, 1923.

Clausen, W. "Callimachus and Latin Poetry." *GRBS* 5 (1964), 181–96.

Coins of the Roman Republic in the British Museum. Edited by H. A. Grueber. London, 1910.

Cole, T. *Democritus and the Sources of Greek Anthropology.* Cleveland, 1967.

Consolo Langher, S. *Contributo alla storia della antica moneta bronzea in Sicilia.* Milan, 1964.

Cornell, T. J. "Aeneas and the Twins: The Development of the Roman Foundation Legend." *PCPS* 21 (1975), 1–32.

Crawford, M. H. Review of *The Last Generation of the Roman Republic* by E. S. Gruen. *JRS* 66 (1976), 214–17.

———. "Greek Intellectuals and the Roman Aristocracy in the First Century B.C." In *Imperialism in the Ancient World.* Edited by P.D.A. Garnsey and C. R. Whittaker, 193–207. Cambridge, 1979.

———. *Coinage and Money under the Roman Republic.* Berkeley, 1985.

Croce, B. *Teoria e storia della storiografia.* 6th ed. Bari, 1948.

Cuntz, O. "Zur Geschichte Siciliens in der cäsarisch-augusteischen Epoche." *Klio* 6 (1906), 466–76.

Derow, P. S. "Polybius, Rome, and the East." *JRS* 69 (1979), 1–15.

Desideri, P. "L'interpretazione dell'impero romano in Posidonio." *RIL* 106 (1972), 481–93.

———. "Posidonio e la guerra mitridatica." *Athenaeum* 51 (1973), 3–29, 237–69.

Diels, H. *Die Fragmente der Vorsokratiker.* 6th ed. Berlin, 1951–1952.

Dodds, E. R. *The Ancient Concept of Progress and Other Essays on Greek Literature and Belief.* Oxford, 1973.

Dolce, C. "Diodoro e la storia di Agathocle." *Kokalos* 6 (1960), 124–66.

Drachmann, A. B. *Diodors römische Annalen bis 302 a. Chr. samt dem Ineditum Vaticanum.* Bonn, 1912.

Drew-Bear, T. "Deux décrets hellénistiques d'Asie Mineure." *BCH* 96 (1972), 435–71.

Drews, R. "Historiographical Objectives and Procedures of Diodorus Siculus." Ph.D. diss., Johns Hopkins University 1960.

———. Review of *Späthellenistische Berichte über Welt, Kultur und Götter: Untersuchungen zu Diodor von Sizilien* by W. Spoerri. *AJP* 83 (1962), 107–8.

———. "Diodorus and His Sources." *AJP* 83 (1962), 383–92.

————. "Ephorus and History Written κατὰ γένος." *AJP* 84 (1963), 244–55.

————. "Ephorus' κατὰ γένος History Revisited." *Hermes* 104 (1976), 497–98.

Eckstein, A. "Polybius, Syracuse, and the Politics of Accommodation." *GRBS* 26 (1985), 265–82.

————. *Senate and General: Individual Decision-making and Roman Foreign Relations, 264–194 B.C.* Berkeley, 1987.

Erim, K. "Morgantina." *AJA* 62 (1958), 79–90.

Ernesti, J.C.T. *Lexicon Technologiae Graecorum Rhetoricae.* Leipzig 1795. Reprint, 1962.

Evans, J. "The Sicilian Coinage of Sextus Pompeius." *ANSMN* 32 (1987), 97–157.

Eyring, N. *Diodori Siculi Bibliothecae Historical Libri Qui Supersunt, e recensione Petri Wesselingii, etc.* 11 vols. Amsterdam, 1793.

Farrington, B. *Diodorus Siculus, Universal Historian.* Inaugaural Lecture. Swansea, 1936.

Fears, J. R. *Princeps a Diis Electus: The Divine Election of the Emperor as a Political Concept at Rome.* Rome, 1977.

Ferguson J. *Utopias of the Classical World.* Ithaca, 1975.

Finley, M. I. *A History of Sicily.* London, 1968.

Fiore, P. "Nuovo contributo all'individuazione archeologia dell'antica Calacta." *Sicilia archeologia* 34 (1977), 63–69.

Fiorentini, G. "Ricerche archeologiche nella Sicilia centro-meridionale." *Kokalos* 26–27 (1980–1981) II, 581–600.

Fornara, C. W. *The Nature of History in Ancient Greece and Rome.* Berkeley, 1983.

Forte, B. *Rome and the Romans as the Greeks Saw Them.* Rome, 1972.

Frank, T. "On the Migration of Romans to Sicily." *AJP* 66 (1935), 61–64.

Fraschetti, A. "Per una prosopografia dello sfruttamento: Romani e Italici in Sicilia (212–44 a.C.)." In *Società romana e produzione schiavistica, I: L'Italia: Insediamenti e forme economiche,* edited by A. Giardina and A. Schiavone, 51–74. Bari, 1981.

Fraser, P. M. *Ptolemaic Alexandria.* 3 vols. Oxford, 1972.

Frier, B. W. *Libri Annales Pontificum Maximorum: The Origins of the Annalistic Tradition.* Rome, 1979.

Gabba, E. *Appiano e la storia delle guerre civili.* Florence, 1956.

————. "Storici greci dell'impero romano da Augusto ai Severi." *RSI* 71 (1959), 361–81.

————. "Considerazioni sulla tradizione letteraria sulle origini della repubblica." In *Les origines de la républic romaine*, Fondation Hardt, *Entretiens* 13, 135–69. Geneva, 1966.

———. *Appiani bellorum civilium liber quintus*. Florence, 1970.

———. "The Perusine War and Triumviral Italy." *HSCP* 75 (1971), 139–60.

———. "Storiografia greca e imperialismo romano (III–I sec. a.C.)." *RSI* 86 (1974), 625–42.

———. "Sulla valorizzazione politica della leggenda delle origini troiane di Roma fra III e II secolo a.C." *CISA* 4 (1976), 84–101.

———. "Sulle strutture agrarie dell'Italia romana fra III e I sec. a.d." In *Strutture agrarie e allevamento transumante nell'Italia romana III–I sec. a.C.*, edited by E. Gabba and M. Pasquinucci, 15–73. Pisa, 1979.

———. "True History and False History in Classical Antiquity." *JRS* 71 (1981), 50–62.

———. "Political and Cultural Aspects of the Classical Revival in the Augustan Age." *CA* 1 (1982), 43–65.

———. "Posidonio, Marcello, e la Sicilia." In *ΑΠΑΡΧΑΙ: Nuove ricerche a studi sulla Magna Grecia e la Sicilia antica in onore di Paolo Enrica Arias*, edited by L. Beschi et al., II, 611–14. Pisa, 1982.

———. "Dionigi, Varrone e la religione senza miti." *RSI* 96 (1984), 855–70.

———. "The Historians and Augustus." In *Caesar Augustus: Seven Aspects*, edited by F. Millar and E. Segal, 61–88. Oxford, 1984.

Gàbrici, E. *La monetazione del bronzo nella Sicilia antica*. Palermo, 1927.

Gauger, J. D. "Phlegon von Tralleis, Mirab. III. Zu einem Dokument geistigen Widerstandes gegen Rom." *Chiron* 10 (1980), 223–61.

Garraffo, S. "Zeus Eleutherios–Zeus Olympios: Note di numismatica siracusana." *AIIN* 23–24 (1976–1977), 9–50.

Gelzer, M. "Nasicas Widerspruch gegen die Zerstörung Karthagos." *Philologus* 86 (1931), 261–99. Also *Kleine Schriften* II, 39–72. Wiesbaden, 1963.

———. *Caesar: Politician and Stateman*. Cambridge, Mass., 1968.

Gentili, B., and G. Cerri. *History and Biography in Ancient Thought*. Amsterdam, 1988.

Gold, B. K. "Pompey and Theophanes of Mytilene." *AJP* 106 (1985), 312–27.

———. *Literary Patronage in Greece and Rome*. Chapel Hill, 1987.

BIBLIOGRAPHY

Gold B. K., ed. *Literary and Artistic Patronage in Ancient Rome.* Austin, 1982.

Goldsberry, M.A.S. "Sicily and Its Cities in Hellenistic and Roman Times." Ph.D. diss., University of North Carolina, 1973.

Goodyear, F.R.D. *The Annals of Tacitus: Books 1–6.* Cambridge, 1972.

Gosling, A. "Octavian, Brutus and Apollo: A Note on Opportunist Propaganda." *AJP* 107 (1986), 586–89.

Gozzoli, S. "Etnografia e politica in Agatarchide." *Athenaeum* 56 (1978), 54–79.

Grant, M. *From Imperium to Auctoritas.* Cambridge, 1946.

Grenfell, B., and A. Hunt. *The Oxyrhynchus Papyrus* XIII. London, 1919.

Gruen, E. S. *Roman Politics and the Criminal Courts.* Cambridge, Mass., 1968.

——. *The Last Generation of the Roman Republic.* Berkeley, 1974.

——. "The Origins of the Achaean War." *JHS* 96 (1976), 46–69.

——. *The Hellenistic World and the Coming of Rome.* 2 vols. Berkeley, 1984.

Habicht, C. *Gottmenschentum und griechische Städte,* 2nd ed. Munich, 1970.

——. "Die augusteische Zeit und das erste Jahrhundert nach Christi Geburt." In *Le culte des souvérains dans l'empire Romaine,* Fondation Hardt, *Entretiens* 19, 39–99. Geneva, 1973.

——. *Pausanias' Guide to Ancient Greece.* Berkeley, 1985.

Hadas, M. *Hellenistic Culture: Fusion and Diffusion.* New York, 1972.

Hadot, M. P. "Chaire d'histoire de la pensée hellénistique et romaine." *Leçon inaugurale,* February 18, 1983. Collège de France, 1983.

Hahn, L. *Rom und Römanismus im griechisch-römischen Osten.* Leipzig, 1906.

Hamilton, J. R. *Plutarch Alexander: A Commentary.* Oxford, 1969.

Hammond, N.G.L. "The Sources for Diodorus Siculus xvi, II: The Sicilian Narrative." *CQ* 32 (1938), 137–51.

Hanslik, R. "Cicero und das erste Triumvirat." *RhM* 98 (1955), 324–33.

Hardie, P. *Virgil's Aeneid: Cosmos and Imperium.* Oxford, 1986.

Harmand, J. "Diodore IV, 19; V, 24; Héraklès, Alesia César le Dieu." *Latomus* 26 (1967), 956–86.

Harmatta, J. "Poseidonios über die römische Urgeschichte." *AC* 7 (1971), 21–25.

Havelock, E. *The Liberal Temper in Greek Politics.* New Haven, 1957.

Heinen, H. "Die Tryphè des Ptolemaios VIII. Euergetes II." In *Althistorische Studien: Hermann Bengtson zum 70. Geburtstag dargebracht von Kollegen und Schülern,* edited by H. Heinen, 116–30. Weisbaden, 1983.

Heinze, R. *Virgils Epische Technik.* 3rd ed. Leipzig, 1928.

Helm, R. *Eusebius Werke: Siebenter band: Die Chronik des Hieronymus.* 2nd ed. Berlin, 1956.

Hill, P. J. "Coin-symbolism and Propaganda during the Wars of Vengeance (44–36 B.C.)." *Numismatica e antichità classiche. Quaderni ticinesi* 4 (1975), 157–90.

Hillscher, A. "Hominum litteratorum Graecorum ante Tiberii mortem in urbe Roma commoratorum historia critica." *Jahrbücher für classische Philologie,* suppl. 18 (1892), 355–444.

Hornblower, J. *Hieronymus of Cardia.* Oxford, 1981.

Horsfall, N. "Some Problems in the Aeneas Legend." *CQ* n.s. 29 (1979), 372–90.

Immerwahr, H. R. *Form and Thought in Herodotus.* Cleveland, 1966.

Jacoby, F. *Apollodors Chronik.* Berlin, 1902.

———. *Die Fragmente der griechischen Historiker.* Vols. I–IIIc. Berlin and Leiden, 1923–1958.

Jenkinson, E. "*Genus scripturae leve*: Cornelius Nepos and Biography at Rome." In *ANRW* I.3, edited by H. Temporini and W. Haase, 703–19. New York, 1979.

Jocelyn, H. D. "The Ruling Class of the Roman Republic and Greek Philosophers." *Bulletin of the John Rylands Library* 59 (1977), 323–66.

Karst J. *Eusebius Werke: Fünfter Band: Die Chronik aus dem armenischen Übersetzt.* Leipzig, 1911.

Kebric, R. B. *In the Shadow of Macedon: Duris of Samos.* Weisbaden, 1977.

Kennedy, G. *The Art of Rhetoric in the Roman World: 300 B.C.–A.D. 300.* Princeton, 1972.

Kidd, I. G. *Posidonius. Vol. II: The Commentary.* 2 vols. Cambridge, 1988.

Kienast, D. "Rom und die Venus vom Eryx." *Hermes* 93 (1965), 478–89.

———. "Augustus und Alexander." *Gymnasium* 76 (1969), 430–56.

Kirchner, J. "Zur Datirung einiger athenischer Archonten." *RhM* 53 (1898), 380–92.

Kleingünther, A. *ΠΡΑΤΟΣ ΕΥΡΕΤΗΣ: Untersuchungen zur Geschichte einer Fragestellung. Philologus suppl.* 26.1 (1933).

Kuhn, T. *The Structure of Scientific Revolutions.* 2nd ed. Chicago, 1970.

Kunz, M. "Zur Beurteilung der Prooemien in Diodors historischer Bibliothek." Diss., Zurich 1935.

Laqueur, R. "Ephorus." *Hermes* 46 (1911), 161–206, 321–54.

———. "Diodorea." *Hermes* 86 (1958), 258–90.

Larsen, J. A. "Roman Greece." In *An Economic Survey of Ancient Rome.* Edited by T. Frank, IV, 259–498. Baltimore, 1938.

Lasserre, F. "Prose grecque classicisante." In *Le classicisme à Rome aux 1ers siècles avant et après J.C,* Fondation Hardt, *Entretiens* 25, 135–73. Geneva, 1979.

Luce, T. J. "The Dating of Livy's First Decade." *TAPA* 96 (1965), 209–40.

Luce, T. J. *Livy: The Composition of His History.* Princeton, 1977.

Ludwich, A. "Ein Diodor-Fragment." *RhM* 34 (1879), 619.

Magie, D. *Roman Rule in Asia Minor to the end of the Third Century after Christ.* Princeton, 1950.

Malitz, J. *Die Historien des Poseidonios.* Munich, 1983.

Manganaro, G. "Iscrizioni latine e greche dal nuovo edificio termale di Taormina." *Cronache di archeologia e di storia dell' arte* 3 (1964), 38–68.

———. "Città di Sicilia e santuari panellenici nel III e II secolo a.C." *Historia* 13 (1964), 414–39.

———. "Über die zwei Sklavenaufstände in Sizilien." *Helikon* 7 (1967), 205–22.

———. "Per una Storia della Sicilia romana." In *ANRW* I:1, edited by H. Temporini, 442–61. New York, 1972.

———. "Una biblioteca storia nel ginnasio di Tauromenion e il P.Oxy. 1241." *PP* 29 (1974), 389–409.

———. "La provincia romana." In *La Sicilia antica* II.2, edited by E. Gabba and G. Vallet, 411–61. Palermo, 1980.

Manni, E. "Diodoro e la storia arcaica di Roma." *Kokalos* 16 (1970), 60–73.

———. "Ancora a proposito di Sileno-Diodoro." *Kokalos* 16 (1970), 74–78.

———. "Diodoro e la storica italiota." *Kokalos* 17 (1971), 131–45.

Marshall, A. J. "Library Resources and Creative Writing at Rome." *Phoenix* 30 (1976), 252–64.

Mattingly, H. B. "Scipio Aemilianus' Eastern Embassy." *CQ* n.s. 36 (1986), 491–95.

Mazza, M. "Economia e società nella Sicilia romana." *Kokalos* 26–27 (1980–1981), 292–353.

———. "Terra e lavoratori nella Sicilia tardo repubblicana." In *Società romana e produzione schiavistica, I: L'Italia: Insediamenti e forme economiche*, edited by A. Giardina and A. Schiavone, 19–50. Bari, 1981.

Mazzarino, S. *Il pensiero storico classico.* 3 vols. Bari, 1966.

McDougall, J. *Lexicon in Diodorum Siculum.* 2 vols. Hildesheim, 1983.

McGing, B. C. *The Foreign Policy of Mithridates VI Eupator King of Pontus. Mnemosyne* suppl. 89. Leiden, 1986.

Meiggs, R. *The Athenian Empire.* Oxford, 1972.

Meister K. "Die sizilische Geschichte bei Diodor von den Anfängen bis zum Tod des Agathokles: Quellenuntersuchungen zu Buch IV–XXI." Diss., Munich, 1967.

———. "Sizilische Dubletten bei Diodor." *Athenaeum* 48 (1970), 84–91.

———. "Absurde Polemik bei Diodor." *Helikon* 13–14 (1973–1974), 454–59.

———. *Historische Kritik bei Polybios.* Wiesbaden, 1975.

Mendels, D. "The Five Empires: A Note on a Propagandistic *Topos*." *AJP* 102 (1981), 330–37.

———. "Greek and Roman History in the *Bibliotheca* of Photius—A Note." *Byzantion* 56 (1986), 196–206.

Michel, D. *Alexander als Vorbild für Pompeius, Caesar, und Marcus Antonius. Archäologische Untersuchungen, Coll. Latomus* 94. Brussels, 1967.

Millar, F. *A Study of Cassius Dio.* Oxford, 1964.

Momigliano, A. "Livio, Plutarco e Giustino su Virtù e Fortuna dei Romani: Contributo alla ricostruzione della fonte di Trogo Pompeo," *Athenaeum* 12 (1934), 45–56. Also *Terzo contributo alla storia degli studi classici e del mondo antico.* I, 499–511. Rome, 1966.

———. Review of *Science and Politics in the Ancient World* by B. Farrington. *JRS* 31 (1941), 149–57. Also *Secondo contributo alla storia degli studi classici e del mondo antico*, 375–88. Rome, 1960.

———. "Terra Marique." *JRS* 32 (1942), 53–64.

———. *Alien Wisdom: The Limits of Hellenization.* Cambridge, Mass., 1975.

———. "The Historians of the Classical World and Their Audiences: Some Suggestions." *The American Scholar* 47 (1978), 193–204. Also *Sesto contributo alla storia degli studi classici e del mondo antico,* I, 361–76. Rome, 1980.

———. "How to Reconcile Greeks and Trojans." *Mededelingen der Koninklijke Nederlandse Akademie van Wetenschappen,* Afd: Letterkunde, n.r. 45, no. 9 (1982), 231–54. Also *On Pagans, Jews, and Christians,* 264–288. Middletown Conn., 1987.

———. "The Origins of Universal History." *Annali della Scuola Normale Superiore di Pisa* 12 (1982), 533–60. Also *Settimo contributo alla storia degli studi classici e del mondo antico,* 77–103. Rome, 1984. Also *On Pagans, Jews, and Christians,* 31–57.

———. "Some Preliminary Remarks on the 'Religious Opposition' to the Roman Empire," in *Opposition et résistances a l'empire d'Auguste e Trajan,* Fondation Hardt *Entretiens* 32 (Geneva, 1986), 103–33. Also *On Pagans, Jews, and Christians,* 120–41.

Mosshammer, A. A. *The Chronicle of Eusebius and Greek Chronographic Tradition.* Lewisburg, Penn., 1979.

Mühl, M. "Diodor über die solonische Gesetzgebung." *WS* 69 (1956), 203–5.

Murray, O. "Philodemus on the Good King according to Homer." *JRS* 55 (1965), 161–82.

———. "Hecataeus of Abdera and Pharaonic Kingship." *JEA* 56 (1970), 141–71.

———. Review of *Filodemo,* edited by T. Dorandi. *JRS* 74 (1984), 235–36.

Neubert, R. *Spuren selbständiger Thätigkeit bei Diodor.* Bautzen, 1890.

Nisbet, R.M.G., and M. Hubbard. *A Commentary on Horace: Odes, Book I.* Oxford, 1970. *Book II.* Oxford, 1978.

Nissen, H. *Kritische Untersuchungen über die Quellen der vierten und fünften Dekaden des Livius.* Berlin, 1863. Reprint, 1975.

Nock, A. D. "Notes on Ruler–Cult I–IV." *JHS* 48 (1928), 21–44. Also Nock, *Essays* I, 134–59.

———. "Posidonius." *JRS* 49 (1959), 1–15. Also Nock, *Essays* II, 853–76.

———. *Arthur Darby Nock: Essays on Religion and the Ancient World.* 2 vols. Edited by Z. Stewart. Oxford, 1972.

Novara, A. *Les idées romaines sur le progrès d' après les écrivains de la République.* Paris, 1982.

Ogilvie, R. M. *A Commentary on Livy, Books 1–5.* Oxford, 1965.

Old Testament Pseudepigraphica: Apocalyptic Literature and Testaments. 2 vols. Edited by J. C. Charlesworth. Garden City, N.Y. 1983, 1985.

Pais, E. "Alcune osservazioni sulla storia e sulla amministrazione della Sicilia durante il dominio romana." *Archivio storico siciliano* 13 (1888), 113–256.

Palm, J. *Über Sprache und Stil des Diodoros von Sizilien.* Lund, 1955.

Parry, A. "Logos and Ergon in Thucydides." Diss., Harvard University, 1957. Reprint, New York, 1981.

Pareti, L. "Due questioni sulla prima guerra servile." *ASSO* 16–17 (1919–1920), 231–47. Also L. Pareti, *Studi minori di storia antica,* 57–72. Rome, 1958–1969.

Passerini, A. "La ΤΡΥΦΗ nella storiografia ellenistica." *SIFC* 11 (1934), 35–56.

Pavan, M. "La teoresi storica di Diodoro Siculo." *RAL* 16 (1961), 19–52, 117–50.

Pearson, L. "The Speeches in Timaeus' History." *AJP* 107 (1986), 350–68.

————. *The Greek Historians of the West: Timaeus and His Predecessors.* Atlanta, 1987.

Pédech, P. *La méthode historique de Polybe.* Paris, 1964.

Peremans, W. "Diodore de Sicile et Agatharchide de Cnide." *Historia* 16 (1967), 432–55.

Perry, B. *Aesopica.* Urbana, Ill., 1955.

Pesely, G. "The Speech of Endius in Diodorus Siculus 13.52.3–8." *CP* 80 (1985), 320–21.

————. "Socrates' Attempt to Save Theramenes." *The Ancient History Bulletin* 2, no. 2 (1988), 31–33.

Peter, H. *Historicorum Romanorum Reliquiae.* 2 vols. 2nd ed. Leipzig, 1906.

Polacco, L. "La posizione del teatro di Siracusa nel quardo dell'archittetura teatrale Greca in Sicilia." In *AΠAPXAI: Nuove ricerche a studi sulla Magna Grecia e la Sicilia antica in onore di Paolo Enrica Arias,* edited by L. Beschi et al., II, 431–43. Pisa, 1982.

Price, S.R.F. *Rituals and Power: The Roman Imperial Cult in Asia Minor.* Cambridge, 1984.

Pritchett, W. K. *Dionysius of Halicarnassus: On Thucydides.* Berkeley, 1975.

Raaflaub, K. A., and L. J. Samons II. "Opposition to Augustus." In *Between Republic and Empire: Interpretations of Augustus and His Princeps,* edited by K. A. Raaflaub and M. Toher. Berkeley, 1990.

Ramage, E. S. "Augustus' Treatment of Julius Caesar." *Historia* 34 (1985), 223–45.

Raubitschek, A. E. "Epigraphical Notes on Julius Caesar." *JRS* 44 (1954), 65–75.

Rawson, E. "The Life and Death of Asclepiades of Bithynia." *CQ* n.s. 32 (1982), 358–70.

———. *Cicero: A Portrait.* Ithaca, 1983.

———. *Intellectual Life in the Late Roman Republic.* Baltimore, 1985.

Reid [Rubincam], C. I. "Diodorus and His Sources." Diss., Harvard University, 1969.

Reinhardt, K. "Hekataios von Abdera und Demokrit." *Hermes* 47 (1912), 492–513.

Reinhold, M. *From Republic to Principate: An Historical Commentary on Cassius Dio's "Roman History" Books 49–52 (36–29 B.C.).* Atlanta, 1988.

Rhodes, P. J. *A Commentary on the Aristotelian Athenaion Politeia.* Oxford, 1981.

Richardson, J. S. "The Spanish Mines and the Development of Provincial Taxation in the Second Century B.C." *JRS* 66 (1976), 139–52.

———. *Hispaniae: Spain and the Development of Roman Imperialism, 218–82 B.C.* Cambridge, 1986.

Rickman, G. *The Corn Supply of Ancient Rome.* Oxford, 1980.

Rizzo, F. P. "Posidonio nei frammenti Diodorei sulla prima guerra servile di Sicilia." In *Studi di storia antica offerti dagli allievi a Eugenio Manni,* edited by G. Bretschweider, 259–93. Rome, 1976.

Robert, L. "Inscriptions." In *Laodicée du Lycos: Le nymphée (campagnes 1961–63).* edited by J. d. Gagniers et al., 247–389. Quebec, 1969.

———. "Théophane de Mytilène à Constantinople." *CRAI* (1969), 42–64.

Roberts, W. R. "The Literary Circle of Dionysius of Halicarnassus." *CR* 14 (1900), 439–42.

Romilly, J. de. "Eunoia in Isocrates or the Political Importance of Creating Good Will." *JHS* 78 (1958), 92–101.

Romilly, J. de. "Thucydide et l'idée de progrès." *Annali della Scuola Normale Superiore di Pisa* 35 (1966), 143–91.

————. *The Rise and Fall of States according to Greek Authors.* Ann Arbor, Mich., 1977.

————. *La douceur dans la pensée grecque.* Paris, 1979.

Rostovtzeff, M. *The Social and Economic History of the Hellenistic World.* 3 vols. Oxford, 1941.

Rubincam, C.I.R. [Reid]. "A Note on Oxyrhynchus Papyrus 1610." *Phoenix* 30 (1976), 357–66.

————. "The Chronology of the Punishment and Reconstruction of Sicily by Octavian/Augustus." *AJA* 89 (1985), 521–22.

————. "The Organization and Composition of Diodorus' Bibliotheke," *EMC/CV* 31, n.s. 6 (1987), 313–28.

————. "Cross-references in the *Bibliotheke Historike* of Diodorus." *Phoenix* 43 (1989), 39–61.

Rusconi, M. "Le notizie romane di Diodoro e gli *Annales maximi*." *CISA* 3 (1975), 105–110.

Rusten, J. *Dionysius Scytobrachion.* Opladen, 1982.

Sacks, K. S. *Polybius on the Writing of History.* Berkeley, 1981.

————. "The Lesser Prooemia of Diodorus Siculus." *Hermes* 110 (1981), 434–41.

————. "Rhetoric and Speeches in Hellenistic Historiography." *Athenaeum* 64 (1986), 383–95.

Saller, R. P. *Personal Patronage under the Early Empire.* Cambridge, 1982.

Sanctis, G. de. "Diocle di Siracusa." *SIFC* 11 (1903), 433–45. Also *Scritti minori* I, 31–42. Rome, 1966.

————. *Ricerche sulla storiografia siceliota.* ΣΙΚΕΛΙΚΑ I. Palermo, 1958.

Santero, J. M. "The *Cultores Augusti* and the Private Worship of the Roman Emperor." *Athenaeum* 61 (1983), 111–25.

Sartori, M. "Note sulla datazione dei primi libri della *Bibliotheca Historica* di Diodoro Siculo." *Athenaeum* 61 (1983), 545–52.

————. "Storia, 'utopia' e mito nei primi libri della *Bibliotheca Historica* di Diodoro Siculo." *Athenaeum* 62 (1984), 492–536.

Schanz, M., and C. Hosius, *Geschichte der römischen Literatur* I. 4th ed. Berlin, 1927.

Scheller, P. *De Hellenistica Historiae Conscribendae Arte.* Leipzig, 1911.

Schepens, G. "Historiographical Problems in Ephorus." In *Historiographia antiqua: Commentationes Lovanienses in honorem W. Pere-*

mans septuagenarii editae, edited by T. Reekmans, 95–118. Louvain, 1977.

Schilling, R. "La place de la Sicile dans la religion romaine." *Kokalos* 10–11 (1964–1965), 259–83.

Schwartz, E. "Hekataeos von Teos." *Hermes* 40 (1885), 223–62.

Scibona, G. "Agira 1." *Archivo storico messinese* 32 (1981), 333–59.

Scott, K. "The Deification of Demetrius Poliorcetes." *AJP* 49 (1928), 137–66, 216–40.

Scramuzza, V. "Roman Sicily." In *An Economic Survey of Ancient Rome*, edited by T. Frank, III, 225–378. Baltimore, 1937.

Seel, O. *Die Praefatio des Pompeius Trogus*. Erlangen, 1955.

———. *Eine römische Weltgeschichte: Studien zum Text der Epitome des Iustinus und zur Historik des Pompejus Trogus*. Nürnberg, 1972.

Seibert, J. *Das Zeitalter der Diadochen*. Darmstadt, 1983.

Sensi Sestito, G. de. "La fondazione di Sibari-Thurii in Diodoro." *RIL* 110 (1976), 243–58.

Shackleton Bailey, D. R., ed. *Cicero's Letters to Atticus*. 1. Cambridge, 1965.

Sherwin-White, A. N. *Roman Citizenship*. 2nd ed. Oxford, 1973.

Simpson, R. H. "Abbreviation of Hieronymus in Diodorus." *AJP* 80 (1959), 370–79.

Sinclair, R. K. "Diodorus Siculus and the Writing of History." *PACA* 6 (1963), 36–45.

———. "Diodorus Siculus and Fighting in Relays." *CQ* n.s. 16 (1966), 249–55.

Sordi, M. *Diodori Siculi Bibliothecae liber sextus decimus*. Florence, 1969.

———. "Timagene di Alessandria: Uno storico ellenocentrico e filobarbaro." In *ANRW* II 30:1, edited by H. Temporini and W. Haase, 775–97. New York, 1982.

Spoerri, W. *Späthellenistische Berichte über Welt, Kultur und Götter: Untersuchungen zu Diodor von Sizilien*. Basel, 1959.

Starr, R. "Cross-references in Roman Prose." *AJP* 102 (1981), 431–37.

Stern, M. *Greek and Latin Authors on Jews and Judaism*. 3 vols. Jerusalem, 1974–1984.

Stone, S. C. III. "Sextus Pompey, Octavian and Sicily." *AJA* 87 (1983), 11–22.

Strasburger, H. "Poseidonios on Problems of the Roman Empire." *JRS* 55 (1965), 40–53.

Sydenham, E. A. *The Coinage of the Roman Republic.* Revised edition by G. C. Haines et al. London, 1952.

Syme, R. *The Roman Revolution.* Oxford, 1939.

———. "Imperator Caesar: A Study in Nomenclature." *Historia* 7 (1958), 172–88.

———. "Livy and Augustus." *HSCP* 64 (1959), 28–87. Also *Roman Papers,* edited by E. Badian, I, 400–54. Oxford, 1979.

———. *Sallust.* Berkeley, 1964.

———. *The Augustan Aristocracy.* Oxford, 1986.

Talbert, R.J.A. *Timoleon and the Revival of Greek Sicily: 344–314 B.C.* Cambridge, 1974.

Taylor, L. R. *The Divinity of the Roman Emperor.* Middletown, Conn., 1931.

———. "Varro's *De Gente Populi Romani.*" *CP* 29 (1934), 221–29.

Theiler W. *Poseidonios: Die Fragmente.* 2 vols. Berlin, 1982.

Thraede, K. "Das Lob des Erfinders." *RhM* 105 (1962), 158–86.

Toulmin, S. *Human Understanding.* 3 vols. Princeton, 1972.

Touloumakos, J. *Zum Geschischtsbewusstsein der Griechen in der Zeit der römischen Herrschaft.* Göttingen, 1971.

Troilo, E. "Considerazioni su Diodoro Siculo e la sua storia universale." *AIV* (1940–1941), 17–42.

Trudinger, K. *Studien zur Geschichte der griechisch-roemischen Ethnographie.* Basel, 1918.

Valk, M. van der. "On Apollodori Bibliotheca." *REG* 71 (1958), 100–68.

Verbrugghe, G. P. "Sicily 210–70 B.C.: Livy, Cicero and Diodorus." *TAPA* 103 (1972), 539–59.

———. "The 'Elogium' from Polla and the First Slave War." *CP* 68 (1973), 25–35.

———. "Narrative Pattern in Posidonius' *History.*" *Historia* 24 (1975), 189–204.

Vittinghoff, F. *Römische Kolonisation und Bürgerrechtspolitik unter Caesar und Augustus.* Acad. d. Wiss. u. d. Lit., Mainz. Abhandlungen d. geistes u. sozialwiss. Kl., no. 14, 1951.

Vogel, F. "Die Veröffentlichung von Diodors Geschichtswerk." In *Verhandlung der einundvierzigsten Versammlung Deutscher Philologen and Schulmänner in München,* 228–36. Leipzig, 1922.

Volkmann, H. "Griechische Rhetorik oder römische Politik?" *Hermes* 82 (1954), 465–76.

————. "Die indirekte Erzählung bei Diodor." *RhM* 98 (1955), 354–67.

Volquardsen, C. A. *Untersuchungen über die Quellen der griechischen und sicilischen Geschichten bei Diodor, Buch xi bis xvi.* Kiel, 1868.

Wacholder, B. Z. "Biblical Chronology in the Hellenistic Chronicles." *HTR* 61 (1968), 451–81.

Wachsmuth, C. *Ueber das Geschichtswerk des sikelioten Diodors.* i. Leipzig, 1892.

Walbank, F. W. "Polybius, Philinus, and the First Punic War." *CQ* 39 (1945), 1–18. Also Walbank, *Selected Papers*, 77–98.

————. "Phalaris' Bull in Timaeus. (Diod. Sic. xiii 90.4–7)." *CR* 59 (1945), 39–42.

————. *A Historical Commentary on Polybius.* 3 vols. Oxford, 1956–1979.

————. *Speeches in Greek Historians*, Third Myres Memorial Lecture. Oxford, 1965. Also Walbank, *Selected Papers*, 242–261.

————. "Political Morality and the Friends of Scipio." *JRS* 55 (1965), 1–16. Also Walbank, *Selected Papers*, 157–80.

————. "The Historians of Greek Sicily." *Kokalos* 14–15 (1968–1969), 476–98.

————. *Polybius.* Berkeley, 1972.

————. "Polybius between Greece and Rome." *Polybe*, Fondation Hardt, *Entretiens* 20. (Geneva, 1974), 1–31. Also *Selected Papers*, 280–97.

————. Review of *The Nature of History in Ancient Greece and Rome* by C. Fornara. *JHS* 105 (1985), 211.

————. *Selected Papers: Studies in Greek and Roman History and Historiography.* Cambridge, 1985.

Wallace-Hadrill, A. "The Golden Age and Sin in Augustan Ideology." *Past and Present* 95 (1982), 19–36.

————. *Suetonius. The Scholar and His Caesars.* London, 1983.

Wallace-Hadrill, D. S. "The Eusebian Chronicle: The Extent and Date of Composition of Its Earliest Editions." *JTS* 106 (1955), 248–53.

The Weber Collection. Edited by L. Forrer. London, 1922–1929.

Weinstock, S. *Divus Julius.* Oxford, 1971.

Wessling, P. *Diodori Siculi Bibliothecae Historicae Libri Qui Supersunt*: see N. Eyring in Texts and Editions, above.

West, S. "Lycophron Italicised." *JHS* 104 (1984), 127–51.

Westlake, H. D. *Essays on Greek Historians.* Manchester, 1969.

Westlake, H. D. "Diodorus and the Expedition of Cyrus." *Phoenix* 41 (1987), 241–54.

Wilhelm, A. "Zu einem Beschlusse der Amphiktionen." *WS* 61–62 (1943–1947), 167–89.

Will, E. *Histoire politique du monde hellénistique.* 2nd ed., 2 vols. Nancy, 1979 and 1982.

Willers, H. "Ein neuer Kämmereibericht aus Tauromenion." *RhM* 60 (1905), 321–60.

Williams, G. "Phases of Political Patronage of Literature in Rome." In *Literary and Artistic Patronage in Ancient Rome*, edited by B. K. Gold, 3–27. Austin, 1982.

Wiseman, J. "Corinth and Rome I: 228 B.C.–A.D. 267." In *ANRW* II 7.1, edited by H. Temporini and W. Haase, 438–548. New York, 1979.

Wiseman, T. P. *Clio's Cosmetics: Three Studies in Greco-Roman Literature.* Leicester, 1979.

————. "*Pete nobiles amicos*: Poets and Patrons in Late Republican Rome." In *Literary and Artistic Patronage in Ancient Rome*, edited by B. K. Gold, 28–49. Austin, 1982.

Woodman, A. *Rhetoric in Classical Historiography.* Portland, Or., 1988.

Yavetz, Z. *Julius Caesar and His Public Image.* London, 1983.

————. "*Res Gestae* and Augustus' Public Image." In *Caesar Augustus: Seven Aspects*, edited by F. Millar and E. Segal, 1–36. Oxford, 1984.

Zecchini, G. "L'atteggiamento di Diodoro verso Cesare e la composizione della 'Bibliotheca Historica.' " *RIL* 112 (1978), 13–20.

————. "Asinio Pollione: Dall' attività politica alla riflessione storiografica." *ANRW* 30.2, edited by H. Temporini and W. Haase, 1265–96. New York, 1982.

Zegers, N. "Wesen und Ursprung der tragischen Geschichtsschreibung." Diss., Cologne, 1959.

Zetzel, J.E.G. *Latin Textual Criticism in Antiquity* New York, 1981.

Ziegler, K. *Plutarchos von Chaironeia.* Stuttgart, 1949.

INDEX OF SIGNIFICANT
PASSAGES IN DIODORUS

INDEX OF SIGNIFICANT
PASSAGES IN OTHER AUTHORS

236

INDEX OF SIGNIFICANT
GREEK TERMS

GENERAL INDEX

Achaean War, 137–42
Aeneas, 154–57
Agatharchides, 19n.32, 21, 37, 50–51, 84–86, 110–11
Agathocles, 17, 21, 96–97
Agyrium, 60, 129–31, 165–67, 192
Alexander the Great, 14–17, 75, 172n.59, 179
Apollodorus of Athens, 109
Arrian, 67–68
Artapanus, 73n.87
Artemidorus, 59n.21, 86, 110–11
Athenaeus, 145n.111
Athens, 42–43, 49, 51–52, 79n.116
Augustus, 75, 129, 156n.156, 160–203; suppression of freedom of speech, 198–201; treatment of Sicily, 207–10

benefactions, 61–82, 103–6, 124
benefit, 23–36. *See also* character assessments
Bibliotheke, Hellenistic language, 11; Latinisms, 118n.3; *Nachleben*, 162–64; name, 3n.2, 77; period of composition, 167–72; *Quellenforschung*, 3–4, 7–8; terminal dates, 169–72
Bull of Phalaris, 113–15

Caecilius of Calacte, 142n.101, 189
Caesar, C. Iulius, 73–76, 81, 104, 117n.1, 124, 138, 156n.155, 160–84, 197; deification of, 171–72, 180–84, 195–96
Callias of Syracuse, 114–15

Carthage, 21, 46, 104–7, 127–37, 194–95
Castor of Rhodes, 65–66
chance. *See* fortune
character assessments, 23–36, 96–97, 75–76. *See also* παρρησία
Clodius, Sextus, 189, 190n.140
chronological references, 91–93
chronology, 64–66
Cicero, M. Tullius, 44, 60, 98
Constantine Porphyrogenitus, 47, 132n.61, 144
Corinth, 44–45, 137–42, 195
cosmogony, 56–82
criticism of other historians, 108–16
cross-references, 83–91
culture, development of, 55–82
culture heroes, 61–82

decadence, 46–54, 143–44, 147. *See also* πλεονεξία
deification, 70–82, 179–84. *See also* ἡμίθεοι; ἡρωικοί; θεός; ἰσόθεοι; σωτήρ
Demetrius of Scepsis, 156
democracy, 20n.36, 167
Diodorus, life, 161–68, 185–90; travels, 161; use of autopsy, 110–16
Dionysus, 67, 70, 74–75, 179
Dionysius of Halicarnassus, 24n.2, 29, 119–20, 185n.109, 187, 190
Dionysius Scytobrachion, 70
Diyllus, 36n.56
Duris, 51, 94–95

240

241

Diodorus Siculus
and the First Century
KENNETH S. SACKS

"This work is by far the most sustained and comprehensive account of the Diodoran elements in the thought of the *Bibliotheke*, as well as a reconstruction of the political and intellectual background to it."
—*Catherine Reid Rubincam,*
University of Toronto

Living in Rome during the last years of the Republic, Diodorus of Sicily produced the most expansive history of the ancient world that has survived from antiquity— the *Bibliotheke*. Whereas Diodorus himself has been commonly seen as a "mere copyist" of earlier historical traditions, Kenneth Sacks explores the complexity of his work to reveal a historian with a distinct point of view indicative of his times.

Sacks focuses on three areas of Diodorus's history writing: methods of organization and style, broad historical and philosophical themes, and political sentiments. Throughout, Diodorus introduced his own ideas or refashioned those found in his sources. In particular, his negative reaction to Roman imperial rule helps to illuminate the obscure tradition of opposition historiography and to explain the shape and structure of the *Bibliotheke*. Viewed as a unified work reflecting the intellectual and political beliefs of the late Hellenistic period, the *Bibliotheke* will become an important source for interpreting first-century moral, political, and intellectual values.

"Sacks's book is an original and valuable contribution to the intellectual history of the late Hellenistic period. His discussion of Diodorus' historical ideas and practice helps to clarify the character of this genre